VMware vSphere 5.x Datacenter Design Cookbook

Over 70 recipes to design a virtual datacenter
for performance, availability, manageability, and
recoverability with VMware vSphere 5.x

Hersey Cartwright

[PACKT] enterprise

PUBLISHING   professional expertise distilled

BIRMINGHAM - MUMBAI

VMware vSphere 5.x Datacenter Design Cookbook

First published: January 2014

Production Reference: 1200114

Published by Packt Publishing Ltd.
Livery Place
35 Livery Street
Birmingham B3 2PB, UK.

ISBN 978-1-78217-700-5

www.packtpub.com

Cover Image by Jeet Shah (rave2600@gmail.com)

Credits

Author
Hersey Cartwright

Reviewers
Takashi HOSHINO
Matthew Marlowe
Nilesh Pawar
Greg Swallow
Bingfeng Zhao

Acquisition Editors
Sam Birch
Kartikey Pandey
Gregory Wild

Lead Technical Editor
Vaibhav Pawar

Technical Editors
Mrunal Chavan
Dennis John
Sebastian Rodrigues

Copy Editors
Tanvi Gaitonde
Dipti Kapadia
Insiya Morbiwala
Kirti Pai

Project Coordinator
Shiksha Chaturvedi

Proofreaders
Sandra Hopper
Elinor Perry-Smith

Indexer
Rekha Nair

Graphics
Valentina Dsilva
Disha Haria
Yuvraj Mannari
Abhinash Sahu

Production Coordinator
Arvindkumar Gupta

Cover Work
Arvindkumar Gupta

About the Author

Hersey Cartwright has worked in the technology industry since 1996 in many roles, from helpdesk support to IT management. He began working with VMware technologies in 2006. He was the key sponsor of the virtualization initiative at ABNB Federal Credit Union and played a key role in the design, implementation, and management of virtual infrastructure of the ABNB.

In his current role as the Senior Virtualization Engineer at ABS Technology Architects, he is responsible for the design and implementation of VMware environments that support a wide range of business applications. He does most of his work with small- and medium-sized environments with 3 to 10 hosts, but he has also been involved with several large, multisite deployments. He has had experience working with a wide variety of server and storage platforms.

Since January 2011, he has been an instructor with the VMware IT Academy program at the Tidewater Community College, where he teaches the VMware Install, Configure, and Manage vSphere 5 and the Optimize and Scale vSphere 5 courses. He has designed and implemented the lab environment used by the students in the virtualization and security programs offered at the Chesapeake Campus of Tidewater Community College. He enjoys teaching and learns a lot by teaching others about the benefits of virtualization.

Along with VMware certifications, he also holds certifications from Citrix for XenApp and XenDesktop and the Information Storage Associate (EMCISA) certification from EMC.

He actively participates in the VMware community and has been awarded the vExpert title in both 2012 and 2013. He has presented multiple articles at `professionalvmware.com` on vBrownBags on vSphere administration, vSphere design, and vSphere disaster recovery. He regularly blogs about virtualization and other technologies at `http://www.vhersey.com/`.

Acknowledgments

I want to thank my family, especially my wife Sandy, for putting up with the long hours I work and supporting everything I do. You guys are my everything, and your support and encouragement means the world to me.

I also want to thank the great VMware community. There are a lot of great folks there who are always willing to help. A special thanks to the `#vCoffee` crew group on Twitter: Shane, Susan, Matt, and Todd.

Finally, I want to thank my employer, ABS Technology Architects, and my supervisor, Rob, for the opportunities and flexibility.

About the Reviewers

Takashi HOSHINO works at Cybozu Labs, Inc. and is interested in database and storage systems. He is developing vmbkp: an open source VMware vSphere backup tool.

Nilesh Pawar has a Bachelor's degree in Information Technology and has successfully completed learning .NET programming. He has a complete understanding of the life cycle of software development projects. He has spent part of his career as a programmer (.NET, MS-SQL, and Crystal Reports). He is a VMware Certified Professional, Red Hat Certified Engineer, and is Citrix Xenserver Certified, along with a strong knowledge of networks. He is well versed with IaaS, PaaS, and SaaS cloud delivery models.

He designs public and private Cloud Infrastructure and Services. He has a deep understanding of network and firewall policies. He has strong impact analysis and debugging skills. He has knowledge of e-mail solutions, security (AV and anti-spam), e-mail archiving and compliances, and two-factor authentication.

He has a good knowledge of Windows clustering and Hyper-V environments. He also likes to learn and excel in new technologies. His resume can be referred to for additional information on his experience. His profile can be found at `www.nileshpawar.info`. He can be reached anytime via his cell phone at +91-99208 29266.

Greg Swallow, an Indiana boy, currently lives in Indianapolis with his wife, Nami, and two children, Noah and Madeline. He has worked as a system administrator since 1997. His career has included running the State of Indiana website for NIC, starting up a hosted IaaS platform that runs VMware vSphere for Expedient, and managing over 2,000 Linux VMs with a team of just two persons at a large Orange company (ExactTarget), where he lives. He is currently employed at Indigo Biosystems as a DevOps engineer, which is a fancy title for a system administrator who likes to work directly with a dev team and can write scripts.

When he's not working, he usually marches with his family through the woods until they beg him to stop, and then they turn around and march back to the car. Otherwise, if they don't want to go, he leaves them behind and grabs his running shoes or his bike and does the same thing on his own.

I would like to thank Expedient for sending me to VCP training. The training has paid off fivefold. I would also like to thank Packt Publishing for offering me the opportunity to review this book. It's been fun!

Bingfeng Zhao is a system programmer. He has a Bachelor's degree in Chemistry from Inner Mongolia University, but he finally found that programming is much more fun and a better way to raise his standard of living. He uses C/C++ mostly and devotes more time to the virtualized digital world. He works for the EMC company as a Principal Software Engineer, and he helps to design and implement unified storage systems. He lives in Beijing, China with his lovely wife Jing Lai.

www.PacktPub.com

Support files, eBooks, discount offers, and more

You might want to visit www.PacktPub.com for support files and downloads related to your book.

Did you know that Packt offers eBook versions of every book published, with PDF and ePub files available? You can upgrade to the eBook version at www.PacktPub.com and as a print book customer, you are entitled to a discount on the eBook copy. Get in touch with us at service@packtpub.com for more details.

At www.PacktPub.com, you can also read a collection of free technical articles, sign up for a range of free newsletters and receive exclusive discounts and offers on Packt books and eBooks.

http://PacktLib.PacktPub.com

Do you need instant solutions to your IT questions? PacktLib is Packt's online digital book library. Here, you can access, read and search across Packt's entire library of books.

Why subscribe?

- Fully searchable across every book published by Packt
- Copy and paste, print and bookmark content
- On demand and accessible via web browser

Free access for Packt account holders

If you have an account with Packt at www.PacktPub.com, you can use this to access PacktLib today and view nine entirely free books. Simply use your login credentials for immediate access.

Instant updates on new Packt books

Get notified! Find out when new books are published by following @PacktEnterprise on Twitter, or the *Packt Enterprise* Facebook page.

Table of Contents

Preface

VMware is the industry leader in datacenter virtualization. Its vSphere 5.x suite of products provides a robust and resilient platform for virtualizing server and application workloads. The features available in vSphere 5.x simplify the management of resources, increase the availability of applications, and guarantee the performance of workloads deployed in the virtualized datacenter.

This book provides recipes for creating a virtual datacenter design using the features of vSphere 5.x by guiding you through the process of identifying the design factors and applying them to the logical and physical design process.

The book provides steps that walk you through the design process from beginning to end, right from the discovery process to creating the conceptual design; calculating the resource requirements of the logical storage, compute, and network design; mapping the logical requirements to a physical design; and finally creating the design documentation.

The recipes in the book provide guidance for making design decisions to ensure the successful creation, and ultimately the successful implementation of a VMware vSphere 5.x virtual datacenter design.

What this book covers

Chapter 1, *The Virtual Datacenter*, provides an introduction to the benefits of the virtual datacenter, the VMware vSphere products, and basic virtualization concepts. The chapter identifies the differences between a datacenter administrator and a datacenter architect. An overview of the VMware Certified Advanced Professional Datacenter Design (VCAP-DCD) certification is also covered.

Chapter 2, *The Discovery Process*, explains how to identify stakeholders, conduct stakeholder interviews, and perform technical assessments to discover the business and technical goals of a virtualization project. The chapter covers how to use tools, the VMware Capacity planner and Windows Performance Monitor, to collect resource information during the discovery process.

Chapter 3, *The Design Factors*, explains how to identify and document design requirements, constraints, assumptions, and risks. The chapter details how to use these design factors to create the conceptual design.

Chapter 4, *The vSphere Management Design*, describes the vCenter Server components and their dependencies. Recipes are included for determining the vCenter Server deployment option and Windows Server or virtual appliance, to determine the type of database to use based on the deployment size.

Chapter 5, *The vSphere Storage Design*, covers the logical storage design. Recipes are included to calculate the storage capacity and performance requirements for the logical storage design. The chapter also covers the details to select the correct RAID level and storage connectivity to support a design.

Chapter 6, *The vSphere Network Design*, provides details on the logical network design. This chapter explains how to calculate bandwidth requirements to support a vSphere design. Details on selecting a virtual switch topology, designing for network availability, and the network requirements to support vMotion and IP-connected storage are also covered.

Chapter 7, *The vSphere Compute Design*, provides recipes for calculating the CPU and memory requirements to create the logical compute design. The chapter also covers cluster design considerations for High Availability (HA) and the Distributed Resource Scheduler (DRS).

Chapter 8, *The vSphere Physical Design*, explains how to satisfy the design factors by mapping the logical management, storage, network, and compute designs to hardware, to create the physical vSphere design. The chapter also provides details on creating a custom installation, on ISO to install ESXi, and on the best practices for host BIOS configurations.

Chapter 9, *The Virtual Machine Design*, looks at the design of virtual machines and application workloads running in the virtual datacenter. Recipes are provided for right-sizing virtual machine resources, enabling the ability to add virtual machine resources, and creating virtual machine templates. The chapter details the use of affinity and anti-affinity rules to improve application efficiency and availability. Converting or migrating physical servers to virtual machines is also covered in this chapter.

Chapter 10, *Disaster Recovery and Business Continuity*, covers options for backup, recovery, and continued operations in the event of a system failure. The chapter covers how to create backups of vSphere configurations so they can be quickly restored. The protection of virtual machines using VMware products for backup and replication is also covered in this chapter.

Chapter 11, *The Design Documentation*, covers documenting a vSphere design. The documentation includes the architecture design document, the implementation plan, the installation guide, the validation and test plan, and operational procedures. This chapter also provides tips for presenting the design to stakeholders and using the design documentation to implement the design.

What you need for this book

The software requirements for this book are as follows:

- VMware vSphere ESXi 5.x
- VMware vSphere vCenter Server 5.x
- VMware PowerCLI 5.x
- VMware vCLI 5.x

Who this book is for

If you are an administrator or consultant interested in designing virtualized datacenter environments using VMware vSphere 5.x and the supporting components, this book is for you. The book will help both new and experienced architects deliver professional VMware vSphere virtual datacenter designs.

Conventions

In this book, you will find a number of styles of text that distinguish between different kinds of information. Here are some examples of these styles and an explanation of their meaning.

Code words in text, database table names, folder names, filenames, file extensions, pathnames, dummy URLs, user input, and Twitter handles are shown as follows:

A URL is set as follows:

```
http://www.vmware.com/
```

File extensions are set as follows:

```
.vmx
```

Any command-line input or output is written as follows:

```
esxcli storage nmp satp set -default-psp=<psp policy to set>
--satp=<SATP_name>
```

New terms and **important words** are shown in bold. Words that you see on the screen, in menus or dialog boxes for example, appear in the text like this: "A template of the **Data Collector Set** can be created to easily import the **Data Collector Set** on other servers/workstations".

[Warnings or important notes appear in a box like this.]

[Tips and tricks appear like this.]

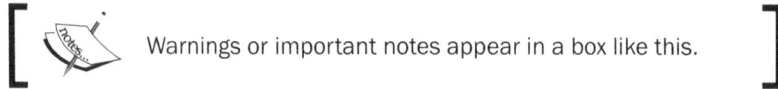

Reader feedback

Feedback from our readers is always welcome. Let us know what you think about this book—what you liked or may have disliked. Reader feedback is important for us to develop titles that you really get the most out of.

To send us general feedback, simply send an e-mail to `feedback@packtpub.com`, and mention the book title via the subject of your message.

If there is a topic that you have expertise in and you are interested in either writing or contributing to a book, see our author guide on `www.packtpub.com/authors`.

Customer support

Now that you are the proud owner of a Packt book, we have a number of things to help you to get the most from your purchase.

Errata

Although we have taken every care to ensure the accuracy of our content, mistakes do happen. If you find a mistake in one of our books—maybe a mistake in the text or the code—we would be grateful if you would report this to us. By doing so, you can save other readers from frustration and help us improve subsequent versions of this book. If you find any errata, please report them by visiting `http://www.packtpub.com/submit-errata`, selecting your book, clicking on the **errata submission form** link, and entering the details of your errata. Once your errata are verified, your submission will be accepted and the errata will be uploaded on our website, or added to any list of existing errata, under the Errata section of that title. Any existing errata can be viewed by selecting your title from `http://www.packtpub.com/support`.

Piracy

Piracy of copyright material on the Internet is an ongoing problem across all media. At Packt Publishing, we take the protection of our copyright and licenses very seriously. If you come across any illegal copies of our works, in any form, on the Internet, please provide us with the location address or website name immediately so that we can pursue a remedy.

Please contact us at `copyright@packtpub.com` with a link to the suspected pirated material.

We appreciate your help in protecting our authors, and our ability to bring you valuable content.

Questions

You can contact us at `questions@packtpub.com` if you are having a problem with any aspect of the book, and we will do our best to address it.

1

The Virtual Datacenter

In this chapter, we will cover:

- ▶ Becoming a virtual datacenter architect
- ▶ Using a holistic approach to datacenter design
- ▶ Passing the VMware VCAP-DCD exam

Introduction

This chapter focuses on many of the basic concepts and benefits of virtualization. It provides a quick overview of VMware virtualization, introduces the virtual datacenter architect, and lays some of the groundwork necessary for creating and implementing a successful virtual datacenter design using VMware vSphere 5.x.

We will also take a look at the **VMware Certified Advanced Professional-Data Center Design** (**VCAP-DCD**) certification, including a few tips that should help you prepare for and successfully complete the certification exam.

If you are already familiar with virtualization, this chapter will provide a review of many of the benefits and technologies of virtualization.

Since the focus of this book is on design, we will not go into great detail discussing the specifics of how to configure resources in a virtual datacenter. Most of you probably already have a good understanding of VMware's virtualization architecture, so this section will provide just a basic overview of the key VMware components that are the building blocks to the virtual datacenter.

Virtualization creates a layer of abstraction between the physical hardware and the virtual machines that run on it. Virtual hardware is presented to the virtual machine granting access to the underlying physical hardware, which is scheduled by the hypervisor's kernel. The hypervisor separates the physical hardware from the virtual machine as shown in the following diagram:

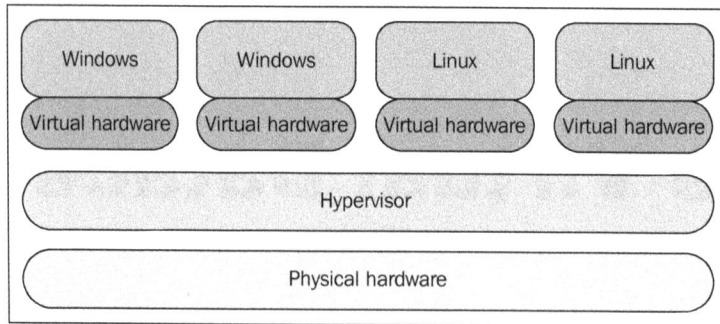

The hypervisor

At the core of any virtualization platform is the hypervisor. The VMware hypervisor is named vSphere ESXi, simply referred to as ESXi. ESXi is a Type 1 or bare-metal hypervisor. This means it runs directly on the host's hardware to present virtual hardware to the virtual machines. In turn, the hypervisor schedules access to the physical hardware of the hosts.

ESXi allows multiple virtual machines with a variety of operating systems to run simultaneously, sharing the resources of the underlying physical hardware. Access to physical resources, such as memory, CPU, storage, and network, used by the virtual machines is managed by the scheduler or **Virtual Machine Monitor** (**VMM**) provided by ESXi. The resources presented to the virtual machines can be overcommitted; this means more resources than are available can be allocated to the virtual machines on the physical hardware. Advanced memory sharing and reclamation techniques, such as **Transparent Page Sharing** (**TPS**) and ballooning, along with CPU scheduling allow for overcommitment of these resources to be possible, resulting in greater virtual to physical consolidation ratios.

ESXi is a 64-bit hypervisor that must be run on a 64-bit hardware. An ESXi installation requires less than 150 MB of space for installation. It can be installed on a hard disk locally, a USB device, a **Logical Unit Number** (**LUN**) on a **Storage Area Network** (**SAN**), or deployed stateless on hosts with no storage. The small footprint of an ESXi installation provides a reduction in the management overhead associated with patching and security hardening.

With the release of vSphere 5.0, VMware retired the ESX hypervisor. ESX had a separate Linux-based service console for the management interface of the hypervisor. Management functions were provided by agents running in the service console. The service console has since been removed from ESXi and agents now run directly on ESXi's VMkernel.

To manage a standalone host running ESXi, a **Direct Console User Interface** (**DCUI**) is provided for basic configuration and troubleshooting. A shell is available that can either be accessed locally from the console or remotely using **Secure Shell** (**SSH**). The esxcli and other commands can be used in the shell to provide advanced configuration options. An ESXi host can also be accessed directly using the vSphere Client. The ESXi DCUI is shown in the following screenshot:

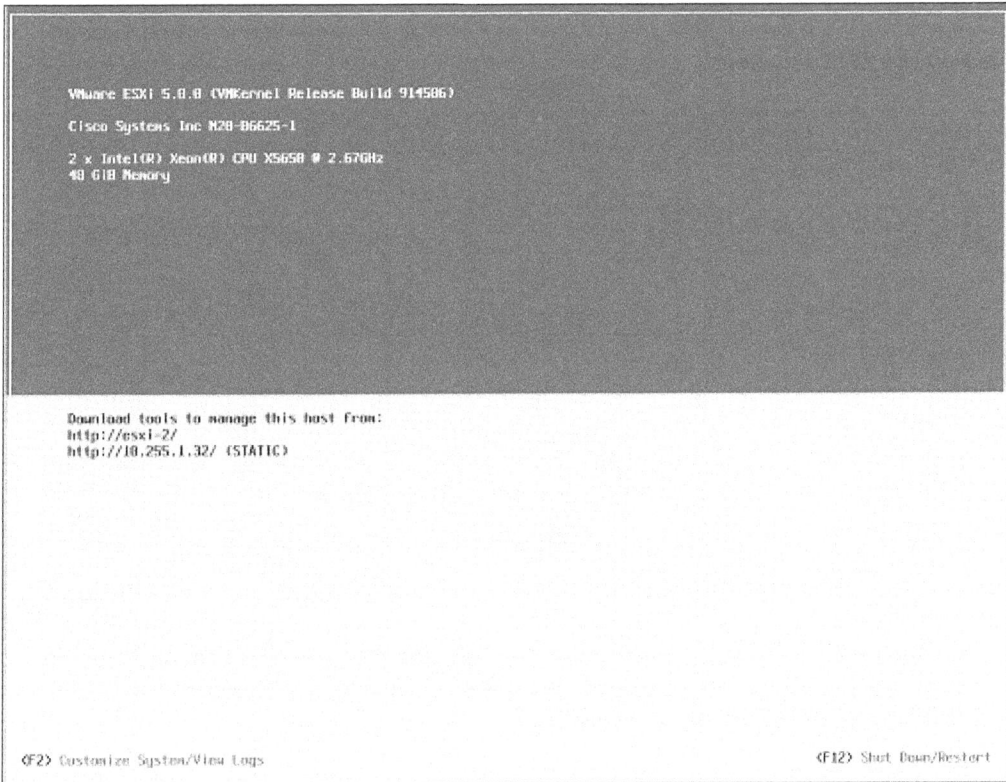

> The DCUI can be accessed remotely using SSH by typing the command dcui in the prompt. Press *Ctrl* + *C* to exit the remote DCUI session.

Virtual machines

A virtual machine is a software computer that runs a guest operating system. Virtual machines are comprised of a set of configuration files and datafiles stored on local or remote storage. These configuration files contain information about the virtual hardware presented to the virtual machine. This virtual hardware includes the CPU, RAM, disk controllers, removable devices, and so on, and emulates the same functionality as the physical hardware. The following screenshot depicts the virtual machine files that are stored on a shared **Network File System** (**NFS**) datastore:

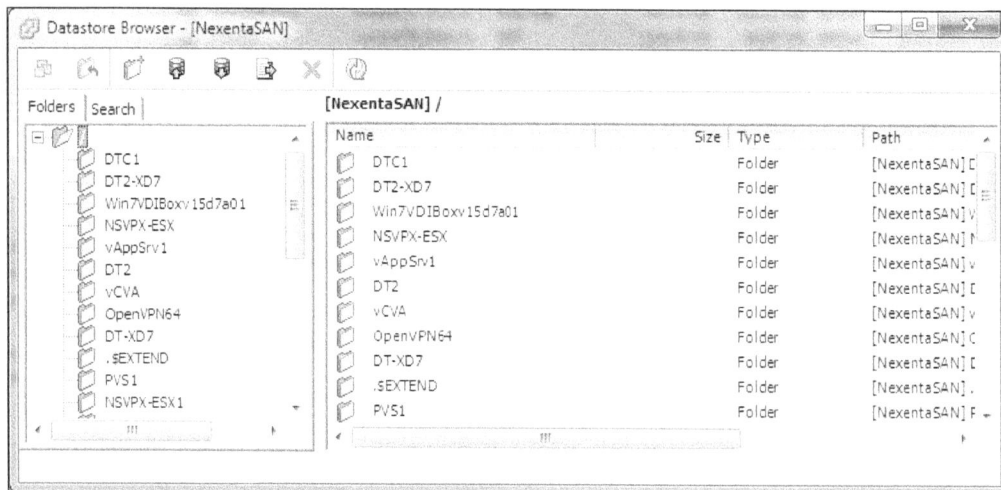

The files that make up a virtual machine are typically stored in a directory set aside for the particular virtual machine they represent. These files include the configuration file, virtual disk files, NVRAM file, and virtual machine logfiles.

The following table lists the common virtual machine file extensions along with a description of each:

File extension	Description
.vmx	This is a virtual machine configuration file. It contains the configurations of the virtual hardware that is presented to the virtual machine.
.vmdk	This is a virtual disk descriptor file. It contains a header and other information pertaining to the virtual disk.
-flat.vmdk	This is a preallocated virtual disk. It contains the content or data on the disk used by the virtual machine.

File extension	Description
`.nvram`	This is a file that stores the state of a virtual machine's **Basic Input Output System** (**BIOS**) or **Extensible Firmware Interface** (**EFI**) configurations.
`.vswp`	This is a virtual machine swap file. It gets created when a virtual machine is powered on. The size of this file is equal to the amount of memory allocated minus any memory reservations.
`.log`	This is a virtual machine logfile.
`.vmsd`	This is a virtual machine file used with snapshots to store data about each snapshot active on a virtual machine.
`.vmsn`	This is a virtual machine snapshot data file.

Virtual machines can be deployed using a variety of methods as follows:

- Using the New Virtual Machine Wizard in the vSphere Client
- By getting converted from a physical machine using the VMware Converter
- By getting imported from an **Open Virtualization Format** (**OVF**) or **Open Virtualization Alliance** (**OVA**)
- By getting cloned from an existing virtual machine
- By getting deployed from a virtual machine template

When a new virtual machine is created, a guest operating system can be installed on the virtual machine. VMware vSphere 5 supports more than 80 different guest operating systems. These include many versions of the Windows server and desktop operating systems, many distributions and versions of Linux and Unix operating systems, and Apple Mac OS operating systems.

Virtual appliances are preconfigured virtual machines that can be imported to the virtual environment. A virtual appliance can be comprised of a single virtual machine or a group of virtual machines with all the components required to support an application. The virtual machines in a virtual appliance are preloaded with guest operating systems and the applications they run are normally preconfigured and optimized to run in a virtual environment.

Since virtual machines are just a collection of files on a disk, they become portable. Virtual machines can be moved from one location to another by simply moving or copying the associated files. Using VMware vSphere features such as vMotion, Enhanced vMotion, or Storage vMotion, virtual machines can be migrated from host to host or datastore to datastore while a virtual machine is running. Virtual machines can also be exported to an OVF or OVA to be imported into another VMware vSphere environment.

Virtual infrastructure management

VMware vCenter Server provides a centralized management interface to manage and configure groups of ESXi hosts in the virtualized datacenter. The vCenter Server is required to configure and control many advanced features, such as the **Distributed Resource Scheduler** (**DRS**), Storage DRS, and **VMware High Availability** (**HA**). The vCenter Server is accessed using either the vSphere Client or the vSphere Web Client. Many vendors provide plugins that can be installed to allow third-party storage, network, and compute resources to be managed using the vSphere Client.

The vCenter Server can be installed on a 64-bit Windows server. It can be run on dedicated physical hardware or as a virtual machine. When the vCenter Server is deployed on the Windows server, it requires either a Microsoft SQL or an Oracle database to store configuration and performance information. IBM DB2 databases are supported with vSphere 5.1, but this support was removed in vSphere 5.5.

SQL Express can also be used for small environments of less than five hosts and 50 virtual machines. The database can either be installed locally on the same server as the vCenter Server or on a remote database server.

Another option for deploying the vCenter Server is the **vCenter Server Appliance** (**VCSA**). The VCSA is a preconfigured, Linux-based virtual machine preinstalled with the vCenter Server components. The appliance includes an embedded database suitable for small deployments or a remote Oracle database.

Several other management and automation tools are available to aid the day-to-day administration of a vSphere environment: the **vSphere Command-Line Interface** (**vCLI**); vSphere PowerCLI provides a Windows PowerShell interface; vCenter Orchestrator can be used to automate tasks; and the **vSphere Management Assistant** (**vMA**) is a Linux-based virtual appliance that is used to run management and automation scripts against hosts. These tools allow an administrator to use command-line utilities to manage hosts from remote workstations.

VMware provides a suite of other products that benefit the virtualized datacenter. These datacenter products, such as vCenter Operations Manager, Site Recovery Manager, and vCloud Director, can each be leveraged in the virtual datacenter to meet specific requirements related to management, disaster recovery, and cloud services. At the core of these products is vSphere suite, which includes ESXi and the vCenter Server.

Understanding the benefits of virtualization

The following table provides a matrix of some of the core VMware technologies and the benefits that can be realized by using them. This is not meant to be an exhaustive list of all VMware technologies and features, but it does provide an insight into many of the technologies commonly deployed in the enterprise virtual datacenter.

VMware technology	Primary benefits	Description
vSphere ESXi	▶ Server consolidation ▶ Resource efficiency	ESXi is VMware's bare-metal hypervisor that hosts virtual machines, also known as guests, and schedules virtual hardware access to physical resources.
HA	▶ Increased availability	HA restarts virtual machines in the event of a host failure. It also monitors and restarts the virtual machines in the event of a guest operating system failure.
vMotion and the VMware DRS	▶ Resource efficiency ▶ Increased availability	vMotion allows virtual machines to be live-migrated between hosts in a virtual datacenter. DRS determines the initial placement of the virtual machine on the host resources within a cluster and makes recommendations, or automatically migrates the virtual machines to balance resources across all hosts in a cluster.
Resource pools	▶ Resource efficiency	These are used to guarantee, reserve, or limit the virtual machine's CPU, memory, and disk resources.
VMware Fault Tolerance (FT)	▶ Increased availability	FT provides 100 percent uptime for a virtual machine in the event of a host hardware failure. It creates a secondary virtual machine that mirrors all the operations of the primary. In the event of a hardware failure, the secondary virtual machine becomes the primary and a new secondary is created.

VMware technology	Primary benefits	Description
Thin provisioning	▸ Resource efficiency	This allows for storage to be overprovisioned by presenting the configured space to a virtual machine but only consuming the space on the disk that the guest actually requires.
Hot add CPU and memory	▸ Resource efficiency	This allows for the addition of CPU and memory resources to a virtual machine while the virtual machine is running.
Storage vMotion	▸ Portability	This moves virtual machine configuration files and disks between storage locations that have been presented to a host.
vSphere Data Protection (**VDP**)	▸ Disaster recovery	This provides agentless image-level backup and recovery of virtual machines.
vCenter Server	▸ Simplified management	This provides a single management interface to configure and monitor the resources available to virtual datacenters.
vCenter Server Linked Mode	▸ Simplified management	This links multiple vCenter Servers together to allow them to be managed from a single client.
Host Profiles	▸ Simplified management	This maintains consistent configuration and configuration compliance across all the hosts in the environment.

There are many others, and each technology or feature may also have its own set of requirements that must be met in order to be implemented. The purpose here is to show how features or technologies can be mapped to benefits, that can then be mapped to requirements and ultimately mapped into a design. This is helpful in ensuring that the benefits and technologies that virtualization provides, satisfy the design requirements.

Identifying when not to virtualize

Not all applications or server workloads are good candidates for virtualization. It is important that these workloads are identified early on in the design process.

There are a number of reasons a server or application may not be suitable for virtualization. Some of these include the following:

- Vendor support
- Licensing issues
- Specialized hardware dependencies
- High resource demand
- Lack of knowledge or skill sets

A common reason to not virtualize an application or workload is the reluctance of a vendor to support their application in a virtual environment. As virtualization has become more common in the enterprise datacenter, this has become uncommon; but, there are still application vendors that will not support their products once virtualized.

Software and operating systems licensing in a virtual environment can also be a challenge, especially when it comes to physical server to virtual machine conversions. Many physical servers are purchased with **Original Equipment Manufacturer** (**OEM**) licenses, and these licenses, in most cases, cannot be transferred to a virtual environment. Also, many licenses are tied to hardware-specific information, such as interface MAC addresses or drive signatures. Licensing issues can usually be overcome. Many times the primary risk becomes the cost to upgrade or acquire new licensing. As with other potential design risks, it is important that any issues and potential impacts licensing may have on the design be identified early on in the design process.

Some applications may require the use of specialized hardware. Fax boards, serial ports, and security dongles are common examples. There are ways to provide solutions for many of these, but often with the risks associated with the ability to support the application or with the loss of one or more of the potential benefits of virtualizing the application, the better solution may be to leave the application on dedicated physical hardware. Again, it is important that these types of applications be identified very early on in the design process.

Physical servers configured with a large amount of CPU and memory resources where applications are consuming a large amount of these resources may not be good candidates for virtualization. This also holds true for applications with high network utilization and large storage I/O requirements. vSphere 5.1 supports virtual machines configured with up to 64 **Virtual CPUs** (**vCPUs**) and 1 TB of RAM, but the high utilization of these configured resources can have a negative impact on other workloads in the virtual environment. These high-utilization workloads will also require more resources to be reserved for failover. The benefits of virtualizing resource-intensive applications must be weighed against the impact placed on the environment. In many cases, it may be better to leave these applications on dedicated physical hardware.

Many administrators may lack knowledge of the benefits or skills to manage a virtualized datacenter. The administrator of a virtual environment must be well-versed with storage, networking, and virtualization in order to successfully configure, maintain, and monitor a virtual environment. Though this may not necessarily be a reason not to leverage the benefits of a virtualized environment, it can be a substantial risk to the acceptance of a design and the implementation. This is especially true with smaller IT departments where the roles of the server, application, storage, and network administrators are combined.

Each of these can introduce risks in the design. We will discuss how risk impacts the design process in much more detail in *Chapter 2, The Discovery Process*, and *Chapter 3, The Design Factors*.

Becoming a virtual datacenter architect

The virtual datacenter architect or architect is someone who identifies requirements, designs a virtualization solution to meet those requirements, and then oversees the implementation of the solution. Sounds easy enough, right?

How to do it...

The primary role of the architect is to provide solutions that meet customer requirements. At times, this can be difficult since the architect may not always be part of the complete sales process. Many times customers may purchase hardware from other vendors and look to us to help them "make it all work". In situations such as this, the purchased hardware becomes a constraint on the design. Identifying and dealing with constraints and other design factors will be discussed in more detail in *Chapter 2, The Discovery Process*, and *Chapter 3, The Design Factors*.

The architect must also be able to identify requirements, both business and technical, by conducting stakeholder interviews and analyzing current configurations. Once the requirements have been identified, the architect must then map the requirements into a solution by creating a design. This design is then presented to the stakeholders, and if approved, it is implemented. During the implementation phase, the architect ensures that configurations are done to meet the design requirements and the work done stays within the scope of the design.

The architect must also understand best practice. Not just best practice for configuring the hypervisor, but for management, storage, security, and networking. Understanding best practice is the key. The architect not only knows best practice but understands why it is considered best practice. It is also important to understand when to deviate from what is considered best practice.

The large part of an architect's work is "customer facing". This includes conducting interviews with stakeholders to identify requirements and ultimately presenting the design to decision makers. Besides creating a solid solution to match the customer's requirements, it is important that the architect gains and maintains the trust of the project stakeholders. A professional appearance and, more importantly, a professional attitude are both helpful in building this relationship.

Using a holistic approach to datacenter design

The virtual datacenter architect must be able to take a holistic approach to datacenter design. This means that for every decision made, the architect must understand how the environment as a whole will be impacted.

An architect is required to be, at the very least, familiar with all aspects of the datacenter. They must understand how the different components of a datacenter, such as storage, networking, computing, security, and management, are interconnected, as shown in the following diagram:

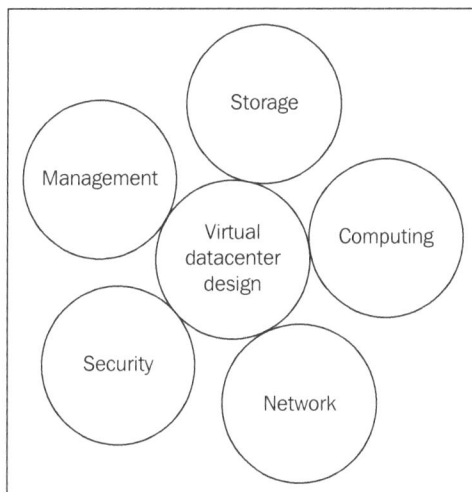

It has become very important to understand how any decision or change will impact the rest of the design. Identifying dependencies becomes an important part of the design process. If a change is made to the network, how are computing, management, and storage resources affected? What other dependencies will this introduce in the design? Failing to take a holistic approach to design can result in unnecessary complications during the design process and potentially costly fixes after the design is implemented.

How to do it...

You have been engaged to design a virtualization solution for a financial organization. The solution you are proposing is using 10 GB **Converged Network Adapters** (**CNA**) to provide connectivity to the organization's network in three 1U rackmount servers. The organization needs to separate a **Virtual Local Area Network** (**VLAN**) that is currently configured to be delivered over the CNA onto a physically separate network to satisfy a new compliance requirement. A 1 GB network will provide sufficient bandwidth for this network, and the network should be highly available. Single points of failure should be minimized.

To support this compliance requirement, you, the architect, must take a holistic approach to the design by answering a number of questions about each design decision, as follows:

- ▶ Are there available network ports in the current rackmount servers or will a network card need to be added? If a card must be added, are there available **Peripheral Component Interconnect** (**PCI**) slots?

- ▶ Will a dual port network card provide sufficient redundancy, or will the network need to be separated across physical cards? Are there onboard network ports available that can be used with a PCI network card to provide in-box redundancy?

- ▶ Has the physical separate switch's hardware been obtained? If not, how long before the equipment is received and deployed? Will this have an impact on the implementation schedule?

- ▶ How will the virtual switch need to be configured to provide the connectivity and redundancy that is required?

How it works...

The impact can be fairly significant, depending on some of the answers. For example, let's say the 1U rackmount server will not support the required network adapters needed to satisfy the requirement and a different 2U rackmount server must be used. This then raises more questions, such as is there sufficient space in the rackmount to support the new server footprint.

What if the requirement had been that the applications connected to this network be virtualized on separate physical server hardware and storage? What parts of the design would have to change? The architect must be able to understand the dependencies of each part of the design and how a change in one place may affect other areas of the design.

As you think through these questions, you should be able to see how a change to a requirement can have a deep impact on many other areas of the design. It becomes very important to identify requirements early on in the design process.

Passing the VMware VCAP-DCD exam

For vSphere 4 and vSphere 5, VMware released advanced exams testing the ability of a person to administer and design complex virtual environments. The exams for vSphere 5 are the **VMware Certified Advanced Professional 5-Data Center Administration** (**VCAP5-DCA**) exam, which focuses on administering a VMware vSphere environment, and the **VMware Certified Advanced Professional 5-Data Center Design** (**VCAP5-DCD**) exam, which focuses on designing a VMware vSphere environment.

The VCAP5-DCD exam tests your ability to design enterprise virtualized environments. To be successful, you must have an in-depth understanding of VMware's core components and the relationship they share with other components of the datacenter, such as storage, networking, and application services, along with a mastery of VMware's datacenter design methodologies and principles. All the exam objectives, including study resources, can be found in the exam blueprint. The exam blueprint can be found on the VCAP5-DCD page at `http://www.vmware.com/go/vcapdcd`.

Getting ready

Before you are eligible to take the VCAP5-DCD exam, you should have obtained the **VMware Certified Professional 5–Data Center Virtualization** (**VCP5-DCV**) certification. Besides the training required for the VCP5-DCV certification, there is no other required training that must be completed in order to sit the VCAP5-DCD exam. When you are ready to schedule your VCAP5-DCD exam, you must submit an exam authorization request to VMware. When you submit the exam authorization request, VMware will verify that you have met the certification prerequisites and provide you with the access necessary to schedule the exam. It typically takes less than two business days to receive the exam authorization.

The exam consists of 100 questions and is scored using a scaled scoring system. You have 4 hours to complete the exam, and the exam has a scoring scale of 100-500 with a minimum passing score of 300. The questions are comprised of a mixture of multiple-choice, drag-and-drop, and design scenarios. Once you have submitted an answer for a question, you are not allowed to return to that question. It is important to note that there is also no way to flag an item for later review.

How to do it...

The VCAP-DCD exam is one of the most challenging exams I have ever taken. Here are a few tips to help you prepare for and successfully sit the VCAP-DCD exam:

> ▶ **Study the material on the exam blueprint**: The exam blueprint lists all the objectives of the exam, along with links to documentation related to each exam objective.

▸ **Schedule your exam**: Scheduling your exam sets a goal date for you to work towards. Setting the date can provide motivation to help you stay on track with your studying efforts.

▸ **Watch the APAC vBrownBag DCD5 Series**: The APAC vBrownBag did a series of podcasts focusing on the VCAP-DCD exam for vSphere 5 exam objectives. These podcasts are very helpful and provide a valuable study resource. The podcast can be found at the following link:

    http://www.professionalvmware.com/brownbags

▸ **Get familiar with the exam design interface**: On VMware's VCAP Certification page for the DCD exam, there is a UI Demo that will help get you familiar with the design interface that is used on the exam.

▸ **Practice time management**: It is very important that you are aware of the amount of time you are taking on a question, and how much time remains. If you get hung up on a multiple-choice question, take your best guess and move on. Conserve time for the more complex, drag-and-drop and design scenario questions.

▸ **Answer every question**: A question left unanswered will be marked incorrect and will not benefit your score in any way. A guess has some chance of being correct.

▸ **Study the material on the exam blueprint**: I know this has already been mentioned once, but it is worth mentioning again. The exam blueprint contains all the testable objectives. Study it!

There's more...

For up-to-date information on the VCAP-DCD certification, to download the exam blueprint, to view the Exam UI Demo, and to book your VCAP-DCD exam, visit the VMware VCAP Certification page at http://www.vmware.com/go/vcap.

2
The Discovery Process

In this chapter, we will cover:

- ▸ Identifying the design factors
- ▸ Identifying stakeholders
- ▸ Conducting stakeholder interviews
- ▸ VMware Capacity Planner
- ▸ Using Windows Performance Monitor
- ▸ Identifying dependencies

Introduction

This chapter will introduce you to the design factors and focus on the discovery phase of the design process.

The following image displays the phases of the design process:

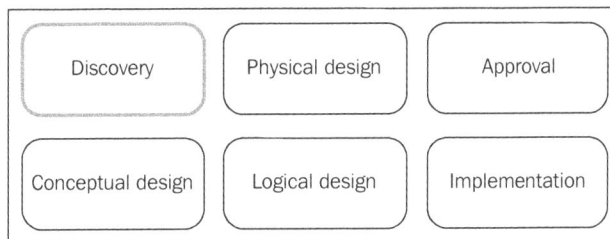

Discovery is the most important phase of the design process. It is also the most time-consuming. The discovery process includes a meeting with the stakeholders to determine business requirements that the design must meet. It also includes current state assessments to determine the technical requirements that the design must satisfy in order to meet the customer requirements, which in turn become the design requirements.

During the discovery process, an architect must interact with many different individuals in an organization to collect the necessary information that is needed to begin creating the conceptual design. Decision makers, strategic planners, facilities and maintenance providers, network administrators, storage administrators, application administrators, and application end users can, in some way, be impacted by or gain some benefit from a virtual datacenter design (some directly and others indirectly). Anyone that may be affected by the design should be identified to be included in the discovery process as early as possible.

The current state assessment is the process of collecting information about the physical resources, such as CPU, memory, and storage, currently supporting the environment. Irrespective of whether the environment is physical servers, virtual servers, or a mix of virtual and physical servers, the current state assessment will identify the total resources available and the total resources actually in use.

There are a number of different tools available to perform a current state assessment of an environment. The tool used often depends on the size of the environment. VMware offers a **Capacity Planner** tool that provides a good way to automate this assessment. For a smaller environment of Windows servers, the Windows **Performance Monitor** (**PerfMon**) utility can be used to collect the current state information. For Linux systems, tools such as top, Kinfocenter, and Zabbix can be used to collect and analyze performance data.

Once the design factors have been identified and accepted, the design process continues with the logical and physical designs. The logical design maps the requirements to the resources required to satisfy the requirements. The physical design then maps the logical design onto the physical hardware that will provide these resources.

Identifying the design factors

The design factors are the primary considerations that influence the design. These factors define the function that the design must accomplish, how it should accomplish it, and what may prevent the design from accomplishing it.

How to do it...

The design factors encompass much more than just the physical resources, such as the CPU, memory, and storage, necessary to run workloads in a virtual environment.

Identifying the design factors needs the following requirements:

- ▶ Functional and nonfunctional requirements
- ▶ Constraints
- ▶ Assumptions
- ▶ Risks

How it works...

Requirements define what a design must do and how it should do it. Requirements can be business or technical. There are two types of requirements: functional and nonfunctional. The requirements should be clearly defined. A good design requirement is verifiable, traceable, feasible, and specific.

Functional requirements specify a specific function of the design or simply what a design must do. Functional requirements can be business or technical requirements. The design must provide a capacity for 10 percent growth over the next three years; this is an example of a functional requirement.

Nonfunctional requirements specify how the design must perform or operate. While a functional requirement defines something that the design must do, the nonfunctional requirement defines how or how well it must be done. System response time is an example of a nonfunctional requirement. Nonfunctional requirements become constraints on the design.

Assumptions are considered valid until they have been proven otherwise. These factors are considered to be true, but further discovery is required to validate them. As part of the design process, assumptions should be documented and then proven or disproven. Sufficient bandwidth being available between different sites to support site-to-site replication is an example of an assumption, if the bandwidth available between the sites or the bandwidth required for replication has not yet been identified.

Constraints place limits on the design choices. Constraints can be business policies or technical limitations. Using a specific vendor for a server's hardware is an example of a technical constraint. The project's budget and the deadlines are also common constraints. Nonfunctional requirements, since they specify how the design must perform or behave, will also become constraints on the design.

Risks may prevent the design from being successful. Risks should be clearly identified to minimize surprises that may prevent the successful implementation of the design. A good design will address and mitigate the risks.

Since the focus of this chapter is on design discovery, I felt it was important to provide this brief introduction to the design factors. We will dive much deeper into determining and defining the requirements, constraints, assumptions, and risks in *Chapter 3, The Design Factors*.

Identifying stakeholders

A stakeholder is anyone who has an interest in or benefits from the design. A virtual datacenter design will have at least some impact on many, if not all, areas of an organization and not just those associated with technology.

How to do it...

Identify the key stakeholders, including the following:

- Project sponsors
- Application owners and providers
- System, network, and storage administrators
- Application users

How it works...

Understanding the role of the stakeholders helps an architect to identify who can provide the information necessary to design a successful virtual datacenter solution. The details of the stakeholders and their roles are specified in the following table:

Stakeholders	Roles
C-level executives	- Strategic planning for the organization - Setting up business policies and goals - Budget approval - Project sponsorship
Business unit managers or directors	- Strategic planning for the business unit - Managing day-to-day operations - Influencing business policies and goals - Make and/or influence decisions
Application owners	- Consumers of IT infrastructure - Document the application and dependencies - Manage the application functions - Provide day-to-day support for the application

Stakeholders	Roles
IT	▶ Technical **Subject Matter Experts** (**SMEs**)
	▶ Network administrators
	▶ System administrators
	▶ Storage administrators
	▶ Help desk
Application or end users	▶ Consumers of application services
	▶ Rely on the infrastructure and applications to accomplish tasks efficiently

Project sponsors are typically C-level executives, vice presidents (VPs), or directors. The project sponsor may also be a committee formed by an organization to evaluate the solutions to business problems or to explore new business opportunities. These stakeholders are often the best resource for obtaining the business requirements that a design must satisfy. If there is a project or a need to explore opportunities, there is a business goal or need driving it. Project sponsors may make the final decision on whether a design has to be approved and accepted for implementation, or they may provide the recommendations for acceptance.

There's more...

Stakeholders or the project team will ultimately be the ones that sign off on or approve the design factors that will be the basis for the logical and physical design. These design factors are identified by analyzing the data collected from the stakeholder interviews and the current state assessments.

The stakeholder's consensus and acceptance of the design factors must be obtained before proceeding with the design process. If you skip this step, you will end up wasting your time and the time of the stakeholders, having to rework areas of the design when requirements are missed, changed, added, or removed.

Define the design factors and obtain acceptance from the project team or stakeholders before taking the next steps in the design process.

Conducting stakeholder interviews

During the discovery process, the primary source of information will be the stakeholder interviews. These interviews can be face-to-face meetings or can be done over the phone (or the Web). Interviews are not only helpful in collecting information about the business needs and technical requirements, but also keep the stakeholders engaged in the project.

How to do it...

Following are examples of the questions that should be asked in order to determine the business requirements that will influence the design:

- What are the business initiatives, challenges, and goals?
- Are there **Service-Level Agreements** (**SLAs**) in place? What are they?
- What are the **Recovery Time Objective** (**RTO**) and **Recovery Point Objective** (**RPO**) requirements?
- Are there any compliance requirements?
- Who are the SMEs associated with the project?
- Who are the stakeholders?
- Who are the decision makers?
- Are there deadlines that the project must meet?
- Is there a budget for the project? What is the budget for the project?

Following are examples of the questions that should be asked in order to determine the technical requirements that will influence the design:

- Are there any current issues or technical pain points within the environment?
- What are the technology initiatives, challenges, and goals?
- How many servers will be virtualized as part of this project?
- Is there a preferred vendor for the server, network, or storage?
- Have any servers already been virtualized? What hypervisor is being used to host the already-virtualized servers?
- What type of growth is expected over the next 3-5 years?
- What **Operation-Level Agreements** (**OLAs**) are in place?
- Is there a current network, system, storage, application documentation?

How it works...

Meetings and interviews with stakeholders should maintain some type of structure or formality. Even if it is just a quick call, you should have some type of agenda. I know this may sound like overkill, but it will help you keep the call or meeting on track and, more importantly, help to ensure that you collect the information you need from the call or meeting.

There are some key items that will help determine the design factors, which are explained as follows:

- **Service-Level Agreements (SLAs)**: These are a part of a service contract where a service, its availability (uptime and access), and its performance (application response and transaction processing) are defined
- **Service-Level Objective (SLO)**: This defines specific objectives that must be achieved as part of the SLA
- **Recovery Time Objective (RTO)**: This is the amount of time in which a service must be restored after a disruption or disaster
- **Recovery Point Objective (RPO)**: This is the maximum amount of data loss acceptable due to a disruption or disaster
- **Operation-Level Agreements (OLAs)**: This is an internal agreement that defines relationships between support groups

Do not expect to complete the discovery in a single meeting or interview, especially for a large enterprise project. There will be follow-up questions that may need to be asked, and there will likely be questions that require more research to be answered.

In situations where more research is required, make sure that someone has been assigned with the responsibility to complete the research. Set an expectation on when the research should be completed and the information should be available. You want to avoid the "I thought so-and-so was getting that" situations and also keep the discovery process moving forward.

VMware Capacity Planner

VMware's Capacity Planner is an inventory and planning tool available to VMware partner organizations, which collects resource utilization information from systems, analyzes the data against industry-standard reference data, and provides the information needed to successfully consolidate the servers into a virtualized environment.

How to do it...

Follow these steps to complete a Capacity Planner engagement:

1. Determine the amount of time for which the Capacity Planner engagement should run based on the business cycle.

2. Choose the type of Capacity Planner assessment to be run: a **Consolidation Estimate** (**CE**) or a **Capacity Assessment** (**CA**).

3. Deploy the Capacity Planner collector in the environment to be assessed.

4. Verify whether the collector is collecting performance metrics for the systems to be analyzed.

5. Collect metrics for the duration of the business cycle.

6. Generate Capacity Planner reports.

How it works...

A Capacity Planner engagement should typically run for at least 30 days to ensure that it covers a complete monthly business cycle. Thirty days is considered typical since this covers a monthly business cycle where the demand for resources increases during the end-of-month or beginning-of-month processing. It is important that the Capacity Planner capture these increases. The time frame for a Capacity Planner engagement can vary depending on the size and nature of the business.

There are two types of Capacity Planner assessments: the CE and the CA. The CE assessment provides the sizing estimates of the current environment, while the CA assessment provides a more detailed analysis of the current environment. The CE assessment helps demonstrate what can be achieved by virtualizing physical workloads, and the CA assessment provides guidance on how systems may be virtualized.

A Capacity Planner collector is installed in the environment that is being assessed. The collector runs as a Windows service and is configured using the VMware Capacity Planner Data Manager. The collector must be installed on a Windows machine, but inventory and performance data can be collected from both Windows and Linux/Unix servers. More than one collector may need to be installed for larger environments. A single collector can collect data from a maximum of 500 systems. The following screenshot depicts the VMware Capacity Planner Data Manager:

The collector or collectors discover systems in the environment and collect inventory and performance data from the systems. The inventory includes information about the installed physical hardware, operating systems, and installed software.

> [💡 If running the VMware Capacity Planner Data Manager on a Windows 7 workstation, use **Run as Administrator**.]

Performance data metrics are collected on CPU utilization, RAM utilization, disk capacity, and disk I/O. This data is then sent securely to the VMware Capacity Planner Dashboard at `https://optimize.vmware.com/` to be analyzed. The following screenshot shows the VMware Capacity Planner Data Manager processor utilization report:

System Name	Current Value	Previous Val...	Running Avg.	Arith. Mean	Geom. Mean	Min	Max
DB-CITRIX	0.646	3.217	0.779	0.304	0.116	0.000	9.155
XA1	29.027	0.126	4.713	1.656	0.036	0.000	40.613
VC51	0.736	0.162	0.437	0.273	0.241	0.000	1.750
PVS1	0.427	1.628	0.760	0.250	0.009	0.000	5.019
DC	3.909	8.181	3.269	1.373	0.687	0.000	18.288
ENTERPRISEA	99.255	55.973	18.174	6.749	0.301	0.000	100.000
DTC1	0.620	2.267	1.996	0.976	0.664	0.000	11.924
SQLDB	0.354	0.255	0.521	0.170	0.007	0.000	4.370
VC1	29.420		29.420	29.420	29.420	9.920	55.355

% Total Processor Utilization

Number of Records: 9 of 9 Time Left: Done

Export... Set Account... Activate Deactivate Close

There can be some challenges to setting up the VMware Capacity Planner. Issues with setting up the correct credentials required for data collection and configuring Windows Firewall and services to allow the data collection are common issues that may be encountered.

The following table includes the services and ports that must be open on target systems to allow the Capacity Planner collector to collect data:

Service	Port
Remote Procedure Call (**RPC**)	TCP/135
NetBIOS Name Service (**NBNS**)	TCP/137
NetBIOS Datagram Service (**NBDS**)	TCP/138
NetBIOS Session Service (**NBSS**)	TCP/139
Microsoft-DS	TCP/445
Secure Shell (**SSH**) (Unix/Linux only)	TCP/22

In order to collect data from Windows systems, **Windows Management Instrumentation** (**WMI**), Remote Registry, and PerfMon must be enabled on the target system. For data collection on Linux or Unix systems, port 22 must be open and the **Secure Shell Daemon** (**SSHD**) must be running. Account credentials provided must have at least local administrator rights on the target systems.

There's more...

Once the inventory and performance data has been collected, the results can be analyzed and reports can be generated. Some of this information can be viewed and exported from the VMware Capacity Planner Data Manager, but detailed analysis reports are generated from the VMware Capacity Planner Dashboard at the following link:

```
https://optimize.vmware.com/
```

If server hardware constraints have been identified during the discovery process, report settings can be adjusted. These constraints will then be applied to the Capacity Planner reporting to determine and show the consolidation ratios that can be obtained using the different hardware configurations. The following screenshot shows the report settings:

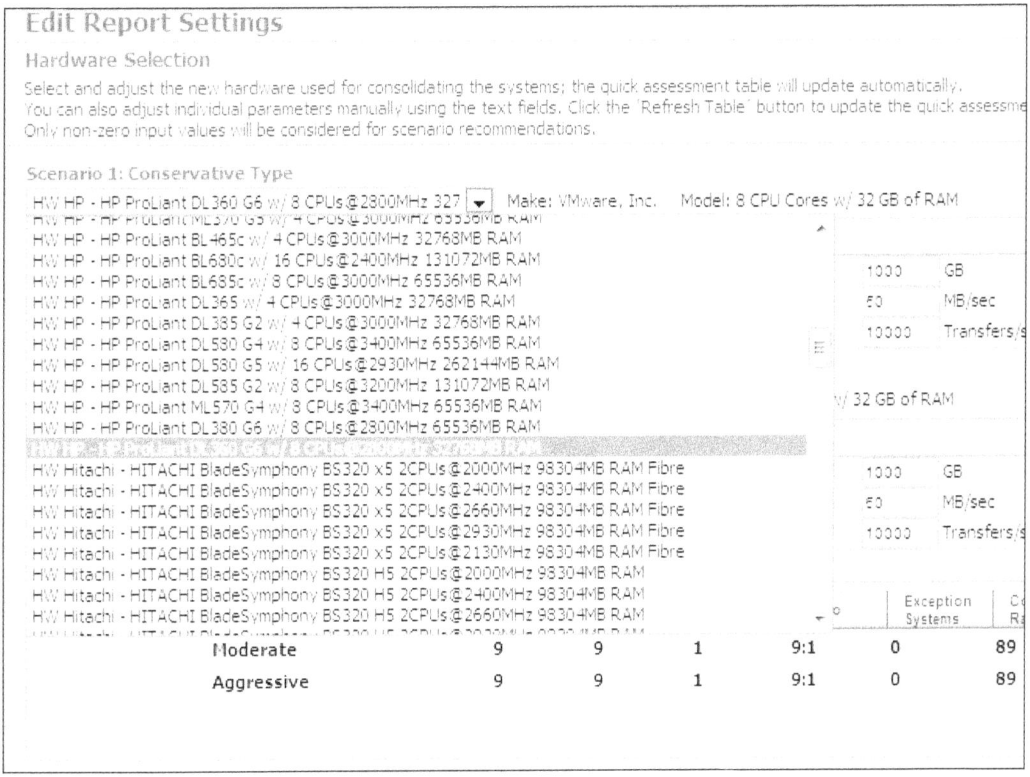

The reports that are available include the Progress Report, which provides an overview of the status of the assessment; the Executive Summary Presentation, which provides a high-level summary of the assessment; and the Assessment Report, which provides information on consolidation ratios and recommendations. Custom reports can also be generated. The following screenshot shows the consolidation recommendations:

System Consolidation Recommendation

Before Virtualization			With VMware Virtualization						
Total Systems	Eligible Systems	Consolidation Scenario and Platform	ESX Hosts	ESX CPU Utilization	ESX Memory Utilization	Average Memory Per VM	Racks Saved	Eligible System Consolidation Ratio	Total System Consolidation Ratio
9	9	Conservative Type	1	23.04%	56.27%	3.25 GB	0	89%	89%
9	9	Aggressive Type	1	23.04%	56.27%	3.25 GB	0	89%	89%

Conservative Type

Make: VMware, Inc.
Model: 8 CPU Cores w/ 32 GB of RAM
CPU: 8
Memory: 32 GB

Aggressive Type

Make: VMware, Inc.
Model: 8 CPU Cores w/ 32 GB of RAM
CPU: 8
Memory: 32 GB

Using Windows Performance Monitor

The Microsoft Windows PerfMon can be used to collect performance information, such as CPU utilization, memory utilization, and disk I/O utilization of the Windows servers.

How to do it...

In this example, Microsoft Windows PerfMon is used to collect disk I/O metrics using the following steps:

1. Open **Performance Monitor** and use the **Data Collector Set** wizard to create a user-defined data collector as displayed in the following screenshot:

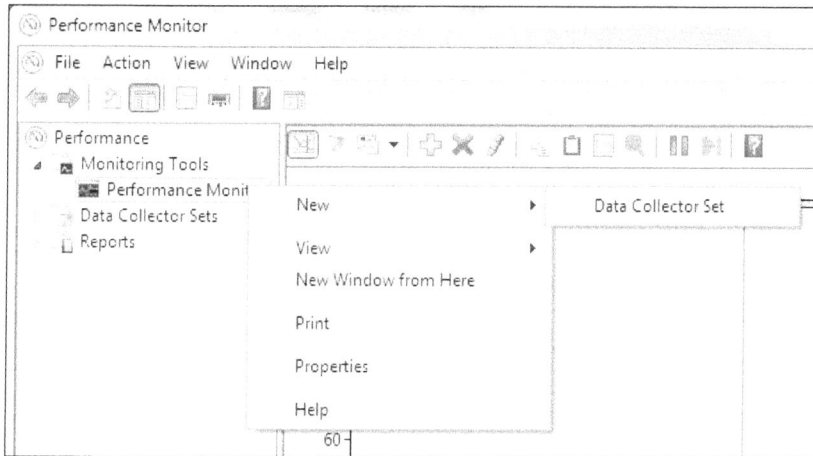

2. Once the **Data Collector Set** application has been created, add a new **Data Collector** to the **Data Collector Set** as shown in the following screenshot:

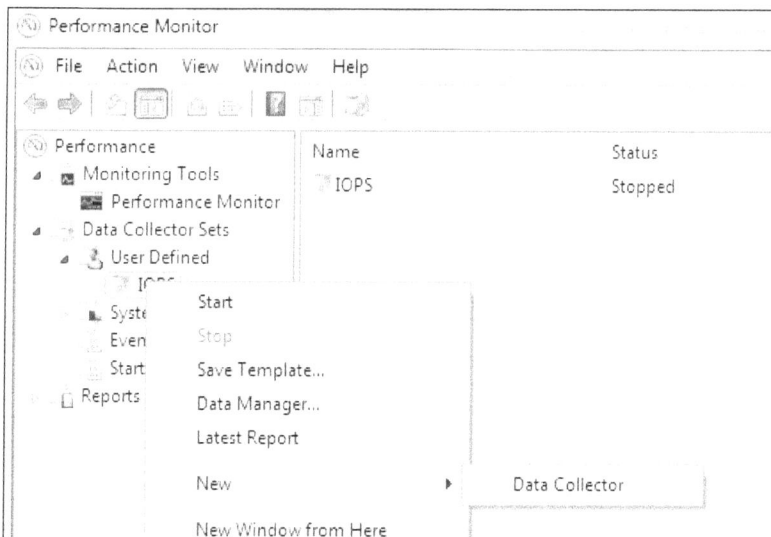

3. Name the new **Data Collector** and select the **Performance counter data collector** radio button as shown in the following screenshot:

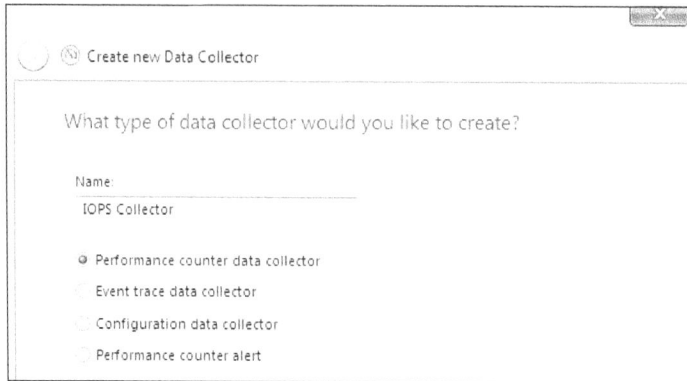

Add the following counters for the `object _Total` instance to the data collector:

- ❏ `\LogicalDisk\Avg. Disk Sec/Read`
- ❏ `\LogicalDisk\Avg. Disk Sec/Write`
- ❏ `\LogicalDisk\Disk Bytes/Sec`
- ❏ `\LogicalDisk\Disk Reads/Sec`
- ❏ `\LogicalDisk\Disk Writes/Sec`
- ❏ `\LogicalDisk\Split IO/sec`
- ❏ `\LogicalDisk\Disk Transfers/sec`

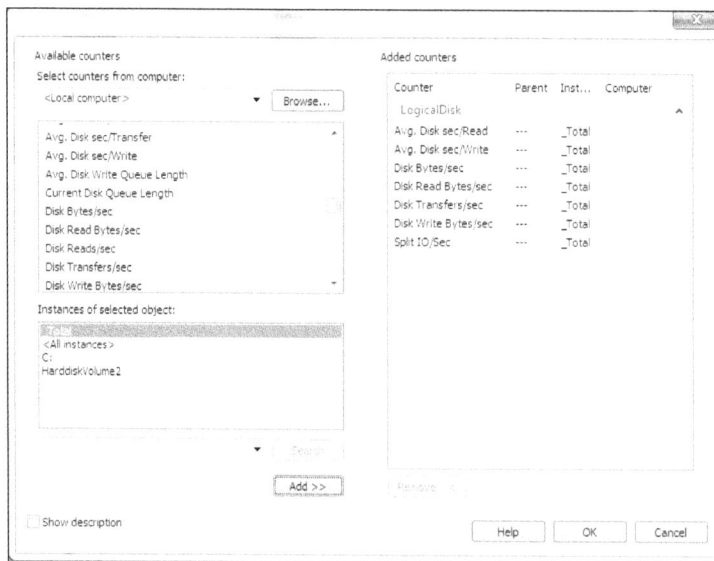

4. Right-click on the new Data Collector set, select the **Stop Condition** tab, and change the stop condition to the period of time for which you want to monitor the **Input/Output Operations Per Second** (**IOPS**), as shown in the following screenshot:

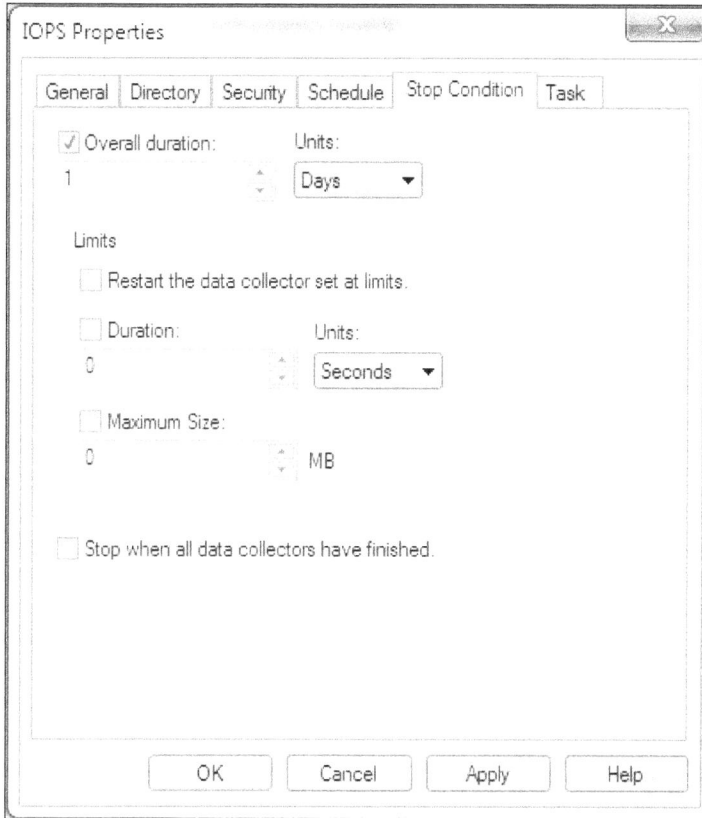

5. Data collection for the **Data Collector Set** can be configured to start manually or can be scheduled to start at a future date or time. The following screenshot displays the setting of a schedule for the **Data Collector Set**:

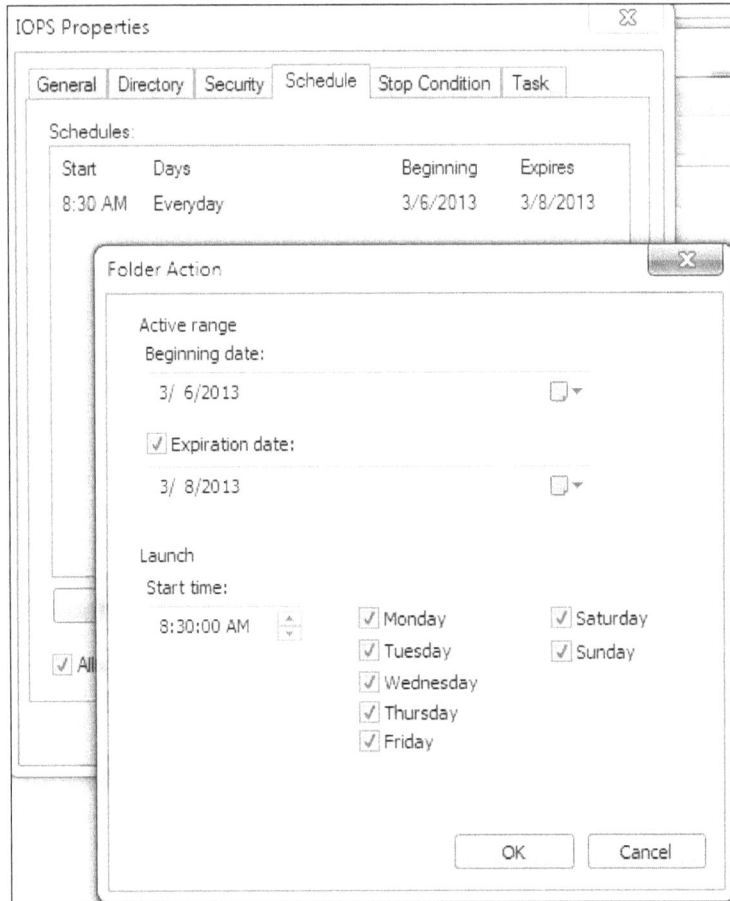

IOPS Properties	☒

| General | Directory | Security | Schedule | Stop Condition | Task |

Schedules:

Start	Days		Beginning	Expires
8:30 AM	Everyday		3/6/2013	3/8/2013

Folder Action ☒

Active range
Beginning date:

3/ 6/2013

☑ Expiration date:

3/ 8/2013

Launch
Start time:

8:30:00 AM

☑ Monday	☑ Saturday
☑ Tuesday	☑ Sunday
☑ Wednesday	
☑ Thursday	
☑ Friday	

OK   Cancel

6. Once the collection process has been completed, you can view the report using the **Reports** section of **Performance Monitor**. The following screenshot shows a sample report:

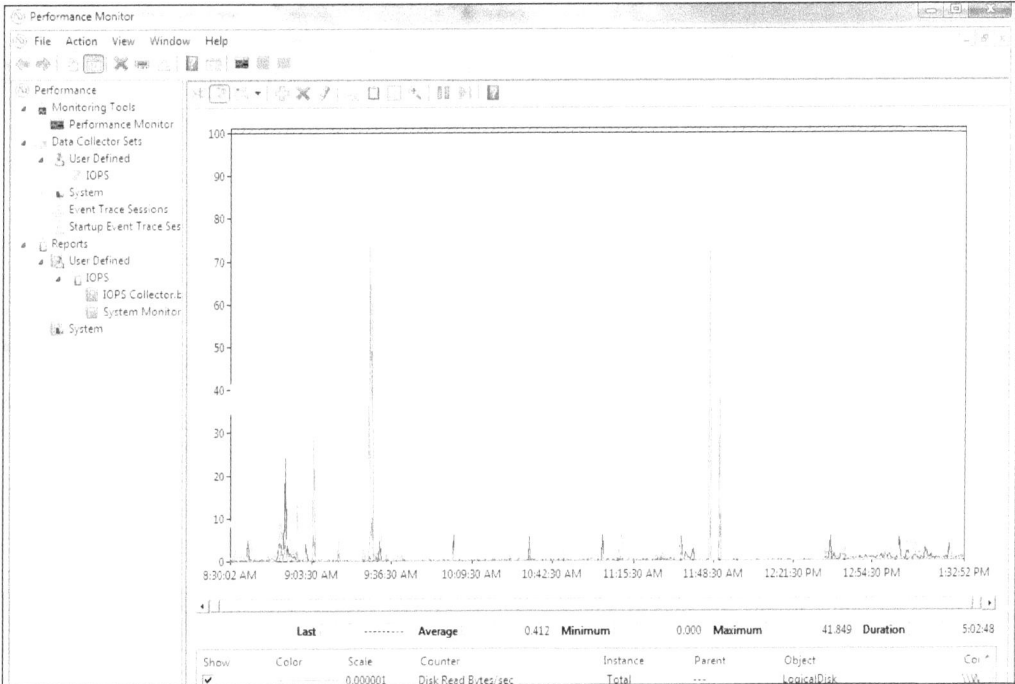

7. A template of the **Data Collector Set** application can be created in order to easily import the **Data Collector Set** on other servers/workstations. This is shown in the following screenshot:

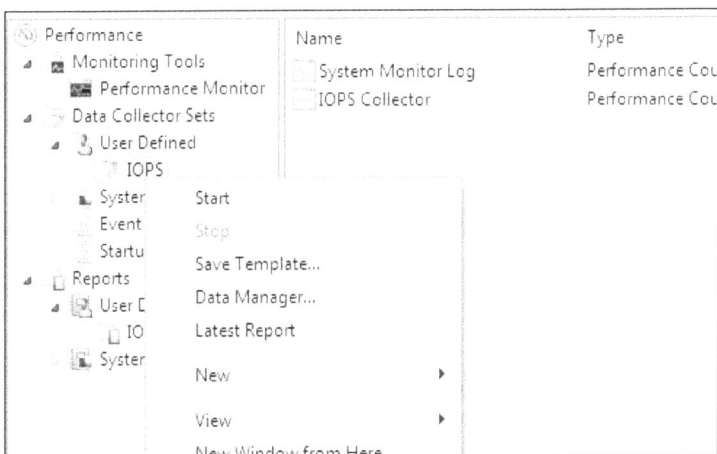

How it works...

The total number of IOPS and the I/O profile of a server are necessary to architect the storage required for a virtualized environment correctly. The IOPS and I/O profile are helpful in determining which **Redundant Array of Independent Disks** (**RAID**) level to use with the number of and the type of disk to be used in order to support the server storage workload.

Windows PerfMon can also be configured to collect metrics associated with CPU and memory usage by simply adding the associated counters to the Data Collector Set.

There's more...

Most organizations will have some form of network-or resource-monitoring system in place, such as Nagios, SolarWinds, or Splunk. The information monitored and collected by these systems will be useful for the current state assessments. The SMEs should be asked if there is monitoring in place and for access to the data collected by these systems.

Many vendors also perform free infrastructure assessments. Often, these free assessments are not thorough enough to provide the details necessary for a complete current state assessment, but they can provide some good information. Again, the project SMEs will be asked if any type of assessments have been done.

Identifying dependencies

A dependency is a relationship among systems or services. During the discovery process, dependencies should be identified and documented. In *Chapter 1, The Virtual Datacenter*, we discussed the importance of taking a holistic view when designing a virtualized environment. Identifying dependencies is the key to the holistic approach of designing.

How to do it...

An architect must identify dependencies in order to understand what effect a design decision or change may have on other services. The architect should identify the following dependencies:

- Identify physical infrastructure dependencies
- Identify application and service dependencies

How it works...

Dependencies can be service-to-service; for example, a web application depends on a frontend web server and a backend database. Dependencies can be service-to-infrastructure; for example, the web application requires a static IP address and a minimum of 10 MB of network bandwidth.

Physical and infrastructure dependencies are generally easier to discover and are commonly documented. Applications will have dependencies, which include server resources, network resources, and storage resources. Infrastructure dependencies that are not documented are often readily discovered as part of the current state assessment. The following table is an example of how physical application dependencies can be documented.

Application	OS	CPU cores	Speed (GHz)	RAM (GB)	Network (GBps)	Network (VLAN)	Storage
IIS	Win2k8 R2	4	2.7	16	1	22	50 GB
SQL database	Win2k8 R2	8	2.7	32	1	22	1 TB

Service-to-service or application-to-service dependencies can be a bit more difficult to discover. Application owners, application developers, application documentation, and application vendors will be the best sources for determining these dependencies.

The following diagram is an example of how service dependencies can be mapped and documented:

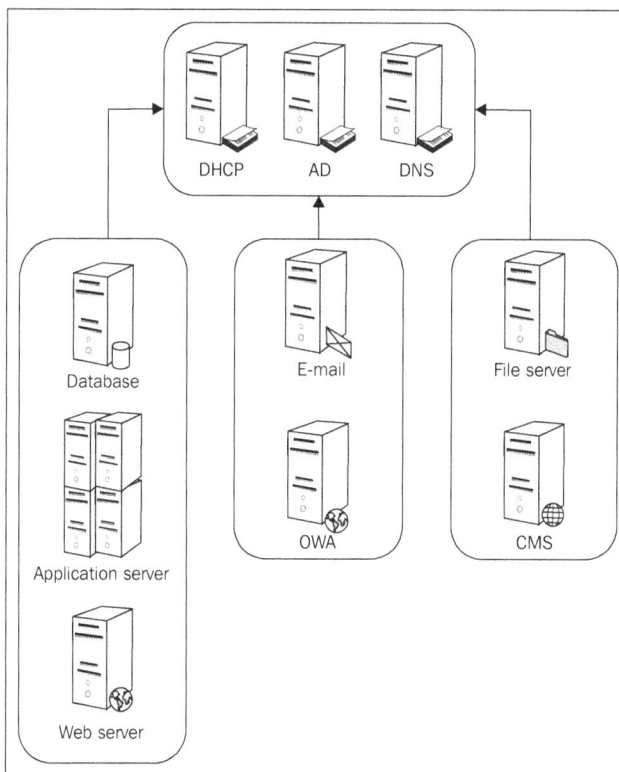

Understanding the dependencies will help an architect to understand how a change made to one area of the design may have an effect on another area of the design. Mapping and documenting application dependencies will provide the necessary information to properly design a solution for business continuity and disaster recovery. Understanding the dependencies will also aid in troubleshooting issues with the design implementation.

Beware that there may be undocumented dependencies that are not easily discovered. This can often be a risk to the design, especially in an organization with a legacy of unsupported applications or applications developed in-house that have not been properly documented.

I have seen issues where a specific configuration such as an IP address or a file location has been hardcoded into an application and not documented. A change is made to the environment and hence the application becomes unavailable. Dependencies of this type can be extremely difficult to plan for and discover.

3
The Design Factors

In this chapter, we will cover:

- ▸ Identifying design requirements
- ▸ Identifying design constraints
- ▸ Making design assumptions
- ▸ Identifying design risks
- ▸ Creating the conceptual design

Introduction

During the discovery process, information is collected on the business and technical goals of the virtualization project. This information must be analyzed in order to determine the design factors.

The design factors that must be determined are as follows:

- ▸ Requirements
- ▸ Constraints
- ▸ Assumptions
- ▸ Risks

Determining the requirements, making and proving assumptions, determining constraints, and identifying risks form the conceptual design. Business and technical design factors identified as part of the conceptual design will be mapped to the resources that are necessary to satisfy them during the logical design process.

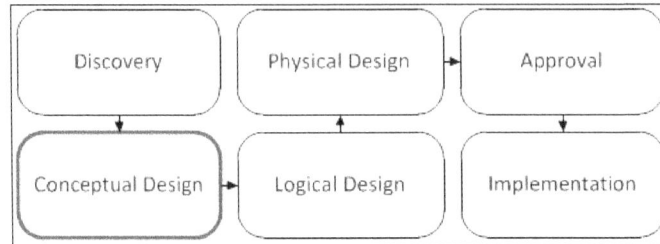

```
┌──────────────┐   ┌──────────────────┐   ┌──────────────┐
│              │   │                  │   │              │
│  Discovery   │   │ Physical Design  │◀──│   Approval   │
│              │   │                  │   │              │
└──────┬───────┘   └─────────▲────────┘   └──────▲───────┘
       │                     │                   │
       ▼                     │                   ▼
┌──────────────┐   ┌──────────────────┐   ┌──────────────┐
│              │   │                  │   │              │
│ Conceptual   │──▶│  Logical Design  │   │Implementation│
│   Design     │   │                  │   │              │
└──────────────┘   └──────────────────┘   └──────────────┘
```

In our example design, after conducting interviews with stakeholders and performing technical assessments of the environment, the following information has been collected about the project's goals, current environment, and business factors that will influence the design:

▶ Currently, there are 100 physical servers, each hosting a single application. Each application services 10 customers.

▶ The business expects to add 50 new customers over the next year.

▶ Support growth over the next five years.

▶ Application uptime and accessibility is very important.

▶ Consolidate physical servers to reduce hardware costs associated with the maintenance and deployment of new application servers.

▶ Not more than 20 application servers or 200 customers should be affected by a hardware failure.

▶ There should be a one-hour maintenance window each month for application and hardware maintenance. Hardware maintenance is currently a challenge. Since hardware and application maintenance cannot be performed at the same time, the maintenance window does not typically provide the time required to perform both application and hardware maintenance.

▶ Application servers run Microsoft Windows 2008 R2 as the operating system.

▶ Each application server is configured with 8 GB of memory. The peak usage of a single application server is approximately 65 percent or approximately 5.2 GB.

▶ Each application server is configured with two dual-core 2.7 GHz processors. The peak usage of a single application server is approximately 10 percent of the total or approximately 1 GHz.

▶ Each application server is configured with 100 GB of disk space. Peak disk capacity usage of a single application server is approximately 65 percent of the total or 65 GB. Peak disk performance of a single application server is 50 IOPS with an I/O profile of 90 percent read and 10 percent write.

- Currently, the stakeholders are using HP DL360 servers. The infrastructure team is very familiar with the management and maintenance of these servers and wants to continue using them.

- Currently, there is no shared storage. The current system and infrastructure administrators are unfamiliar with the shared storage concepts and protocols.

- Cisco switches are used for network connectivity. Separate VLANs exist for management connectivity and production application connectivity.

- Currently, each physical server contains a single gigabit network interface card. Peak network usage is 10 Mbps.

- Server logs are auditable and must be retained for six months. All logs should also be sent to a central Syslog server that is already in place.

- If an application server fails, the current recovery time is around 8 hours. The solution should reduce this time to less than 4 hours.

- The management team expects the implementation to be completed before the third quarter.

- There is an approved project budget of $200,000.

In this chapter, we will use this information to determine the design factors in order to create the conceptual design. Throughout the design process, each design decision is mapped back to these design factors.

Identifying design requirements

The design requirements specify the functions that the design must perform and the objectives that the design must meet.

There are two types of requirements, functional requirements and nonfunctional requirements. Functional requirements specify the objectives or functions that a design must meet. Nonfunctional requirements define how the design accomplishes the functional requirements.

Typical functional requirements include the following:

- Business goals
- Business rules
- Legal, regulatory, and compliance requirements
- Application system requirements
- Technical requirements
- Administrative functions

Typical nonfunctional requirements include the following:

- ▸ Performance
- ▸ Security
- ▸ Capacity
- ▸ Availability
- ▸ Manageability
- ▸ Recoverability

When identifying and defining the requirements, separate the functional requirements from the nonfunctional requirements; nonfunctional requirements are design constraints and will be documented separately.

Since functional requirements define what the design must accomplish, once identified and approved, these requirements typically cannot be easily changed during the design process.

How to do it...

1. Analyze the business and technical information collected during the discovery process.
2. Determine the functional and nonfunctional requirements of the design.
3. Document the design requirements.

How it works...

When defining the requirements, each requirement should be clearly stated and specified. Define requirements individually; multiple requirements should not be combined into a single requirement.

During the discovery process, the following information about the current size of the existing environment was identified:

- ▸ Currently, there are 100 physical servers, each hosting a single application. Each application services 10 customers.
- ▸ Not more than 20 application servers or 200 customers should be affected by a hardware failure.
- ▸ Consolidate physical servers to reduce the hardware costs associated with maintaining and refreshing the hardware of the existing application servers.

One of the goals of the project is to consolidate the physical servers in order to reduce hardware costs. An example design requirement to support this might be as follows:

- ▸ Consolidate existing physical servers

This requirement is vague and with the information available from the discovery, the requirement should be more specific. Based on the number of existing physical servers and the maximum number of customers that should be impacted during a hardware failure, a better requirement example may be as follows:

▸ Consolidate the existing 100 physical application servers down to five servers

Information about the expected growth of the environment was also discovered:

▸ The business expects to add 50 new customers each year
▸ Support growth over the next five years

Based on this information, there is a requirement that the environment must be designed to provide the capacity necessary to support future growth. An example requirement to support this might be:

▸ Provide sufficient capacity to support growth

Again this requirement is very vague and does not provide any information about how much the growth will be or over what period of time is growth expected. From the discovery, it is known that the business expects to add 50 new customers over the next year. Each server hosts a single application, which will provide service for 10 customers. The solution should support growth over the next five years.

Using this information, a requirement that specifies the growth that should be supported and the time period over which this growth is expected is as follows:

▸ Provide capacity to support growth for 25 additional application servers over the next five years

The architect can also determine the availability of requirements for hardware maintenance and application resiliency:

▸ A one-hour maintenance window each month for application and hardware maintenance. Hardware maintenance is currently a challenge. Since hardware and application maintenance cannot be performed at the same time, the maintenance window does not typically provide the time required to perform both application and hardware maintenance.
▸ Application uptime and accessibility is very important.
▸ Not more than 20 application servers or 200 customers should be affected by a hardware failure.

From this information, the requirement that might be identified is that the server hardware maintenance should not affect application uptime, and redundancy should be maintained during hardware maintenance operations.

The problem with this requirement is that it includes two separate requirements; one requirement is for application uptime, and another requirement is for redundancy. These requirements should be split into two individual requirements.

> Server hardware maintenance should not affect application uptime.
>
> Provide *N+2* redundancy to support a hardware failure during normal and maintenance operations.

There's more...

Once the functional requirements have been identified and defined, the requirements should be recorded in the design documentation as part of the conceptual design. There are a number of formats that can be used, such as bulleted lists and numbered lists, but a simple table works well. Assigning an ID to each requirement makes it easier to reference the requirement later in the design document.

ID	Requirement
R001	Consolidate the existing 100 physical application servers down to five servers
R002	Provide capacity to support growth for 25 additional application servers over the next five years
R003	Server hardware maintenance should not affect application uptime
R004	Provide *N+2* redundancy to support a hardware failure during normal and maintenance operations

Identifying design constraints

The design constraints are factors that restrict the options the architect can use to satisfy the design requirements. Once the functional and nonfunctional requirements have been identified, they are separated. The nonfunctional requirements that define how requirements must be satisfied become the constraints on the design.

Design constraints include the following:

- Technology constraints such as hardware vendors, software solutions, and protocols
- Operational constraints such as performance and accessibility
- Financial constraints such as budgets

Unlike functional requirements, the constraints and nonfunctional requirements may change during the design process. This holds true especially if the constraint introduces risks into the design. For example, if an identified constraint that requires a specific model of hardware to be used prevents the design from satisfying a functional requirement, the constraint may need to be changed or adjusted.

How to do it...

1. Analyze the business and technical information collected during the discovery process.
2. Determine the nonfunctional requirements of the design.
   - ❑ Nonfunctional requirements are constraints on the design
3. Identify any other constraints on the design.
4. Document the design constraints.

How it works...

As with functional requirements, when defining the nonfunctional requirements or constraints, they should be clearly stated and specified. Define each constraint individually; do not combine multiple nonfunctional requirements into a single constraint.

- ▸ Currently, HP DL360 servers are used. The infrastructure team is very familiar with the management and maintenance of these servers and wants to continue using them.

This statement does not identify something the design must do. It is placing a constraint on the design by providing a specific type of hardware that should be used. Following is an example of the constraint that can be formed from this statement:

- ▸ HP DL360 servers should be used for compute resources

Budgetary constraints affect nearly all the projects. There will likely be a limit on the amount of money a company will want to spend to accomplish a goal.

> If a budget has not been established for a project, it is likely that the business has not committed to the project. Beware of the infinite budget.

During the design discovery, the following budget was identified for this project:

- ▸ There is an approved project budget of $200,000

This budget constraint can simply be stated as: A project budget of $200,000.

Operational constraints are also common. Often, there will be existing processes or policies in place that will need to be factored into the design. Often, you will need to accommodate the existing monitoring and management applications in the design. An example of an operational requirement is as follows:

> ▸ Server logs are auditable and must be retained for six months. All logs should also be sent to a central Syslog server that is already in place.

Here, a functional and nonfunctional requirement can be identified. The functional requirement is that the server logs are auditable and must be retained for six months. This functional requirement defines something the design must do, but there is also a constraint on how the design must accomplish this, and that is by using Syslog to send logs to a central server. Based on this information, the constraint is as follows:

> ▸ Syslog should be used to send server logs to an existing central Syslog server

There's more...

Constraints should be documented as part of the conceptual design. Just as you used a table to document the design requirements, using a simple table works well when documenting the design constraints. Each constraint is assigned an ID, so it can be easily referenced later in the design document.

ID	Constraint
C001	HP DL360 servers should be used for compute resources
C002	A project budget of $200,000
C003	Syslog should be used to send server logs to an existing central Syslog server

Making design assumptions

Assumptions are made by the architect and have not yet been validated. Assumptions are accepted as a fact until they have been validated or not. As part of the design process, each assumption needs to be validated as a fact. If an assumption cannot be validated, a risk will be introduced into the design.

How to do it...

Any assumptions that are made will need to be defined and documented as follows:

1. Identify any assumptions that have been made about the design.
2. Document the design assumptions.

How it works...

Common assumptions relate to power, space, and cooling. A common example of an assumption that an architect may make is as follows:

- ▸ There is sufficient power, cooling, and floor/rack space available in the datacenter to support both the existing and consolidated environment during the migration

When working through the physical design, the power, cooling, and space requirements will need to be identified and the assumption validated. A goal of this project is to consolidate the existing physical servers. The overall need for power, cooling, and space will be reduced once the project is complete, But enough of these resources need to be available to support both the existing physical environment and the new consolidated environment during the consolidation process.

A requirement was identified based on the discovery information to provide *N+2* redundancy.

R004	Provide *N+2* redundancy to support a hardware failure during normal and maintenance operations

This requirement was defined based on the following discovery information:

- ▸ A one-hour maintenance window each month for application and hardware maintenance. Hardware maintenance is currently a challenge. Since hardware and application maintenance cannot be performed at the same time, the maintenance window does not typically provide the time necessary to perform both application and hardware maintenance.
- ▸ Application uptime and accessibility is very important.

What assumption may have been made when defining this requirement?

An assumption was made based on the importance of application uptime and accessibility that there should be sufficient resources to provide redundancy not only during normal operations but also in the event of a host failure, when a host may be unavailable due to maintenance being performed.

- ▸ Resources should be provided to support a host failure during both normal and host maintenance operations

A requirement to support growth in the environment was also defined:

- ▸ The business expects to add 50 new customers over the next year
- ▸ Support growth over the next five years

R002	Provide capacity to support growth for 25 additional application servers over the next five years

An expected growth of 50 customers over the next year was identified, but the design is expected to support growth over the next five years. To create this requirement, an assumption was made that growth would be the same over years two through five.

> ▶ Growth is calculated based on the addition of 50 new customers each year over the next five years.

The company may have a forecast for growth that exceeds this. If this assumption is incorrect, the design may not meet the defined requirement.

There's more...

Assumptions should be documented in the design document. As with documenting design requirements and constraints, use a table for this. Each assumption is assigned an ID, so that it can be easily referenced later in the design document.

ID	Assumption
A001	Sufficient power, cooling, and floor/rack space is available in the datacenter to support the existing and consolidated environment during the migration
A002	Resources should be provided to support a host failure during both normal and maintenance operations
A003	Growth is calculated based on the addition of 50 new customers each year over the next five years

Identifying design risks

Risks include anything that may prevent the design from satisfying the requirements.

Design risks include the following:

> ▶ Technical risks
>
> ▶ Operational risks
>
> ▶ Financial risks

Risks are often introduced through constraints or assumptions that have not been proven. Risks resulting from assumptions are mitigated by validating them.

How to do it...

Throughout the design process, design decisions should mitigate or minimize risks by following this process:

1. Identify any risks associated with the design requirements or assumptions.

2. Validate assumptions to reduce the risks associated with them.

3. Determine how design decisions will help mitigate or minimize risks.

How it works...

There are a few risks in the design based on the discovery information, assumption, and constraints.

As part of the discovery process, the following risk was noted:

▸   Currently, there is no shared storage. The current system and infrastructure administrators are unfamiliar with the shared storage concepts and protocols.

These operational risks were identified during discovery. The operational risks can be minimized by providing implementation and operational documentation.

There is a technical constraint that may also introduce risks is as follows:

C001	HP DL360 servers should be used for compute resources

This constraint may introduce some risks to the environment if the capabilities of the HP DL360 servers are not able to fulfill the requirements. Can the servers be configured with the processing and memory required by the requirements? Are there enough expansion slots to support the number of network ports or HBAs required? It may be necessary to remove or change this constraint if the HP DL360 server is not able to fulfill the technical requirements of the design.

An assumption was also made with regards to the growth of the environment over the next five years.

▸   Growth is calculated based on the addition of 50 new customers each year over the next five years

If this assumption is not validated and growth is forecasted by the company to be higher in two to five years, the design will be at risk to not meet the growth requirements. Validating this assumption will mitigate this risk.

Creating the conceptual design

The conceptual design is created with the documentation of the requirements, constraints, and assumptions. The design documentation should include a list of each of the design factors. The conceptual design guides the design. All logical and physical design elements can be mapped back to the conceptual design in order to provide justifications for design decisions.

How to do it...

To create the conceptual design, follow the given steps:

1. Use the design factors to form the conceptual design.
2. Organize the design factors to be easily referenced during the design process.
3. Create high-level diagrams that document the functional blocks of the design.

How it works...

The conceptual design should include a brief overview that describes the key goals of the project and any factors that may drive the business decisions related to the project. The conceptual design includes all the identified requirements, constraints, and assumptions.

The following paragraphs explain an example of conceptual design:

The primary goal of this project is to lower hardware cost through the consolidation of physical application servers. The design will increase application uptime and resiliency and reduce application recovery time.

The design will attempt to adhere to the standards and best practices when these align with the requirements and constraints of the design.

Design requirements

Requirements are the key demands on the design. The design requirements are as follows:

ID	Requirement
R001	Consolidate the existing 100 physical application servers down to five servers
R002	Provide capacity to support growth for 25 additional application servers over the next five years
R003	Server hardware maintenance should not affect application uptime
R004	Provide $N+2$ redundancy to support hardware failure during normal and maintenance operations

Design constraints

Constraints limit the logical decisions and physical specifications. Constraints may or may not align with the design objectives. The design constraints are as follows:

ID	Constraint
C001	HP DL360 servers should be used for compute resources
C002	A project budget of $200,000
C003	Syslog should be used to send server logs to an existing central Syslog server

Assumptions

Assumptions are the expectations of a system that have not yet been confirmed. If the assumptions are not validated, risks may be introduced. Assumptions are as follows:

ID	Assumption
A001	There is sufficient power, cooling, and floor/rack space available in the datacenter to support the existing and consolidated environments during the migration
A002	Resources should be provided to support a host failure during both normal and maintenance operations
A003	Growth is calculated based on the addition of 50 new customers each year over the next five years

There's more...

The conceptual design can also include diagrams that provide high-level overviews of the proposed design. Conceptual diagrams of the functional blocks of the design include the virtualization infrastructure, storage, servers, and networking. A conceptual diagram does not include specifics about resources required or hardware vendors. The following is an example of a conceptual diagram that shows how the virtualization infrastructure will leverage the existing physical network:

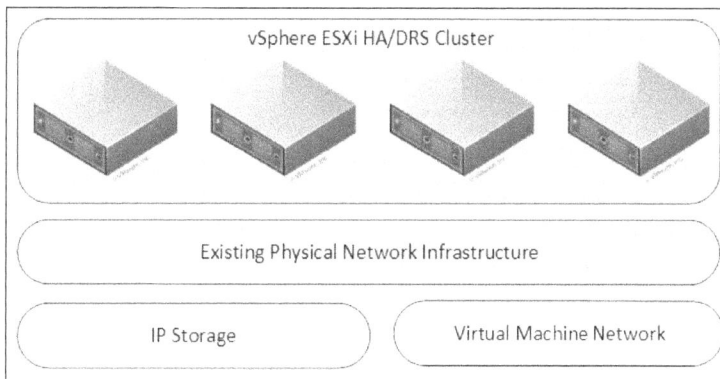

The diagram shows, at a very high level, how servers will be placed in a **vSphere High Availability (HA) / Distributed Resource Scheduler (DRS)** cluster. The existing physical network infrastructure will be leveraged to provide connectivity for IP Storage and the virtual machine networks. The diagram does not include any specifics about the type of servers, type of array, or the resources required, but it does provide an overview of how the different parts of the design will work together.

4
The vSphere Management Design

In this chapter, we will cover:

- ▸ Identifying vCenter components and dependencies
- ▸ Selecting a vCenter deployment option
- ▸ Determining the vCenter system requirements
- ▸ Selecting a database for vCenter deployment
- ▸ Determining database interoperability
- ▸ Choosing a vCenter Single Sign-On deployment mode
- ▸ Designing for management availability
- ▸ Backing up the vCenter Server components
- ▸ Using vCenter Server Heartbeat to provide vCenter availability
- ▸ Securing the management components
- ▸ Designing a separate management cluster

Introduction

This chapter discusses the design considerations that should be taken into account when designing the management layer of the virtual infrastructure. We will look at the different components that make up vCenter and how to size them correctly. This chapter also covers the different deployment options for vCenter and its components as well as the importance of availability, recoverability, and security of these components. The following diagram displays how management design is integrated into the design process:

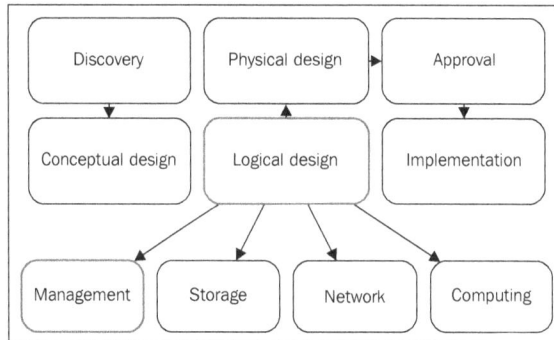

Questions that the architect should ask and answer during the management design process are as follows:

- ▸ What components are necessary to manage the virtual environment?
- ▸ How will management components be deployed?
- ▸ What resources are required to support the management components?
- ▸ What impact will the loss of a management component have on the environment?
- ▸ How to recover from the loss of a management component?

Identifying vCenter components and dependencies

The vCenter Server provides the central configuration and management of the ESXi servers and the services provided by the virtual infrastructure. vCenter 5.1 is composed of several components and services such as the VMware **Single Sign-On** (**SSO**) server, the vCenter Inventory Service, the vCenter Server, and the vSphere Web Client.

How to do it...

Identify the following core components and services of vCenter 5.1:

- ► **VMware SSO**: This provides identity management for administrators, users, and applications that interact with the VMware vSphere environment. Multiple **Active Directory** (**AD**) domains and **Open Lightweight Directory Access Protocol** (**OpenLDAP**) authentication sources can be added to provide authentication to the vCenter management components.

- ► **VMware vCenter Inventory Service**: This maintains application and inventory data, so inventory objects including datacenters, clusters, folders, and virtual machines can be searched and accessed.

- ► **VMware vCenter Server**: This provides the configuration, access control, and performance monitoring of ESXi/ESX hosts and virtual machines that have been added to the inventory of the vCenter Server.

- ► **VMware vSphere Web Client**: This allows the connections made to vCenter to manage objects in its inventory, using a web browser. Many of the new features and capabilities in Version 5.1 can only be configured and managed using the VMware vSphere Web Client.

How it works...

Each vCenter Server component or service has a set of dependencies. The following diagram illustrates these dependencies:

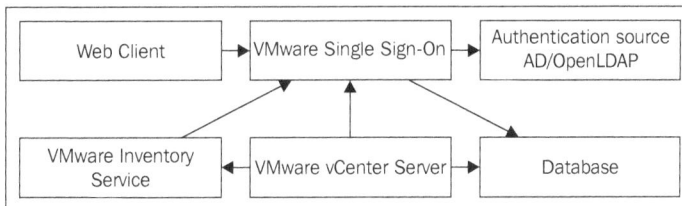

There's more...

The vCenter 5.1 installation CD includes several other tools that provide support and automation to deploy, manage, patch, and monitor the vSphere virtual environment. These tools can be installed on the same server as other vCenter Server components or on a separate server. The tools included in the vSphere virtual environment are as follows:

- ► **VMware vSphere Update Manager (VUM)**: This provides a central automated patch and version management for ESXi hosts and virtual appliances

- ► **ESXi Dump Collector**: This collects memory dumps over the network in the event of an ESXi host encountering a critical error

- ► **VMware vSphere Syslog Collector**: This enables network logging and combines the logs from multiple hosts

- ► **VMware vSphere Auto Deploy**: This provides the automated deployment and configuration of ESXi hosts

- ► **VMware vSphere Authentication Proxy**: This allows hosts to join a domain without using AD credentials

Selecting a vCenter deployment option

There are a number of deployment options available for deploying vCenter. The vCenter Server can be deployed on a dedicated physical server running a 64-bit Windows server operating system, on a virtual machine running a 64-bit Windows server guest operating system, or on a Linux-based virtual appliance. All vCenter components can be installed on a single server, or the components can be installed on separate virtual or physical machines.

How to do it...

Regardless of the deployment option selected, the vCenter Server components must be installed and configured in a specific order so that the service dependencies are met.

The order of installation of the vCenter Server components is as follows:

1. vCenter SSO
2. VMware vCenter Inventory Service
3. VMware vCenter Server
4. VMware vSphere Web Client
5. Other vCenter tools and plugins (VUM, third-party plugins, and so on)

The following diagram illustrates the order of installation of the vCenter Server components:

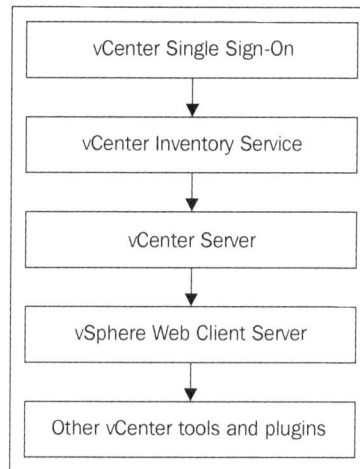

How it works...

Deploying the vCenter Server components on a virtual machine is a VMware recommended practice. When vCenter is deployed on a virtual machine, it is possible to take advantage of the portability and availability provided by the virtual infrastructure. One of the primary advantages of deploying vCenter components on virtual machines is that **VMware High Availability** (**HA**) can be leveraged to protect the management environment from a hardware failure or a virtual machine crash.

vCenter Server Appliance (**VCSA**) is a preconfigured Linux-based virtual machine that has been optimized to run the vCenter Server and the associated services. It includes a PostgreSQL-embedded database that can be used for small deployments of five hosts and 50 virtual machines. A remote database connection can be configured to support larger deployments.

Limitations of the VCSA are as follows:

- ▸ Microsoft SQL is not supported as a remote database.
- ▸ VUM must be installed on a separate Windows server.
- ▸ vCenter Linked Mode is not supported.
- ▸ If the VCSA SSO server is used, it is configured in the basic mode. SSO must be installed on a separate Windows server if high availability or multisite modes are required.

The vCenter Linked Mode creates groups of vCenter Servers that can be managed centrally. Logging into one member of the vCenter Linked Mode group allows an administrator to view and manage the inventories of all the vCenter Servers in the group. VMware SSO now provides a similar functionality to all the vCenter Servers that are registered with the same SSO server, when managing them through the Web Client. The vCenter Linked Mode is available only when deploying the vCenter Server on a virtual or physical Windows server. The vCenter Linked Mode is not available with the VCSA.

The SSO server, vCenter Inventory Services, vCenter Server, vSphere Web Client server, and VUM can all be installed on a single Windows server, or each component can be installed on a separate server. Installing all the components on a single server simplifies deployment, while installing each component on a separate server allows the resources for each service to be adjusted as necessary. This flexibility may be useful in larger deployments but it adds complexity to the deployment.

Determining the vCenter system requirements

The minimum system requirements for the vCenter Server service are two CPUs of 2.0 GHz or faster and 4 GB of memory. When other services are installed on the vCenter Server or in larger environments, these minimum requirements may not provide the resources necessary to support vCenter deployment.

The size of the vCenter inventory, the number of hosts, and the number of virtual machines also have an impact on the amount of CPU and memory resources required. The minimum system requirements will support a small deployment of up to five hosts and 50 virtual machines.

How to do it...

The following steps will help you to determine the vCenter system requirements:

1. Estimate the number of host and virtual machines that will be managed by the vCenter Server.

2. Determine whether all the vCenter Server components will be installed on a single server or on separate servers.

3. Size the vCenter Server to support the managed inventory.

How it works...

The vCenter Server 5.1 system requirements based on inventory size are given in the following table:

Inventory size	Number of 2 GHz CPU cores	Memory	Size of database
50 hosts / 500 virtual machines	2	4 GB	5 GB
300 hosts / 3000 virtual machines	4	8 GB	10 GB
1,000 hosts / 10,000 virtual machines	8	16 GB	10 GB

If the vCenter Server has been deployed on a Windows virtual machine, enable **Memory Hot Add** and **CPU Hot Plug** in the virtual machine configuration. This will allow the CPU and memory resources to be added to the virtual machine without impacting the virtual machine uptime. This is shown in the following screenshot:

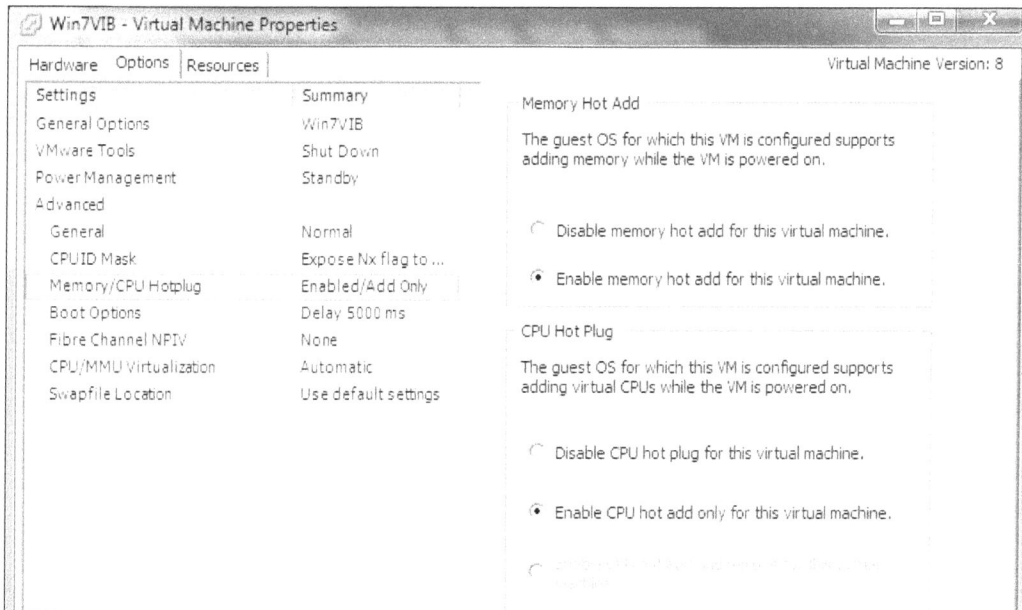

The vCenter Server components can be installed on separate physical or virtual machines. The following table lists the minimum requirements for each component, if the services are installed on separate physical or virtual machines:

Component	2 GHz CPU cores	Memory	Disk size
VMware SSO	2	3 GB	2 GB
Inventory Service	2	3 GB	60 GB
Web Client	4	2 GB	2 GB

If the SSO, vCenter Inventory Service, and vCenter Server are all installed on the same machine, the recommended minimum requirements are two CPUs of 2 GHz and 10 GB of RAM. If the databases are installed on the same machine, additional CPU, memory, and disk resources will be necessary.

The vCenter Server 5.1 virtual appliance is deployed with a configuration of 2 vCPUs and 8 GB of memory. The default can be adjusted based on the size of the inventory the appliance has to manage.

The vCenter Server virtual appliance memory requirements are given in the following table:

Inventory size	Memory
10 hosts / 100 virtual machines	4 GB
100 hosts / 1,000 virtual machines	8 GB
400 hosts / 4,000 virtual machines	16 GB
> 400 hosts / > 4,000 virtual machines	24 GB

All the necessary vCenter components are preinstalled and optimized on the vCenter Server virtual appliance. This includes the VMware SSO service, the vCenter Inventory Services, the vCenter Server, and the Web Client Server. The appliance also includes vSphere, the Syslog Collector, and the ESXi Dump Collector.

VUM cannot be deployed on the vCenter Server virtual appliance. If VUM is required in an environment managed by the virtual appliance, it must be installed on a separate physical or virtual environment supported by the Windows server.

There's more...

VMware and third-party plugins may require their own resources. For example, if VUM is installed on the same machine as other vCenter components, the CPU, memory, and disk size requirements will need to be adjusted to support the additional resources required.

Selecting a database for vCenter deployment

The vCenter SSO, vCenter Server, and VUM each require a supported database to be deployed.

How to do it...

Perform the following steps to select a database for the vCenter deployment:

1. Estimate the number of host and virtual machines that will be managed by the vCenter Server.

2. Choose a supported database platform that is suitable to support the vCenter inventory.

How it works...

The database stores configuration and performance information. The three database deployment options are as follows:

- Use the embedded database on the VCSA or the bundled SQL Express database if installing vCenter on a Windows server

- Install a full database server locally on the same server as the vCenter Server components

- Connect to a database hosted on a remote server

The embedded database on the vCenter Server virtual appliance or the SQL Server Express, which can be deployed as part of the vCenter Server Windows install, is intended for small deployments of up to five hosts and 50 virtual machines. If the beginning inventory size is greater than five hosts and 50 virtual machines or there is expected growth beyond five hosts and 50 virtual machines, a different database option should be selected.

Reasons to use the embedded or SQL Express database are as follows:

- A small environment of less than five hosts and 50 virtual machines with no expected growth

- Easy to install and configure

- Free! No need to license a separate database server software

> Databases are created as part of the installation process when using the bundled SQL Express or embedded database option with the SSO and vCenter Server. If a full installation of a database server is used, these databases and the ODBC connections required for them are manually created.

Installing a full SQL or Oracle database locally on the same Windows server as the vCenter components is supported, but this increases the amount of resources necessary for the vCenter Server. Additional memory up to 4 GB may be required depending on the size of the vCenter inventory. Hosting the database locally on the same server is fully supported and can provide faster access since the access to the database does not rely on network resources.

Reasons to choose a locally installed database are as follows:

- Fast database access, which is not dependent on network resources
- If using a SQL database, the vCenter Server components and the required databases can be protected using vCenter Server Heartbeat

A full installation of SQL or Oracle can also be performed on a separate physical or virtual machine. The vCenter components access the databases hosted on the remote database server. The creation of the databases and the configuration of the vCenter components is the same as with a full database installation on the same server as vCenter. Accessing the databases requires network resources; because of this, a network congestion or a network outage can affect the accessibility of the databases.

Reasons to choose a remotely installed database are as follows:

- Leverage an existing database server already available in the environment.
- Separation of roles is another reason. Database administrators are responsible for administering the database servers, while virtual administrators are responsible for administering the virtual environment.
- High availability to the databases can be provided using Microsoft or Oracle clustering.
- Reduces the amount of resources that need to be allocated to the vCenter Server.

There's more...

If installing the SQL Express database to support the vCenter 5.1 Server on a Windows server, download and install SQL Server 2008 R2 Management Studio Express from Microsoft at `http://www.microsoft.com/en-us/download/details.aspx?id=22985`. This will provide a management interface to the SQL Express databases created by the SSO and vCenter Server installation.

If SQL Express is used and the environment grows beyond five hosts and 50 virtual machines, the databases can be migrated to a Standard, Enterprise, or Datacenter Edition of SQL server installation.

Determining database interoperability

VMware provides an online interoperability matrix in order to make it easy to determine which database versions are compatible and supported with which versions of VMware products.

How to do it...

In order to determine database interoperability with VMware products, perform the following steps:

1. Visit `http://partnerweb.vmware.com/comp_guide2/sim/interop_matrix.php`.

2. Select the **Solution/Database Interoperability** radio button.

3. In the **Select a VMware Product** option, select **VMware vCenter Server** and a **Version** from the respective drop-down boxes.

4. Add database versions using the database drop-down box. You can add multiple database versions.

The database's compatibility with the selected product will be displayed in the table. Hovering over the green check will display more specific information about the supported option.

How it works...

Verifying database product interoperability ensures the supportability of the database and the version that has been selected for use with a specific VMware product. The **VMware Product Interoperability Matrixes** are regularly updated by VMware when new database or VMware product versions are released.

Database and product interoperability should be checked for new installations, and this should be done prior to upgrading VMware products or applying service packs to database servers.

There's more...

The interoperability matrix can be used to determine database operability for all supported VMware products and solutions. It can also be used to determine supported upgrade paths and interoperability between different VMware solutions.

Choosing a vCenter Single Sign-On deployment mode

In vSphere 5.1, there are three deployment modes available for the vCenter SSO server. These are as follows:

- ▸ Basic mode
- ▸ High availability cluster mode
- ▸ Multisite mode

The deployment mode that is chosen depends on the requirements of the design. Is high availability required? Will there be a SSO server located at multiple sites? Will vCenter Linked Mode be used? This recipe takes a look at the different deployment modes and how they are used.

SSO has been rewritten, and the deployment has been simplified in vSphere 5.5. vSphere 5.5 provides a single deployment option for single or multiple sites. The dependency on an external database has also been removed in vSphere 5.5.

How to do it...

To determine the SSO deployment mode for a vSphere 5.1 deployment, follow these steps:

1. Identify the use cases for each SSO deployment mode.
2. Select the SSO deployment mode based on the environment requirements.

How it works...

Basic mode deploys a standalone version of the SSO server. This is the most common deployment option and will meet the requirements of most environments. Multiple AD and OpenLDAP identity sources can be configured on an SSO server installed in basic mode. Local operating system identity sources can also be configured. If the SSO server is used with the vCenter Server virtual appliance, basic mode is the only available option.

Multiple vCenter Servers and multiple vCenter Inventory Services can be registered with the SSO server configured in basic mode. All the registered vCenter Servers can be managed by the vSphere Web Client. However, if the SSO server is unavailable, administrators will not be able to authenticate and will not be able to access the vCenter Server using the vSphere Client or the Web Client.

The following diagram illustrates how vCenter services authenticate against the SSO server deployed in basic mode:

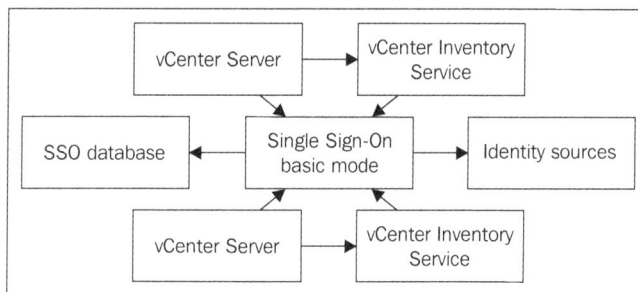

High availability cluster mode installs two or more vCenter SSO servers in a high availability cluster configuration. This is the most complex installation mode since it requires a third-party load balancer to determine if the SSO server has failed and then redirect authentication requests to another SSO server in the cluster.

Each SSO server installed in high availability mode uses the same database and contains the same AD or OpenLDAP identity sources. High availability mode does not support using local operating system user accounts for authentication.

A load balancer that is enabled by a third-party **Secure Sockets Layer** (**SSL**) is required to facilitate failover between the SSO servers configured in high availability cluster mode. The load balancer should be configured to provide failover only. Load balancing between SSO servers configured in high availability mode is not supported.

The following diagram illustrates how vCenter services authenticate against SSO deployed in high availability cluster mode:

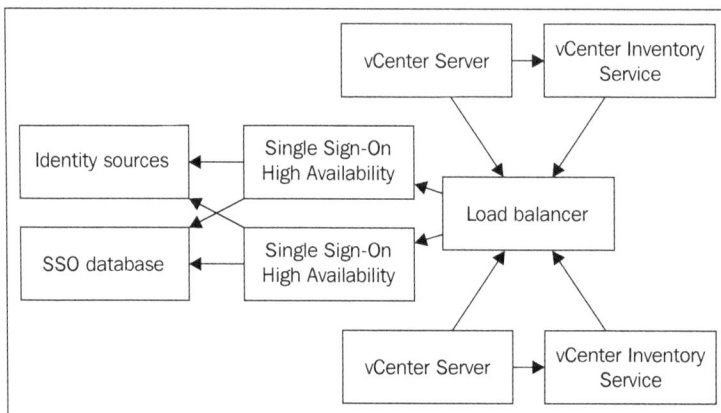

In a deployment where servers are installed at multiple locations, SSO servers can be installed in multisite mode to provide faster access by allowing access to the authentication services that are local to the vCenter Server they support. Each SSO server in a multisite deployment has its own database and is configured to AD and OpenLDAP sources located at the same location. Multisite mode is required when using vCenter Linked Mode between vCenter Servers at multiple sites.

The following diagram illustrates how vCenter services authenticate against SSO deployed in multisite mode:

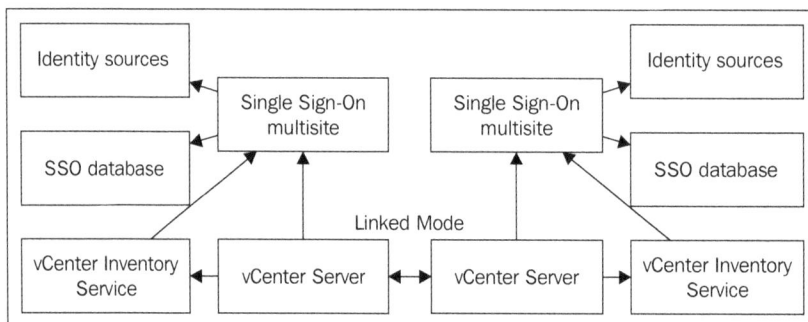

Multisite mode does not provide failover between the SSO servers at different sites. If the SSO server at one site fails, vCenter authentication at that site will also fail even if SSO servers at other sites are still functional.

There's more...

Regardless of the mode chosen, the SSO server database is separated from the vCenter Server database. A periodic of Sign-On configuration and database should be taken, so it can be restored in the event of a system failure or database corruption.

The procedure for backing up and restoring the SSO configuration can be found in this VMware knowledge base article at `http://kb.vmware.com/kb/2034928`. The SSO database should be backed up using the method supported by the database server software.

Designing for management availability

The availability of the management functions of an environment becomes more critical; for example, in virtual desktop environments and other self-service provisioning environments. In these environments, if the vCenter Server is unavailable, so is the ability to provide the provisioning of services.

If the environment does not provide these type of services, the ability to manage the environment, especially during a failure or disaster, is also critical. How can you troubleshoot an issue with a virtual machine or a group of virtual machines if the primary tool that is used to manage the environment is unavailable?

How to do it...

To properly design for management availability, follow these steps:

1. Identify management environment dependencies.
2. Identify the potential single points of failure in the management environment.
3. Create a management design that ensures high availability of the management components.

How it works...

When designing the management network, single points of failure should be minimized. Redundant network connections and multiple network interfaces connected to separate physical switches should be configured to provide connectivity.

The storage that hosts the management components should be configured to support the capacity and performance of the management components. The storage should also be configured to be highly available, so that a disk or path failure does not interrupt management operations.

If the vCenter Server is running on a virtual machine, it can be protected with HA. If the host that vCenter is running on or the operating system crashes, the vCenter Server is restarted on a surviving host. There will be some downtime associated with the failure, but the vCenter Server services will be restored.

In environments where the vCenter Server provides provisioning, such as a virtual desktop or self-service cloud environments, the vCenter uptime is critical. In environments where vCenter is installed on a physical machine and HA is not an option, vCenter Server Heartbeat can be used to protect the vCenter Server. vCenter Server Heartbeat protects the vCenter Server, the supporting components, and the databases from network, hardware, and application failures. Design considerations for using vCenter Server Heartbeat to protect the vCenter Server are covered in detail in the *Using vCenter Server Heartbeat to provide availability* recipe later in this chapter.

Sufficient resources should be dedicated to the vCenter Server and its components. We discussed correct sizing of the vCenter Server earlier in the chapter. Sizing vCenter correctly and reserving resources ensures not only performance but also availability. If a virtual machine is running on the same host as the vCenter Server or one of its components and it consumes too much of the host resources, it may impact the performance and availability of the vCenter Server services. Applying resource reservations to the vCenter Server will prevent resource contention. Another means of preventing resource contention is by designing a separate cluster to host the management components. Management cluster design is discussed in the *Designing a separate management cluster* recipe in this chapter.

Backing up the vCenter Server components

In order to recover the vCenter Server components in the event of an outage that results in data loss or data corruption, it is necessary to perform backups of the databases and the vCenter Server configurations. The vCenter SSO, the vCenter Inventory Service, and the vCenter Server each have specific configuration information that should be backed up.

The frequency of backups depends on the **Recovery Point Objective** (**RPO**) that has been defined for the management environment. The RPO defines the maximum period of data loss that can be tolerated as a result of an outage. If the RPO has been determined to be four hours, this means backups should occur at least every four hours.

How to do it...

If the VCSA with the embedded database is used, a backup of the database can be taken using the following procedure:

1. **Secure Shell** (**SSH**) into the vCenter Server virtual appliance.

2. Change the path to `/opt/vmware/vpostgres/1.0/bin`.

3. Run `./ pg_dump EMB_DB_INSTANCE -U EMB_DB_USER -Fp -c > Backup_Filename`.

4. Enter the **EMB_DB_PASSWORD** when prompted.

5. The configuration file located at `/etc/vmware-vpx/embedded_db.cfg` contains the **EMB_DB_INSTANCE**, **EMB_DB_USER**, and **EMB_DB_PASSWORD** values.

Back up the vCenter SSL certificates using the following steps:

1. The `rui.key` file is the private key, the `rui.crt` file is the certificate, and the `rui.pfx` file is the concatenation of the `rui.key` and `rui.crt` files in the PFX format. All of these files are required and should be backed up.

2. The vCenter SSL certificates' location depends on the operating system on which the vCenter Server has been installed. These files can be stored at the following locations:

   ❑ For Windows Server 2008, these files are located at `C:\ProgramData\VMware\VMware VirtualCenter\SSL`

   ❑ For Windows Server 2003, these files are located at `C:\Documents and Settings\All Users\Application Data\VMware\VMware VirtualCenter\SSL`

   ❑ On the vCenter Server virtual appliance, the files are located at `/etc/vmware-vpx/ssl`

To back up the vCenter Inventory Service on a Windows server, use the following steps:

1. Stop the VMware vCenter Inventory Service using `services.msc`.

2. Open a command prompt and change the path of the folder to that of the vCenter Inventory Service installed at `directory\Infrastructure\Inventory Service\scripts` and run the script `backup.bat` using the following commands:

   ```
   > cd vCenter_Install_Directory\Infrastructure\Inventory Service\
   scripts
   ```

   ```
   > backup.bat -file backup_filename
   ```

3. When the backup is completed, the message **Backup Completed successfully** will be displayed. Start the VMware vCenter Inventory Service using `services.msc`.

To back up the vCenter Inventory Service on the VCSA, complete the following steps:

1. Log in to the vCenter Server virtual appliance as `root`.

2. Stop the vCenter Inventory Service by running the following command:

    ```
    # serviceservicevmware-inventory-service stop
    ```

3. Change the path of the folder to `/usr/lib/vmware-vpx/inventoryservice/scripts/` and run the script `backup.sh` using the following commands:

    ```
    # cd /usr/lib/vmware-vpx/inventoryservice/scripts
    # ./backup.sh -file backup_filename
    ```

4. When the backup is completed, the message **Backup Completed successfully** will be displayed. Restart the vCenter Inventory Service using the following command:

    ```
    # serviceservicevmware-inventory-service start
    ```

To back up the SSO Configuration, follow these steps:

1. Open a command prompt using **Run as administrator**.

2. Change the path of the folder to that of the vCenter SSO installed at `directory\Infrastructure\SSOServer\scripts` and run the `sso-backup.wsf` script using the following commands:

    ```
    >cdSSO_install_directory\Infrastructure\SSOServer\scripts
    > cscript sso-backup.wsf /z
    ```

3. The vCenter SSO configuration backup is stored in a ZIP file, `Single Sign On.zip`, located on the administrator's desktop.

How it works...

How backups are done depends on the database software that is used to host the database. For example, if the database is a Microsoft SQL database, a backup can be performed on demand in the SQL Management Studio or as a scheduled SQL job. Third-party backup tools can also be used to back up the vCenter and SSO databases.

The vCenter Server database and the SSO database should be backed up regularly, depending on the RPO that has been defined for the management components.

SSL certificates are used by the vCenter Server to encrypt communications between the ESXi hosts in the environment. The database password is encrypted using the certificates, so the certificates are also required for vCenter to access its database. These SSL certificates should be regularly backed up.

The vCenter Inventory Service, SSO configurations, and even the database should be backed up to ensure that each of these services can be restored.

There's more...

There are a number of third-party tools available that can be leveraged to back up virtual machines. If the vCenter Server components are installed on a virtual machine or if the vCenter Server virtual appliance is deployed, these third-party tools can be used to take full virtual machine backups. This simplifies the backup and recovery process. These third-party backup tools also simplify backup testing since the full virtual machine can be recovered in an isolated or sandbox environment.

Using vCenter Server Heartbeat to provide vCenter availability

vCenter Server Heartbeat is a separately licensed product available from VMware that provides high availability clustering of VMware vCenter Server. vCenter Server Heartbeat can be used to protect both the vCenter Server components and the vCenter databases from operating system, application, network, and hardware failures. vCenter Server Heartbeat can only be used to protect the vCenter Server deployed on a Windows server. It cannot be used to protect the vCenter Server virtual appliance.

How to do it...

Perform the following steps for using vCenter Server Hearbeat to provide availability:

1. Identify the use cases for protecting the vCenter Server with vCenter Server Heartbeat.
2. Understand the architecture of the vCenter Server Heartbeat cluster.

How it works...

vCenter Server Heartbeat provides multiple methods of protection, which include **Physical-to-Virtual** (**P2V**), **Virtual-to-Virtual** (**V2V**), and **Physical-to-Physical** (**P2P**). Protection can be provided over the **Local Area Network** (**LAN**) for high availability or over the **Wide Area Network** (**WAN**) for disaster recovery.

The vCenter Server Heartbeat software is installed on a primary or production server and a secondary or ready-standby server. The primary server assumes the active role during normal operations, while the secondary server assumes the passive role. The active server is visible on the network using the Principal IP address, and the passive server is hidden from the public network until a switchover or failover operation changes the roles of the primary and secondary servers.

A separate control channel is used to provide communications between the vCenter Servers being protected. Each server requires two IP addresses, one for the control channel and one for management.

The control channels of the communications between the active and passive server and controls failover and data transfers from the active server to the passive server. The control channel is also used by the passive server to monitor the active server's status. The control channel can use the same interface as the principal network, but using a separate dedicated **Network Interface Controller** (**NIC**) for the control channel is recommended. The following diagram shows the network channel between the active and passive servers:

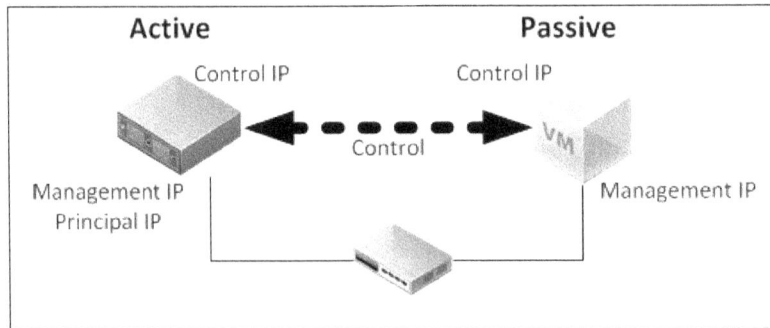

The Principal IP address is used to access the services on the active server. This IP address can be moved between the primary and secondary server when roles are switched from active to passive. When a switch or failover occurs, the Principal IP address is removed from the previously active server and reassigned to the new active server.

The Management IP address is used to access the server when it is in the passive role. The Management IP address is a static address on the same network interface and on the same subnet as the Principal IP address. This address is used by administrators to manage the passive server.

vCenter Server Heartbeat can protect vCenter across the WAN. The requirements for protecting vCenter over the WAN with vCenter Server Heartbeat are as follows:

- A routable IP address for the channel network
- Minimum 1 MB of bandwidth between sites
- Rights to add/update/remove DNS records
- A domain controller at recovery site

Securing the management components

Securing the management components is critical. If the vCenter Server is compromised, a great deal of damage can be done, from powering off virtual machines to completely deleting virtual machines from disks.

We will not dive deep into the configuration of security, instead we will just take a look at some of the key best practices that should be considered when designing the management layer.

How to do it...

There are a number of security practices that can be implemented to harden the management environment as follows:

- Place the vCenter Server and other management components on a separate physical network or **Virtual Local Area Network** (**VLAN**). Providing a network separation of the management components from production networks used by virtual machines makes it easier to configure firewall access to the management components.

- Use VUM to apply critical security patches to hosts. ESXi already has a very small attack service, but critical security patches are released from time to time and should be installed as soon as possible.

- Set permissions on vCenter inventory objects based on roles. Everyone who accesses the vCenter Server should not be set up as an administrator. Use roles and permissions to assign only the necessary permissions that a user needs in order to perform his/her role.

- Replace self-signed certificates with **Certificate Authority** (**CA**) signed user certificates. Communication with and between vCenter components is secured using SSL certificates. The default SSL certificates are self-signed certificates that are created during installation. These self-signed certificates are vulnerable to man-in-the-middle attacks since the certificate warnings are commonly ignored. The PDF document from VMware on replacing SSL certificates can be found at `http://www.vmware.com/files/pdf/techpaper/vsp_51_vcserver_esxi_certificates.pdf`.

- Use ESXi lockdown mode on hosts managed by vCenter. Lockdown mode ensures that all access to ESXi hosts is authenticated by the vCenter Server. Once lockdown mode is enabled, direct access to the host is no longer available except through the **Direct Console User Interface** (**DCUI**).

ESXi lockdown mode is used very rarely, and I do not understand why this is the case. Environment security is greatly increased by limiting the ability to directly access ESXi hosts. Lockdown mode can be enabled when first adding a host to the vCenter inventory. Lockdown mode can be easily disabled and enabled at any time in order to directly access a host if necessary for support or troubleshooting. The following screenshot displays the lockdown mode host configuration in the vSphere Web Client:

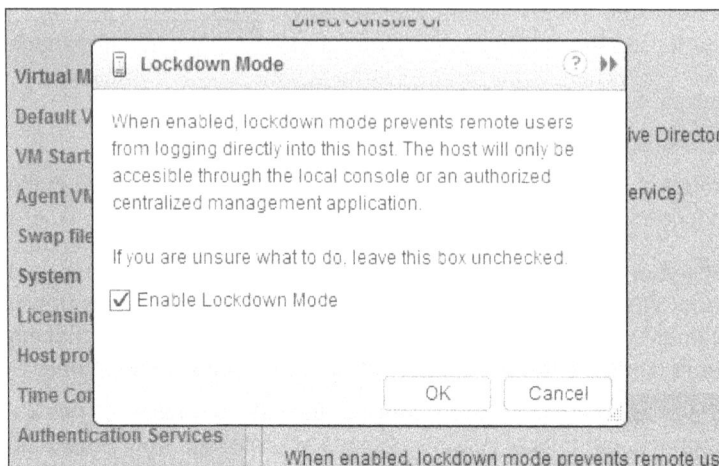

When lockdown mode is enabled, the host can still be managed using the vSphere Client connected to the managing vCenter Server, VMware PowerCLI, or VMware **vSphere Command-Line Interface** (**vCLI**). The only difference is that access is authenticated through the vCenter Server, instead of using a local account on the ESXi host. While lockdown mode is enabled, access to the host through SSH is unavailable.

There's more...

Beyond applying best practice for securing vCenter components, best practice for securing the operating systems hosting the vCenter components should also be applied. This best practice is as follows:

- Unnecessary services should be removed or disabled
- Windows firewall should be correctly configured to allow access to the management services
- Windows security updates should be applied when available
- Access to the operating system should be tightly controlled

Designing a separate management cluster

The management components of a virtual environment can be resource intensive. If you are running vCenter and its dependencies as virtual machines in the same cluster as the cluster managed by the vCenter server, the resources required by the management infrastructure must be factorized into the capacity calculations of the logical design. Creating a separate management cluster separates the resources required by the vCenter components from the resources required by the applications hosted in the virtual infrastructure.

How to do it...

Management cluster best practice is as follows:

- CPU and memory resources to support management applications
- Multiple network interfaces and multiple physical network switches to minimize the single points of failure in the management network
- Multiple paths to the storage in order to minimize the single points of failure in the storage network
- Storage designed to support both the capacity and the performance required for management applications

To correctly size the management cluster, the services that will be hosted in the cluster need to be identified. The following questions also need to be answered:

- Will the cluster also provide the resources needed for the vCenter or SSO databases?
- What about other management tools, such as vCenter Operations Manager, vCenter Log Insight, or other third-party management tools?

How it works...

The design of a management cluster follows the same process as designing a cluster hosting the production applications. Requirements need to be identified and the logical design process for storage, networking, and computing resources must be followed. Functional requirements for the management network will likely include high availability, minimizing single points of failure, and quickly recovering failed components.

There's more...

When vCenter Server Heartbeat is used to protect the vCenter Server running on a virtual machine, anti-affinity rules can be used to ensure that the primary and secondary servers run on separate hosts within the cluster. This prevents both the primary and secondary servers from running on the same host, which reduces the likelihood of a hardware failure impacting the vCenter operations.

Affinity rules can also be used to keep virtual machines together. For example, keeping the virtual machine running the vCenter Server and the virtual machine running the vCenter Server database on the same host reduces the load on the physical network since all communication between the two servers never leaves the internal host network.

If hosting vCenter in the same cluster, affinity and anti-affinity rules can be used to keep the vCenter Server running on specific hosts so that it can be easily located in the event of the vCenter Server being unavailable.

5

The vSphere
Storage Design

In this chapter, we will cover the following topics:

- ▸ Identifying RAID levels
- ▸ Calculating storage capacity requirements
- ▸ Determining storage performance requirements
- ▸ Calculating storage throughput
- ▸ Storage connectivity options
- ▸ Storage path selection plugins
- ▸ Sizing datastores

Introduction

Storage is an essential component of vSphere design and provides the foundation for the vSphere environment. A solid storage design that addresses capacity, performance, availability, and recoverability is the key to a successful vSphere design. The following diagram displays how a storage design is integrated into the design process:

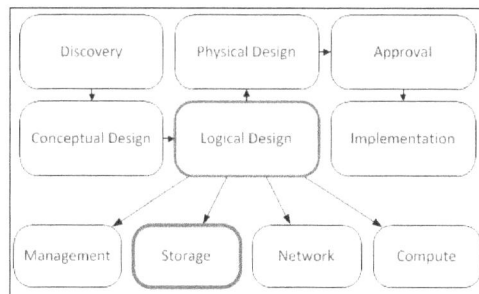

Several storage options and protocols are supported in a vSphere environment. The architecture chosen for a vSphere deployment depends on the capabilities and features needed to meet the design requirements.

This chapter will cover calculating the storage capacity and performance requirements, sizing datastores, and selecting a storage protocol. The calculations for the recipes in this chapter will be based on the following requirements identified in *Chapter 3*, *The Design Factors*:

- ▸ There are 100 application servers
- ▸ Each application server is configured with 100 GB of disk space. The peak disk capacity usage of a single application server is approximately 65 percent of the total or 65 GB. The average disk performance of a single application server is 50 IOPS with an I/O profile of 90 percent read and 10 percent write.
- ▸ Provide capacity to support growth for 25 additional application servers over the next 5 years.

Identifying RAID levels

A **Redundant Array of Independent Disks** (**RAID**) combines multiple physical disks into a single unit of storage. The advantages in speed, reliability, and capacity can be realized depending on which RAID level is selected. RAID provides the first level of protection against data loss due to a disk failure.

How to do it...

In order to select the proper RAID level to support the virtual workloads, you need to perform the following steps:

1. Identify the different RAID levels and capabilities.
2. Select an appropriate RAID level to support a virtualized workload based on capacity and performance requirements.

How it works...

RAID0 stripes disks together to appear as a single disk with a capacity equal to the sum of all the disks in the set. RAID0 provides excellent performance and capacity efficiency, but offers no data protection. If a disk fails in a RAID0 set, the data is lost and must be recovered from a backup or some other source. Since this level offers no redundancy, it is not a good choice for production or mission-critical storage.

The following diagram illustrates the disks in a RAID0 configuration:

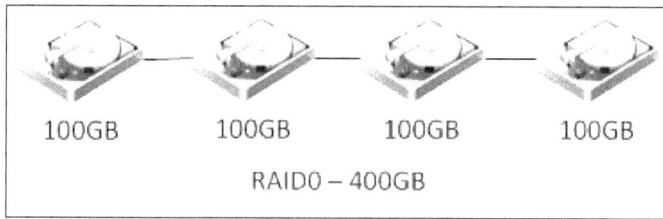

RAID1 duplicates or mirrors data from one disk to another. A RAID1 set consists of two disks and data is written on both the disks, which can then be read from either disk. If one of the disks fails, the mirror can be rebuilt by replacing the disk. The following diagram illustrates disks in a RAID1 configuration:

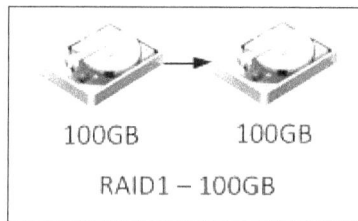

RAID 1+0, RAID1/0, or RAID10 is a stripe of multiple mirrors. RAID10 provides excellent redundancy and performance, making this the best option for mission-critical applications. RAID10 is well-suited for applications with small, random, write-intensive IOs such as high transaction applications, large messaging applications, or large transactional database applications. A RAID10 set can recover from multiple drive failures as long as two drives in the same mirror set do not fail.

Both RAID1 and RAID10 have a capacity efficiency of 50 percent since half of the disks in a RAID1 or RAID10 set are used to store the mirrored data. The following diagram illustrates disks in a RAID10 configuration:

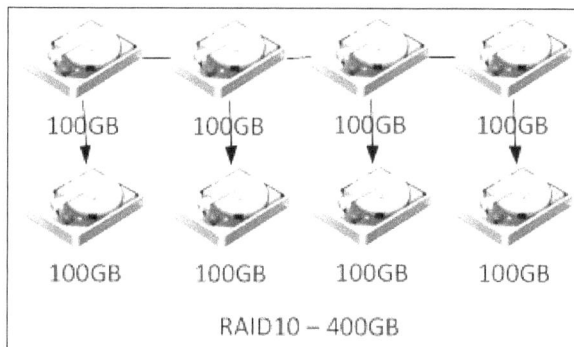

In RAID5, data is striped across several drives and parity is written equally across all the drives in the set. The parity allows for the recovery from a failure of a single drive in the set. This level offers a balance of performance and capacity and is suitable for storing transactional databases, web servers, application servers, file servers, and mail servers. The following diagram illustrates disks in a RAID5 configuration:

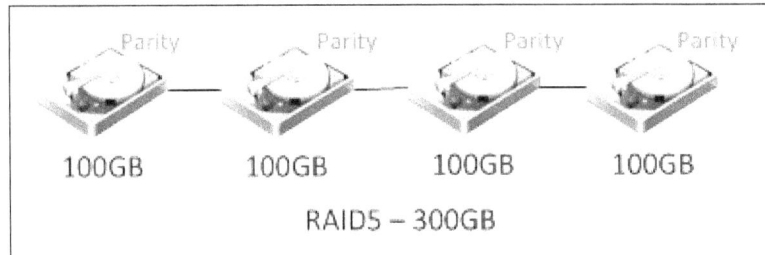

The capacity efficiency of a RAID5 set is calculated using the formula *[(n - 1) / n] * 100*, where *n* is equal to the number of disks in the set. For example, a RAID5 set containing four 100 GB disks would provide 75 percent of the total capacity or 300 GB.

*[(4-1)/4]*100 = 75%*

*(100GB * 4) * .75 = 300GB*

RAID6 is similar to RAID5, except that the two parity blocks are written and distributed equally across all the drives in the set. The second parity increases the write penalty but protects against two drive failures in the set. File archiving and file servers are common workloads hosted on RAID6.

The capacity efficiency of a RAID6 set is calculated using the formula *[(n - 2) / n] * 100*, where *n* is equal to the number of disks in the set. A RAID6 set containing six 100 GB disks would provide approximately 67 percent of the total capacity or 400 GB.

*[(6 - 2) / 6] * 100 = ~67%*

*(100GB * 6) * .67 = ~400GB*

There's more...

To increase the redundancy of a RAID set, hot spares should be configured in the array. The hot spares are used to automatically replace a failed drive in a RAID set temporarily, until the failed drive can be replaced. A single hot spare can be configured to provide protection for multiple RAID sets.

Calculating storage capacity requirements

Capacity is usually measured in **Gigabytes** (**GB**) or **Terabytes** (**TB**). Capacity should include the total space needed to support the current, the space needed to support growth, the space needed for virtual machine swapfiles, and the additional slack space for snapshots and other virtual machine data.

How to do it...

In order to calculate the storage capacity requirements, you need to perform the following steps:

1. Determine the capacity required to support the current workloads.
2. Determine the capacity required to support future growth.

How it works...

Capacity is calculated to support the current and future growth based on the design requirements as follows:

Current Capacity = 100 Virtual Machines x 100 GB = 10 TB

Growth Capacity = 25 Virtual Machines x 100 GB = 2.5 TB

20% Slack space = 12.5 TB x .20 = 2.5 TB

Capacity = 12.5 TB + 2.5 TB = 15 TB

Each virtual machine will have a swapfile or `.vswp` file that is created when the virtual machine is powered on. The size of the `.vswp` file for each virtual machine is equal to the size of the allocated memory minus the memory reservation.

vSwap Capacity = (100 Virtual Machines + 25 Future Virtual Machines) x 8 GB of Memory = 1 TB

The total capacity needed to support the requirements is 16 TB.

There's more...

The application servers are configured with 100 GB of disk space, but the maximum space that is actually consumed by a server is only 65 GB. Resizing the virtual machine disk or using thin provisioning can reduce the required amount of storage capacity significantly.

Since only the actual used space is consumed, thin provisioning virtual machine disks allows for the disk capacity to be over allocated, which means that more capacity can be allocated to the virtual machine disks than what is actually available on the datastore. This increases the amount of management oversight required to monitor the capacity. vCenter datastore alarms can be configured to monitor over allocation and datastore usage to assist in capacity management.

Determining storage performance requirements

Disk performance is measured in Input/Output per Second (IOPS). One disk read request or one disk write request is equal to one I/O.

How to do it...

The IOPS required to support an application is calculated based on the percentage of read I/O, the percentage of write I/O, and the write penalty of the RAID level the workload will be hosted on.

To calculate the IOPS requirements, perform the following steps:

1. Determine the number of IOPS a workload requires.
2. Identify the percentage of read I/O to write I/O for the workload.
3. Determine the write penalty of the RAID level that will host the workload.
4. Calculate the IOPS the storage must be capable of providing to support the workload.

How it works...

To get the total amount of required IOPS, multiply the number of workloads by the number of Functional Application IOPS.

*Total IOPS = (100 current workloads + 25 future workloads) * 65 IOPS = 8125 IOPS*

To calculate the Functional IOPS required for a specific workload, use the following formula:

*Functional Workload IOPS = (Workload IOPS * %Reads) + ((Workload IOPS * %Writes) * Write Penalty)*

The write penalty is based on the number of I/O operations a specific RAID configuration requires for a single write request. Writing data to multiple disks in a mirror or parity calculations in a RAID5 or RAID6 configuration adds I/O operations to the write request. The write request is not completed until the data and parity are written to the disks.

The following table illustrates the write penalty based on the RAID levels:

RAID	Write Penalty
0	1
1	2
5	4
6	6
10	2

Based on the requirements of 50 IOPS per workload with 90 percent reads and 10 percent writes on the storage configured in RAID5, the actual workload IOPS would be 65 IOPS.

*Functional Application IOPS = (50 * .90) + ((50 * .10) * 4) = 65 IOPS*

Each disk in a storage array is able to provide a number of IOPS. The number of IOPS a single disk can deliver is calculated from the average latency and the average seek time of the disk. The formula to calculate disk performance is as follows:

IOPS = 1 / (average latency in milliseconds + average seek time in milliseconds)

The following table lists some approximate IOPS provided, based on the spindle speed and the drive type:

Drive Speed	~ IOPS
SSD	> 2500
15k SAS/FC	175
10k SAS/FC	125
7200 NL-SAS/SATA	75
5400 SATA	50

Based on the number of IOPS required, there will be a need of 47 15k SAS drives to support the workload.

8125 IOPS / 175 IOPS per Drive = 46.4 or 47 15k SAS drives

The same workload on drives configured in RAID10 sets would require 40 15k SAS drives to provide the required IOPS.

*Functional Workload IOPS = (50 * .90) + ((50 * .10) * 2) = 55 IOPS*

*Total IOPS = (100 current workloads + 25 future workloads) * 55 IOPS = 6875 IOPS*

6875 IOPS / 175 IOPS per Drive = 39.3 or 40 15k SAS drives

There's more...

Many arrays provide a caching mechanism using memory or SSD disks to increase the number of IOPS the array can deliver. This allows a few slow drives to deliver a higher number of IOPS. This caching can greatly reduce the number of drives needed to deliver the same number of IOPS by writing to a faster cache instead of writing directly to disks. FAST Cache of EMC and Flash Cache of NetApp are examples of vendor-specific SSD caching technologies that can be used to increase storage I/O performance.

Calculating storage throughput

The data transfer rate or throughput is the rate at which data can be read from or written to the storage device and is typically measured in MB/s.

How to do it...

Throughput should be calculated in order to ensure that the storage controllers and disk can support the required data transfer rates. Throughput is also used to correctly size the storage connectivity bandwidth.

To calculate storage throughput requirements, perform the following steps:

1. Determine the I/O size of the workload.
2. Determine the number of IOPS required to support the workload.
3. Calculate the throughput required.

How it works...

Throughput is calculated by multiplying the I/O size of the workload by the number of IOPS. Transactional databases and application servers typically have an I/O size between 4k and 64k, whereas file archiving applications, backup applications, and media streaming applications typically have larger I/O sizes from 64k to 1024k.

To calculate the throughput, the following formula is used:

*Throughput = Functional Workload IOPS * IO Size*

Using the Functional Workload IOPS from the previous recipe and an I/O size of 8k, the throughput required can be calculated as follows:

*Throughput = 6875 * 8k = 55 MB/s*

Network Interface Card bandwidth is usually expressed in Mbps. To convert MB/s to Mbps, simply multiply by 8.

*Bandwidth Mbps = 55 MB/s * 8 = 440 Mbps*

The array would need to support a throughput of atleast 55 MB/s, and the connectivity bandwidth would need to be sufficient enough to support atleast 440 Mbps.

Storage connectivity options

vSphere supports multiple storage protocols and connectivity options. Storage can be directly connected to a host, or storage can be centralized and shared with multiple hosts. Shared storage is required when implementing many vSphere features such as **VMware High Availability** (**HA**), **VMware Fault Tolerance** (**FT**), and **VMware Distributed Resource Scheduling** (**DRS**).

How to do it...

In order to determine the storage connectivity requirements, perform the following steps:

1. Identify the supported storage protocols and connectivity options.
2. Select the storage protocol and connectivity that supports the design requirements.

How it works...

Performance, availability, and costs are all factors that should be considered when choosing a storage connectivity option. The following table provides a quick overview of the different storage connectivity options and how they compare with each other in terms of performance, availability, and costs:

Protocol	Performance	Availability	Costs
Local Storage	Good	Fair	Low
Fibre Channel	Excellent	Excellent	High
iSCSI	Good	Excellent	Medium
NFS	Good	Good	Low
FCoE	Excellent	Excellent	High

Direct attached or local storage is storage directly attached to a host. Since this storage is not shared, many VMware features will not be available for virtual machines hosted on the local storage.

Best practices when using Direct attached or local storage are as follows:

- ▸ Configure RAID to provide protection against a hard disk failure.
- ▸ Use a hardware RAID controller that is on the VMware HCL.

Fibre Channel (**FC**) is a block-level, low latency, high-performance storage network protocol that is well-suited for workloads with high I/O requirements. The FC protocol encapsulates the SCSI commands into the FC frames. A Fibre Channel **Host Bus Adapter** (**HBA**) is required to connect the host to the storage network or fabric. FC HBAs can provide a throughput of 2, 4, 8, or 16 Gbps depending on the capabilities of the HBA and the FC network. FC uses zoning and LUN masking to configure which hosts can connect to which targets on the SAN.

The cost of deploying FC-connected storage can be significantly higher than other options, especially if an existing FC infrastructure does not already exist.

The best practices when using FC are as follows:

- ▸ Use multiple HBAs in the host to provide multiple paths from load balancing and redundancy.
- ▸ Ensure all HBAs and switches are configured for the same speed. Mixing the speed of HBAs and switches can produce contention at the FC switch and SAN.
- ▸ Use single-initiator single-target zoning. A single HBA, the initiator, is zoned to a single array target, the target. A separate zone is created for each host HBA.
- ▸ Mask LUNs presented to ESXi hosts from other devices.
- ▸ Ensure firmware levels on FC switches and HBAs are up-to-date and compatible.

iSCSI provides block-level storage access by encapsulating SCSI commands in TCP/IP. iSCSI storage can be accessed with the iSCSI software initiator, included with ESXi through a standard network adapter, or using a dependent or independent iSCSI HBA.

- ▸ A dependent iSCSI adapter depends on VMware networking and iSCSI configuration for connectivity and management.
- ▸ An independent iSCSI HBA provides its own networking and configuration for connectivity and management. Configuration is done directly on the HBA through its own configuration interface.

Throughput is based on the network bandwidth, the speed of the network interface card (1 Gbps or 10 GbE), and the CPU resources required to encapsulate the SCSI commands into TCP/IP packets.

The cost of implementing iSCSI is typically significantly lesser than implementing FC. Standard network adapters and network switches can be used to provide iSCSI connectivity. Using dedicated iSCSI HBAs not only increases performance, but also increases cost. The price of 10 GbE switches and 10 GbE adapters continues to drop as the deployment of these becomes more widespread.

The best practices when using iSCSI are as follows:

- Configure multiple vmks bound to multiple vmnics to provide load balancing and redundancy for iSCSI connections.

- Use network cards with **TCP/IP Offload Engine** (**TOE**) enabled, to reduce the stress on the host CPU.

- Use a physically separate network for iSCSI traffic. If a physically separate network is not available, use VLANs to separate iSCSI traffic from other network traffic.

- Enable jumbo frames (MTU 9000) on the iSCSI network.

The **Network File System protocol** or **NFS** can be used to access virtual machine files stored on a **Network Attached Storage** (**NAS**) device. Virtual machine configuration files, disk (VMDK) files, and swap (`.vswp`) files can be stored on the NAS storage. vSphere currently supports NFS Version 3 over TCP. Throughput is based on the network bandwidth, the speed of the network interface card (1 Gbps or 10 GbE), and the processing speed of the NAS. Multiple paths can be configured for high availability, but load balancing across multiple paths is not supported with NFS.

The cost of implementing NFS connectivity is similar to iSCSI. No specialized network hardware is required. Standard network switches and network adapters are used and there is no need for specialized HBAs.

The best practices when using NFS-connected storage are as follows:

- Use a physically separate network for NFS traffic. If a physically separate network is not available, use VLANs to separate NFS traffic from other network traffic.

- Hosts must mount NFS exports with root access.

- Enable jumbo frames (MTU 9000) on the NFS network.

Fibre Channel of Ethernet (**FCoE**) encapsulates Fibre Channel in Ethernet frames. A **Converged Network Adapter** (**CNA**) that supports FCoE is required or a network adapter with FCoE capabilities can be used with the software FCoE initiator included with ESXi.

A common implementation of FCoE is with Cisco UCS blade chassis. The connectivity for TCP/IP network and FCoE storage traffic is converged between the chassis and the Fabric Interconnects. The Fabric Interconnects splits out the traffic and provides the connectivity paths to the TCP/IP network and storage network fabrics.

The best practices when using FCoE are as follows:

- Disable the **Spanning Tree Protocol** (**STP**) on the switch ports connected to FCoE adapters

- Ensure the latest microcode is installed on the FCoE network adapter

- If the FCoE network adapter has multiple ports, configure each port on a separate vSwitch

The **VMware vSphere Storage Appliance** (**VSA**) is a software-based storage solution that allows the local storage across multiple ESXi hosts to be presented as a single shared NFS datastore. The following diagram illustrates how the VSA creates a cluster of localhost storage to provide shared storage to the vSphere environment.

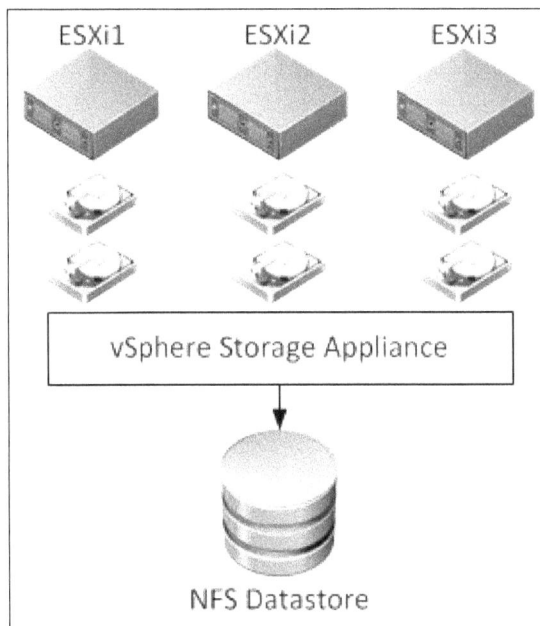

The VSA is deployed as a virtual appliance and runs on several ESXi hosts to provide a VSA cluster access to the local storage resources of the host. A VSA cluster can consist of two or three ESXi hosts. Management of the cluster is accomplished with the VSA Manager plugin that is installed on a vCenter Server. The VSA is managed using the vSphere Client or vSphere Web Client.

Storage path selection plugins

Mutlipathing allows more than one physical path to be used to transfer data between the ESXi hosts and the storage array. In the event of a failure in a storage path, the host or hosts can switch to another available path. Multipathing also provides load balancing by distributing the storage I/O across multiple physical paths.

How to do it...

To determine the multipathing policy, we perform the following steps:

1. Identify the different native multipathing policies available and the capabilities of each policy.

2. Select a multipathing policy based on the number of paths and the array type used.

3. Change the default multipathing policy using the `esxcli` command.

4. Configure the multipathing policy on the storage devices presented to the ESXi host.

How it works...

The VMware **Native Multipathing Plugin** (**NMP**) supports storage arrays listed on the **VMware Hardware Compatibility List** (**HCL**). NMP provides path selection based on the array type by associating a set of physical paths with a storage device or LUN.

The **Storage Array Type Plugin** (**SATP**) monitors the available storage paths, reports changes in the path status, and initiates failover between paths when needed. The **Path Selection Plugins** (**PSP**) determine which available path to use for I/O. There are the following three Native Multipathing PSPs available:

- ▶ **Fixed**: The host always uses a preferred path if the preferred path is available. If the preferred path fails, another available path is selected and used until the preferred path becomes available. This is the default policy for active/active storage devices.

- ▶ **Most Recently Used** (**MRU**): The host uses the most recently used path. If the current path fails, another path is selected. I/O does not revert to the previous path when it becomes available. This is the default policy for active/passive storage devices.

- ▶ **Round Robin** (**RR**): I/O is rotated through all active paths. This provides load balancing across all physical paths available to the hosts. This PSP can be used on active/passive or active/active arrays.

Array vendors may provide their own path selection plugins to provide storage multipathing. The use of third-party MPPs will depend on array-and-vendor best practices. The NMP can be used for any supported array.

The optimal PSP to choose is dependent on the recommendations of the array vendor.

By default, a PSP is set based on the SATP used for the array. The SATP to use is identified by the **Pluggable Storage Architecture** (**PSA**) using a set of claim rules that base the selection on the vendor and model of the array. The SATP then determines the default PSP to be used.

The NMP PSP policies are as follows:

- **VMW_PSP_MRU**: for Most Recently Used
- **VMW_PSP_FIXED**: for Fixed
- **VMW_PSP_RR**: for Round Robin

The default PSP for an SATP can be changed using the following `esxcli` command:

```
esxcli storage nmp satp set –default-psp=<psp policy to set>
--satp=<SATP_name>
```

Using the command line changes the default PSP for all new devices identified by the SATP. The PSP for an individual device or LUN can also be changed. This can be done in the vSphere Client or vSphere Web Client by managing the paths for a single storage device on a host.

To change the PSP of a device using the vSphere Client, navigate to **Host and Clusters** | **Hosts** | **Configuration** | **Storage Adapters**, and select the storage adapter that services the paths you want to modify. In the **Details** section of the **Storage Adapters** window, right-click on the device you want to modify the PSP on and select **Manage Paths**.

The following screenshot displays path management in the vSphere Client:

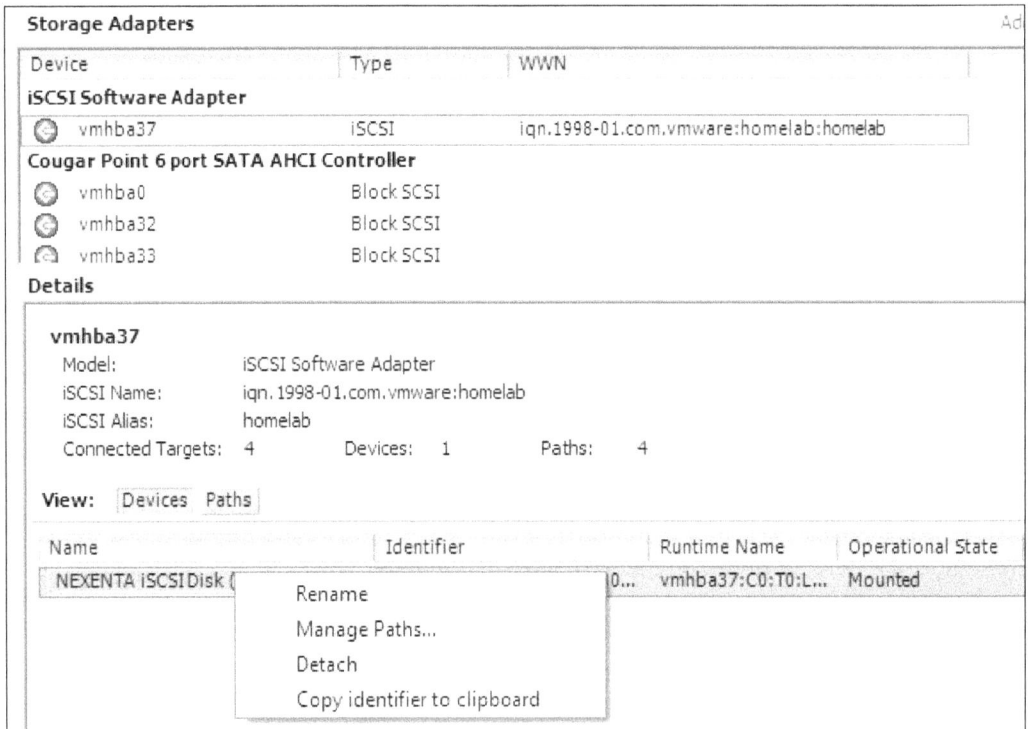

From the **Manage Paths** window, select the **Path Selection** with the drop-down menu and click on **Change**.

The following screenshot displays how to select and change the path selection policy for a device using the vSphere Client:

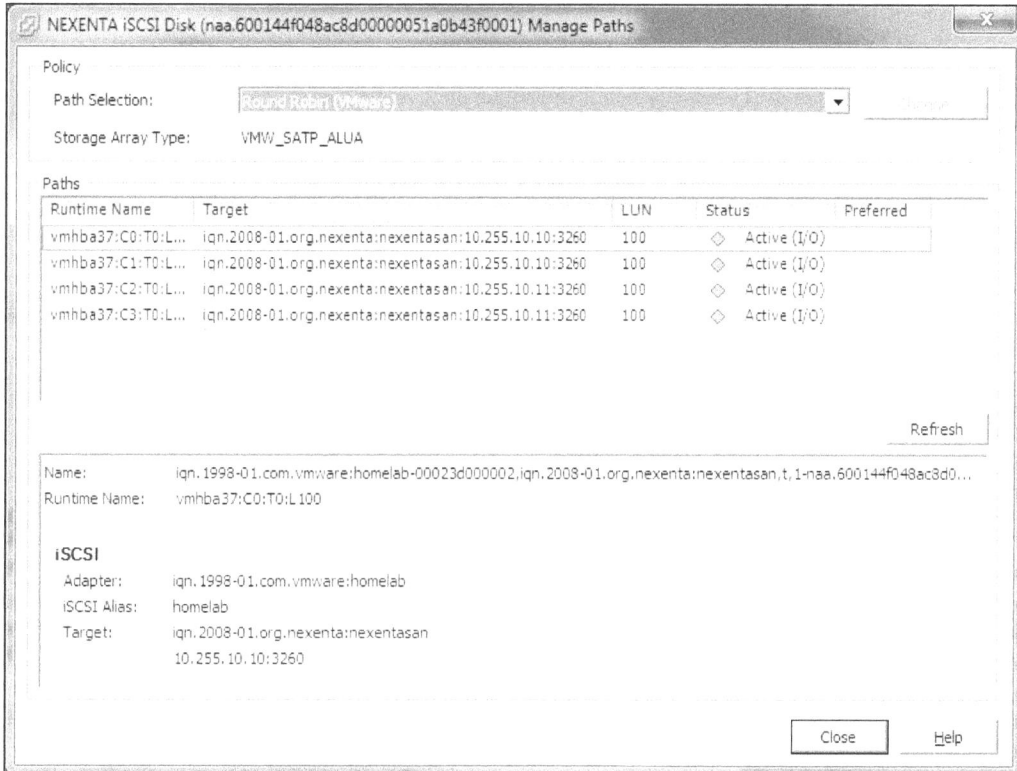

Changing the default PSP for an SATP or the PSP for a device can be done without impacting normal operations. A change made to the PSP for a single device takes effect immediately. Changing the default PSP for the SATP changes only the settings of newly discovered devices and not the PSP settings of the current devices.

Sizing datastores

A datastore is a logical representation of storage presented to an ESXi host where virtual machine files are stored. A datastore can be a VMFS formatted volume, an NFS export, or a path on the local ESXi filesystem.

How to do it...

Design requirements, virtual machine disk size, IOPS, and recovery are all factors that can determine the number of virtual machines to store on a single datastore. The size of the datastore is calculated based on the number of virtual machines per datastore and the size of the virtual machines.

1. Determine the number of virtual machines per datastore based on the capacity, performance, and recovery requirements.
2. Understand the impact the SCSI reservations may have on datastore sizing.
3. Understand how recovery time impacts datastore sizing.

How it works...

A design factor that was identified in *Chapter 3*, *The Design Factors*, specified that no more than 20 application servers should be affected by a hardware failure. Applying the same requirement to datastore sizing would mean that no more than 20 application servers should be hosted on a single datastore.

*Number of VMs per datastore * (VM disk size + .vswp size) + 20% = Minimum datastore size*

The datastore size for 20 application server workloads each with 100 GB of disk storage and 8 GB of RAM with no reservations plus 20 percent for slack would be approximately 2.5 TB.

*20 * (100GB + 8GB) + 20% = 2,592 GB or ~ 2.5TB*

The storage backing the datastore has to provide enough IOPS to support the virtual machines running on it. If a virtual machine generates 50 IOPS and there are 20 virtual machines on the datastore, the storage must be able to support 1000 IOPS.

> The maximum size of a VMFS5 datastore is 64 TB.

Block storage formatted as a VMFS volume is susceptible to SCSI reservations or locking of the entire LUN for a very short period of time by a single host. A few operations that cause SCSI reservations to occur are as follows:

- Creating a VMFS datastore
- Expanding a VMFS datastore
- Powering on a virtual machine
- Creating a template
- Deploying a virtual machine from a template

- ▸ Creating a virtual machine
- ▸ Migrating a virtual machine with vMotion
- ▸ Developing a virtual machine disk
- ▸ Creating or deleting a file

With the introduction of VMFS5 along with the **vStorage APIs for Array Integration** (**VAAI**) hardware-assisted locking feature, the impact of SCSI reservations is minimized. If an array does not support the VAAI hardware-assisted locking feature, then the number of virtual machines per datastore may need to be decreased to reduce the impact of LUN locking for SCSI reservations.

The **Recovery Time Objective** (**RTO**) must also be taken into account when determining the size of a datastore. If the datastore is lost or becomes inaccessible, how long will it take to restore the virtual machines that were running on it?

Size of Datastore / GBs recovered per hour <= RTO

If 500 GB is to be recovered per hour, the time to recover a failed datastore can be calculated as follows:

2.5 TB / 500GB = 5 hours to recover

If the RTO for the applications or workloads running on the datastore is less than 5 hours, the datastore would need to be resized to ensure recovery would take place within the defined RTO.

There's more...

Multiple datastores can be aggregated to create a datastore cluster. A datastore cluster is a collection of the member datastore resources with a shared management interface. vSphere Storage DRS manages the datastore cluster resources to determine the initial placement and on-going balancing of virtual machine VMDKs across the datastores in the cluster. Datastore clusters are supported for both VMFS and NFS datastores.

A few recommended practices when using datastore clusters and Storage DRS are as follows:

- ▸ Cluster datastores with similar IOs and capacity characteristics
- ▸ Use separate datastore clusters for replicated and nonreplicated datastores
- ▸ Do not mix NFS and VMFS datastores in the same cluster
- ▸ Do not place datastores shared across multiple datacenters in a datastore cluster

When a virtual machine is placed on a datastore cluster, Storage DRS determines which datastore in the cluster the files will be stored in, based on space utilization and/or performance. The following diagram is a logical representation of the virtual machines placed on a datastore cluster:

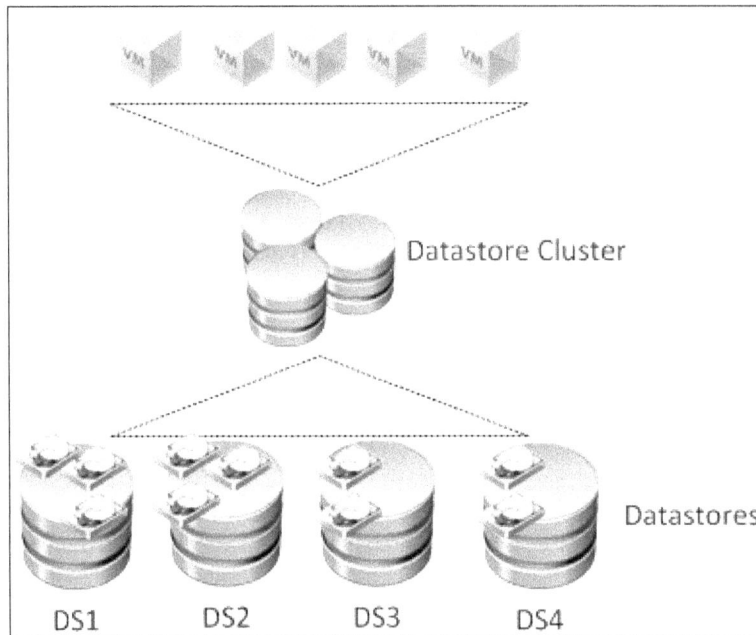

The best practices when using datastore clusters are as follows:

▶ Datastores in a cluster should have similar performance capabilities

▶ Keep similar virtual machine I/O workloads together on the same cluster

▶ Do not mix replicated and nonreplicated datastores in the same cluster

▶ Do not mix NFS and VMFS datastores in the same datastore cluster

▶ Use VMDK affinity rules to keep virtual machine disk files together on the same datastore within the datastore cluster

▶ Use VM anti-affinity rules to ensure virtual machines run on different datastores within the datastore cluster

The VMware vSphere Storage DRS Interoperability whitepaper can be found at `http://www.vmware.com/files/pdf/techpaper/vsphere-storage-drs-interoperability.pdf`. This whitepaper provides an overview of the datastore cluster best practices and interoperability of datastore clusters along with other VMware products.

6
The vSphere
Network Design

In this chapter, we will cover the following topics:

- ▶ Determining network bandwidth requirements
- ▶ Standard or distributed virtual switches
- ▶ Providing network availability
- ▶ Virtual switch security
- ▶ Network resource management
- ▶ Using private VLANs
- ▶ IP storage network design considerations
- ▶ vMotion network design considerations

Introduction

To effectively design a virtual network infrastructure, a design architect must understand the virtual network architecture, including which features are available and how they are configured. This chapter contains recipes a design architect can use to design a virtual network architecture that provides the capacity and availability required to support the virtual infrastructure.

The logical network design includes calculating the network capacity or bandwidth required to support the virtual machines, and determining the capacity required to support VMware technologies such as vMotion and Fault Tolerance. If IP-based storage connectivity is required, the design must account for the networking necessary to support storage traffic as well.

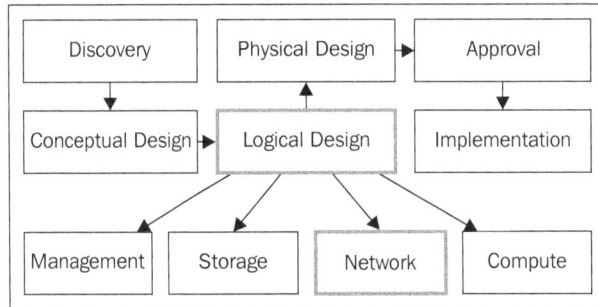

This chapter discusses the different virtual network switch technologies available in vSphere and the different features available in each. This chapter also covers how load balancing and teaming are used to improve network utilization efficiency and increase availability. Network capacity resource management using traffic shaping and network I/O control are also covered.

Determining network bandwidth requirements

Bandwidth refers to the capacity of the network and is measured in either **gigabits per second** (**Gbps**) or **megabits per second** (**Mbps**). The bandwidth required is based on the amount of data transferred or the throughput required by the virtual machines. Most modern networks are capable of transferring data at 1 Gbps or 10 Gbps. Network adapters that support 40 Gbps have recently become available.

The number of physical network adapters in each host required to support a solution is dependent on the amount of bandwidth required to support virtual machine network traffic, the number of virtual switches required, and the network redundancy requirements.

From the case example in *Chapter 3, The Design Factors*, the following information is used to help calculate the network bandwidth requirements:

▶   Cisco switches are used for network connectivity. Separate VLANs exist for management connectivity and production application connectivity.

▶   No more than 20 application servers, or 200 customers, should be affected by hardware failure.

▶   Currently, each physical server contains a single gigabit network interface card. Peak network usage is 10 Mbps.

How to do it...

1. Calculate the total amount of bandwidth required to support virtual machine network traffic using the following formula:

   Total Number or Virtual Machines x Bandwidth per Virtual Machine (Mbps) = Total Bandwidth Requirement (Mbps)

2. Calculate the amount of bandwidth required per host. This is dependent on the maximum number of virtual machines that can be run on a single host.

3. Determine the network requirements for other vSphere services and features, such as vMotion, iSCSI, NFS, and Fault Tolerance.

4. Select the type and number of network adapters to provide the network connectivity required to support design requirements.

How it works...

The physical network infrastructure must be capable of supporting the total throughput requirement of the environment. The total throughput requirement is calculated by multiplying the number of virtual machines by the throughput required by a single virtual machine:

100 Virtual Machines x 10Mbps = 1000 Mbps Total

The throughput required for a single host is calculated by multiplying the number of virtual machines that will run on a host by the throughput required by a single virtual machine:

20 Virtual Machines x 10 Mbps = 200 Mbps per Host

Network adapters are generally capable of delivering throughput equal to approximately 80 percent of the adapter speed, for example, 800 Mbps for a 1-Gbps network adapter. A single gigabit Ethernet connection would provide sufficient bandwidth to support the virtual machine throughput requirements calculated previously. An additional network adapter would be required to support failovers.

There are also network bandwidth requirements to support VMkernel interface network connectivity for management, vMotion, IP storage, and Fault Tolerance. The minimum bandwidth requirements for VMkernel network connectivity are as follows:

- Management: 100 Mb
- vMotion: 1 Gb
- IP storage: This is dependent on the amount of storage throughput required but is limited to the bandwidth of a single path
- Fault Tolerance: 1 Gb

Sufficient physical network connectivity and bandwidth must be included in the design to support these services.

Network connectivity can be provided using multiple 1 Gb network adapters, or 10GbE **Converged Network Adapters** (**CNA**) can be used to carry multiple network traffic types, including virtual machine network traffic and VMkernel (management, vMotion, FT, and IP storage) network traffic on a single 10GbE network adapter.

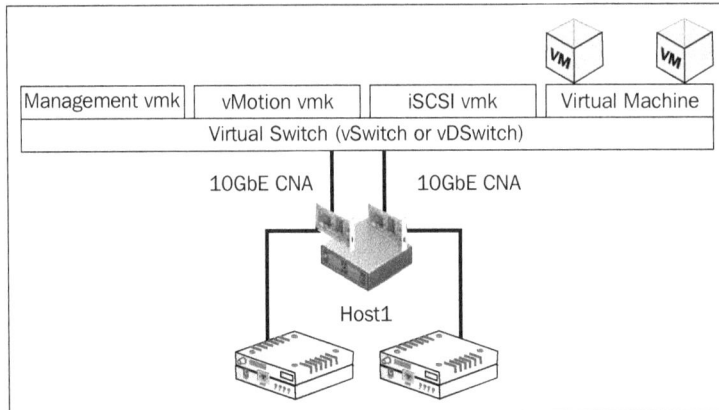

When CNAs are used to provide physical uplink connectivity to virtual switches, **traffic shaping** or **Network I/O Control** (**NIOC**) should be configured to ensure that sufficient network bandwidth is available to each traffic type serviced by the CNAs.

There's more...

For a virtual machine with very high network I/O requirements, **DirectPath I/O** allows a physical network adapter to be passed through directly to the virtual machine.

The following screenshot shows how a virtual machine is provided direct access to a physical network card using DirectPath I/O:

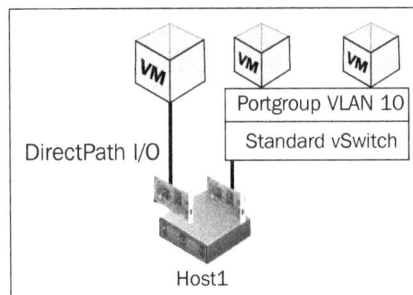

When DirectPath I/O is used, the network adapter is only made available to the virtual machine it is passed to and cannot be shared with other virtual machines. The full bandwidth capacity of the network adapter is available to the virtual machine. Because a virtual machine with DirectPath I/O configured is dependent on the physical network card in the host, it cannot be moved to other hosts using vMotion nor can it be protected using VMware HA. The exception to this is when using a Cisco UCS system that has a supported Cisco UCS **Virtual Machine Fabric Extender** (**VM-FEX**) distributed switch.

Standard or distributed virtual switches

The connectivity of the virtual network to the physical network in a vSphere 5 environment is accomplished using one of two virtual switch technologies: the standard virtual switch (vSwitch) or the virtual distributed switch (vDSwitch). VMware technologies such as VMware HA, VMware DRS, and Fault Tolerance require that virtual switch configurations be consistent across all ESXi hosts in a cluster.

How to do it...

1. Identify the features and capabilities of virtual standard switches and distributed virtual switches.
2. Based on the design requirements, determine which virtual switch technology should be selected to support them.

How it works...

The virtual switch technology chosen is dependent on the connectivity, availability, and manageability requirements and the features available on the virtual switch.

A **standard virtual switch** (**vSwitch**) is configured and managed independently on each ESXi host and supports up to 1024 virtual switch ports per vSwitch. Because vSwitches are configured on each individual host, it increases the administrative overhead required to support large environments. Advance network features such as port mirroring, NetFlow integration, and private VLANs are not available when using standard virtual switches. vSwitches are available at all vSphere license levels.

Several networks can use the same vSwitch, or networks can be separated across multiple vSwitches. Multiple physical uplinks can be associated with a vSwitch to provide redundancy and load balancing. vSwitches can be created with no physical uplinks to keep virtual machine network traffic isolated on a single host.

The following screenshot depicts a common logical network design using standard virtual switches to provide virtual machine network connectivity:

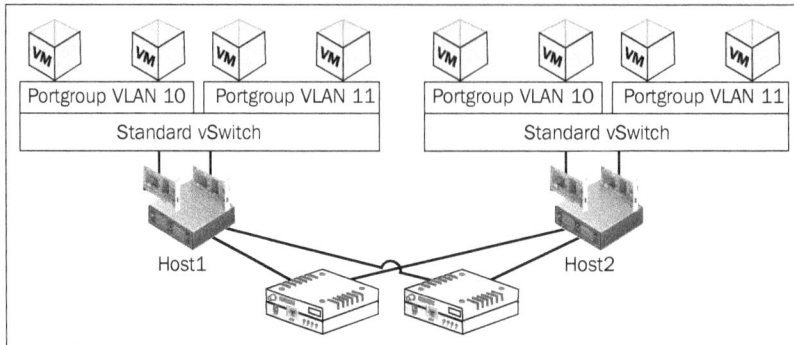

Virtual distributed switches (**vDSwitches**) are configured and managed by vCenter. A vDSwitch guarantees consistent network policy configurations and PortGroup configurations across all hosts with uplinks that are connected to it. In vSphere 5.1, a single vDSwitch can support 500 ESXi hosts and provide up to 60,000 virtual switch ports. **vSphere Enterprise Plus Licensing** is required to use vDSwitches.

Multiple physical uplinks from each host can be associated with a vDSwitch to provide redundancy and load balancing. A vDSwitch will not be available for use by a host without any physical uplinks associated with it:

The following screenshot depicts a logical virtual network design using a virtual distributed switch:

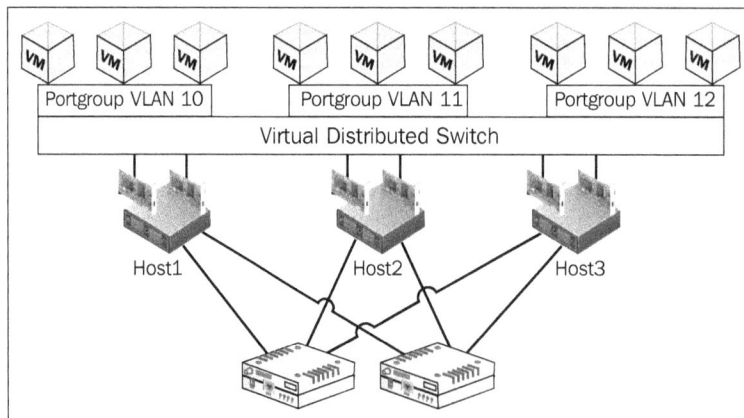

vCenter is required to manage vDSwitches. vCenter controls the configuration state and keeps track of virtual machine connection information for the vDSwitch. If the vCenter Server managing the vDSwitch is unavailable, new connections to the vDSwitch will not be possible.

The features available when using a vDSwitch are as follows:

- The central management of the virtual switch and virtual machine PortGroups
- Link Aggregation Control Protocol (LACP)
- Ingress and egress traffic shaping
- Load balancing based on physical NIC load
- NetFlow integration
- Port mirroring
- Third-party virtual switches (Cisco Nexus 1000v)
- Private VLANs (PVLAN)
- Network I/O Control (NIOC)

There's more...

Third-party virtual switches, such as the Cisco Nexus 1000v, can be used to extend the functionality of a vDSwitch. They provide an interface for provisioning, monitoring, securing, and configuring the virtual network using standard vendor network management tools.

Providing network availability

Network availability is obtained by minimizing **Single Points of Failure** (**SPOF**) and providing sufficient capacity. Multiple network ports, network adapters, and physical switches can be used to minimize single points of failure, and link aggregation can be used to provide load balancing across multiple network adapters.

vSphere virtual network configurations offer multiple NIC teaming and load balancing options. The options used are dependent on the number of network adapters available, the number of virtual machines connected, the physical network's topology, and the amount of bandwidth required.

How to do it...

1. Identify the availability options available on virtual switches and virtual switch PortGroups.
2. Determine the load balancing policies to provide availability based on design requirements.
3. Determine the network adapter teaming policies to provide availability based on design requirements.

How it works...

Load balancing distributes the network load across multiple available adapters. Load balancing policies are configured as part of the NIC **Teaming and failover** options on virtual switches, virtual machine PortGroups, and VMkernel interfaces.

The following screenshot illustrates the **Edit Settings** dialog for configuring **Teaming and failover** options on a virtual machine PortGroup on a standard virtual switch:

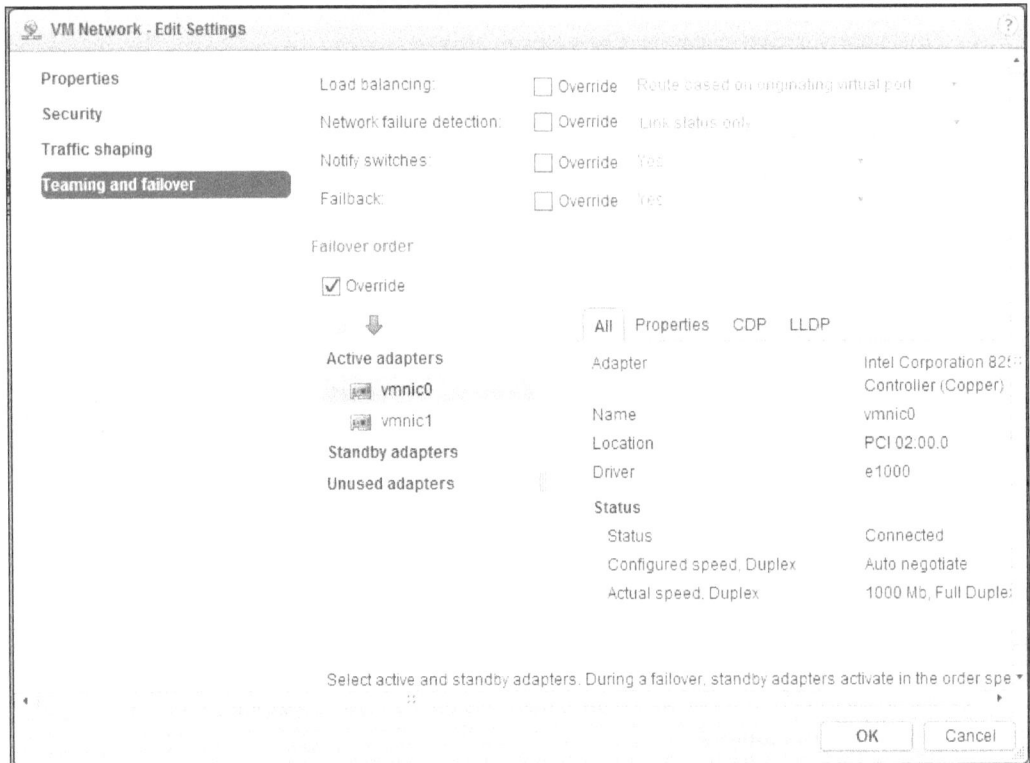

The following load balancing policies can be applied to virtual switches or virtual PortGroups:

▶ **Route based on originating virtual port**: This is the default load balancing policy. When it is being used, the load is balanced based on the number of physical NICs and the number of virtual switch ports in use. Virtual port connections are distributed across the physical NICs available to the virtual switch. A virtual machine connected to the virtual port will always use the same physical NIC unless the NIC becomes unavailable.

- ▸ **Route based on IP hash**: This load balancing policy uses a hashing algorithm that determines the physical path based on the source and destination IP addresses of the virtual machine traffic. A virtual machine's network traffic can use multiple available NICs. This policy is used when using either EtherChannel or the LACP link aggregation.

- ▸ **Route based on source MAC hash**: This load balancing policy is similar to the **Route based on originating virtual port** policy, except that the physical NIC used for virtual machine traffic is based on the virtual network adapter's MAC address and not the virtual port connection.

- ▸ **Use explicit failover order**: This policy is not really a load balancing policy because network traffic always uses the physical NIC uplink that is configured as the highest ordered active physical uplink available.

- ▸ **Route based on physical NIC load**: This is an additional load balancing option offered by vDSwitches that is not available to vSwitches. It is the most efficient because it distributes the load across active uplinks based on the actual workload of the physical NICs.

Redundancy in the virtual network is provided by configuring **Failover order**. These configurations define the physical uplinks that are actively used to pass network traffic, and those that are available stand in the event of an active uplink failing.

The available adapters are as follows:

- ▸ **Active adapters**: These are adapters that are available for use by the virtual switch, a virtual machine network PortGroup, or a VMkernel interface.

- ▸ **Standby adapters**: These are adapters that become active only in the event that an active adapter becomes unavailable.

- ▸ **Unused adapters**: These adapters are unused. They will never be used by the virtual switch, a virtual machine PortGroup, or a VMkernel interface.

The following screenshot shows adapters configured in **Active** and **Standby**. If **Active Adapter** (**vmnic0**) fails, the **Standby Adapter** (**vmnic1**) will become active:

The following screenshot shows an example of an active/standby network configuration commonly used in small environments to provide connectivity and redundancy for the host management and vMotion networks:

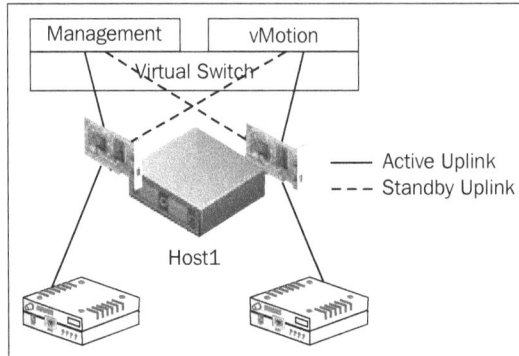

Network Failover Detection and **Failback** are settings that control how a network failure is detected and what happens when an Active adapter is returned to service after a failure.

How network failure is detected is configured using the **Network Failover Detection** option. Two failure detection options are available: **Link Status Only** and **Beacon Probing**. The **Link Status Only** option uses the link state, up or down, of the physical NIC to determine if the uplink is available. The **Beacon Probing** option detects network failures by sending and receiving beacon probes out to all physical uplinks on the virtual switch and can detect link state and switch failures. At least three active uplinks are needed for beacon probing to work effectively. The VMware Knowledge Base article located at `http://kb.vmware.com/kb/1005577` provides more information on how beacon probing works with virtual switches.

The **Failback** setting defines whether or not an Active adapter is returned to service if the adapter becomes available after a failure based on the value set for **Network Failover Detection**. If a physical switch fails and **Failback** is enabled with **Link Status Only** being used for **Failover Detection**, the adapter may become active and will be returned to service before the physical switch is available to pass traffic.

Virtual switch security

Security is an important factor that must be considered when designing virtual networks. Many of the same network practices that are used in the physical network can be applied to the virtual network. The virtual network provides several advantages to security, but it also introduces some challenges.

The security of virtual machine network traffic is critical along with the security of the VMkernel traffic to prevent attacks that may compromise the management, vMotion, Fault Tolerance, and IP storage networks.

How to do it...

1. Identify the available virtual switch security options.

2. Select a virtual switch security configuration based on design requirements.

3. Apply security best practices to create a virtual network design, separating virtual machine services and network traffic into security zones based on design requirements.

How it works...

Separate the virtual machine network traffic based on services and security zones. Use separate vSwitches or VLAN tagging on PortGroups to separate nonproduction, DMZ, Test/Dev, management, vMotion, IP storage, and production virtual machine network traffic. The following are some things to take care of:

▶ The vSphere management network should be separated from other network traffic using a management VLAN or a physically separate network.

▶ vMotion network traffic is transmitted unencrypted. It could be possible for an attacker to obtain the memory contents of a virtual machine during vMotion migration. The recommended practice is for the vMotion network to be on a separate VLAN or physically separated non-routable network from other production traffic.

▶ iSCSI and NFS IP storage traffic is also typically unencrypted. IP-based storage should be logically separated on its own VLAN or on a separate physical non-routable network segment.

The following screenshot shows the **Security** settings that can be applied to a virtual standard switch:

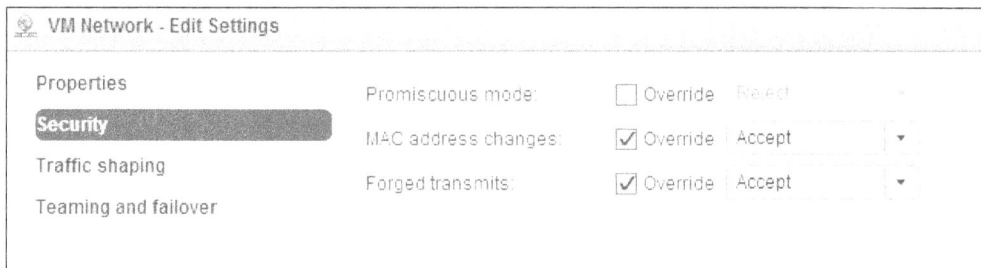

VM Network - Edit Settings			
Properties	Promiscuous mode:	☐ Override Reject	
Security	MAC address changes:	☑ Override Accept	▼
Traffic shaping	Forged transmits:	☑ Override Accept	▼
Teaming and failover			

Virtual switch security settings are as follows:

- **Promiscuous mode**: This policy is set to **Reject** by default. Setting it to **Accept** allows for guest network adapters connected to the virtual switch to detect all network frames passed on the virtual switch.

- **MAC address changes**: If this policy is set to **Reject** and the guest operating system changes the MAC address to a MAC address other than what is defined in the virtual machine configuration file, inbound network frames are dropped.

- **Forged transmits**: Setting this policy to **Reject** will drop any outbound network frame with a source MAC address different from the one currently set on the adapter.

Network resource management

In a vSphere environment, physical network resources are shared across multiple virtual machines and services. The ability to ensure that sufficient capacity is available across shared resources thus becomes important. If a single virtual machine or a VMkernel network service, such as vMotion or Fault Tolerance, saturates the available network capacity, other virtual machines and services, including host management services, may be adversely impacted.

How to do it...

1. Identify the traffic shaping and network resource controls available on the virtual network switches.

2. Determine the network resources required for different traffic types: management, IP storage, vMotion, and virtual machine traffic.

3. Design traffic shaping or Network I/O Control policies to guarantee or limit network resources for the network traffic types based on design requirements.

How it works...

Traffic shaping is used to limit the amount of bandwidth available to virtual switch ports. Network IO Control (NIOC) is used to apply limits and guarantee traffic to different virtual network service types.

Traffic shaping can be configured on vSwitches, vDSwitch uplinks, VMkernel interfaces, and PortGroups to restrict the network bandwidth available to the network ports on the virtual switch. Traffic shaping is applied at all times, regardless of the amount of network capacity available. This means that if traffic shaping is enabled and configured on a virtual switch or PortGroup to limit the peak bandwidth to 1,048,576 Kbps (1 Gbps), only 1,048,576 Kbps of bandwidth will be used even if more bandwidth is available.

The following bandwidth characteristics can be applied to the traffic shaping policy:

▶ **Average bandwidth**: This is the allowed average load measured in Kbits/sec (Kbps)

▶ **Peak bandwidth**: This is the maximum allowed load measured in Kbits/sec (Kbps)

▶ **Burst size**: This is the maximum number of bytes, measured in Kbytes, that can be burst over the specified average bandwidth

Traffic shaping policies on a vSwitch apply only to egress or outbound traffic. vDSwitch traffic shaping policies can be configured for both ingress (inbound) and egress (outbound) traffic.

The following is a screenshot of the configuration screen for applying **Traffic shaping** to a virtual machine PortGroup on a standard virtual switch:

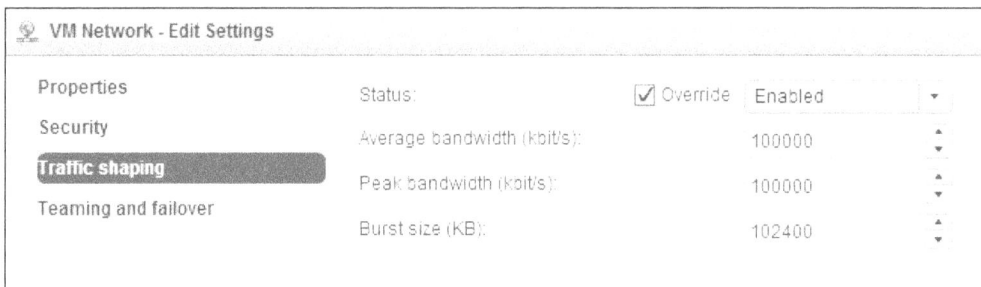

The following screenshot shows the **Ingress traffic shaping** and **Egress traffic shaping** settings that can be applied to a virtual machine PortGroup on a vDSwitch:

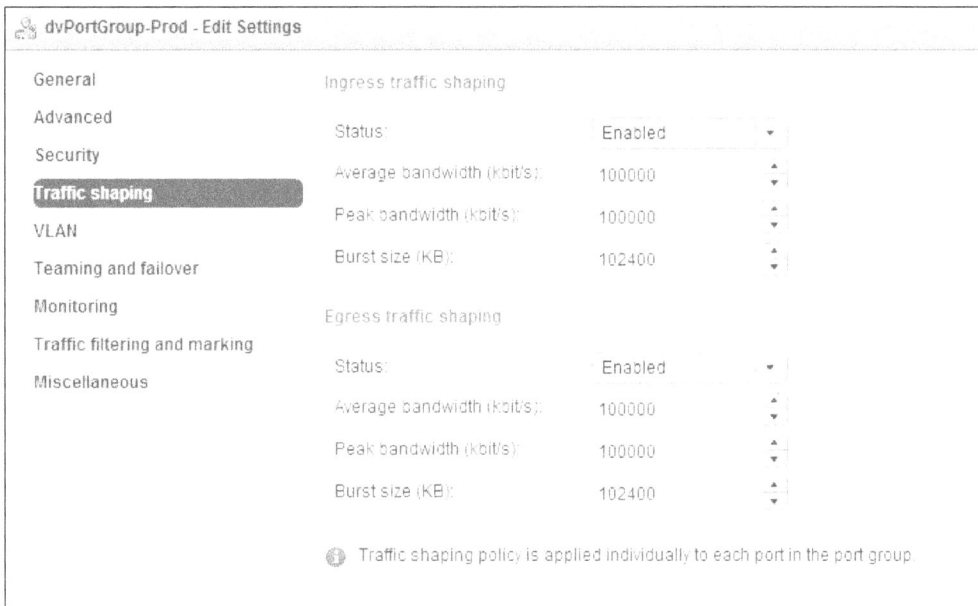

Unlike traffic shaping, NIOC provides control over network bandwidth for specific network protocols only during times of network contention. NIOC can only be enabled on vDSwitches.

Shares, limits, and Quality of Service (QoS) can be applied to network traffic types to limit and guarantee bandwidth to the different network traffic types, including the following:

- Management traffic
- vMotion traffic
- IP storage traffic (NFS/iSCSI)
- Fault Tolerance traffic
- vSphere replication traffic
- Virtual machine traffic

The following screenshot illustrates the Network I/O Control configurations of a vDSwitch:

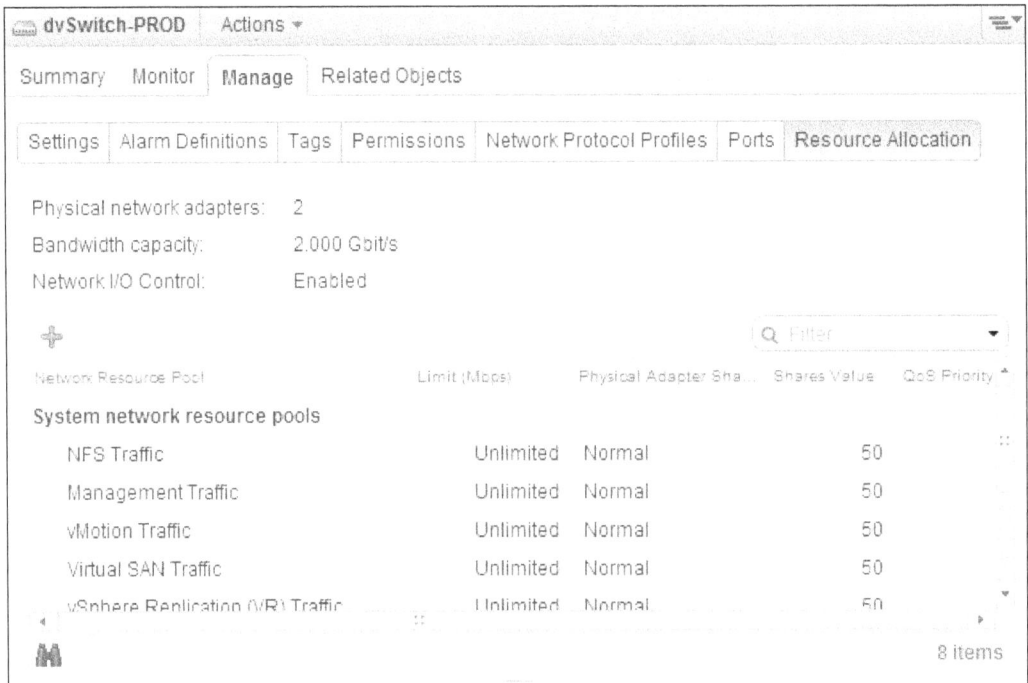

dvSwitch-PROD Actions ▾					
Summary Monitor **Manage** Related Objects					
Settings	Alarm Definitions	Tags	Permissions	Network Protocol Profiles	Ports	**Resource Allocation**

Physical network adapters: 2
Bandwidth capacity: 2.000 Gbit/s
Network I/O Control: Enabled

Network Resource Pool	Limit (Mbps)	Physical Adapter Sha...	Shares Value	QoS Priority
System network resource pools				
NFS Traffic	Unlimited	Normal	50	
Management Traffic	Unlimited	Normal	50	
vMotion Traffic	Unlimited	Normal	50	
Virtual SAN Traffic	Unlimited	Normal	50	
vSphere Replication (VR) Traffic	Unlimited	Normal	50	

8 items

Limit the settings as per the host. The Mbps limit set is applied to all hosts connected to the vDSwitch. Physical adapter shares define the share traffic of the available bandwidth on a physical NIC attached to the vDSwitch; a specific traffic type is allocated during a time of network bandwidth contention.

The percentage of bandwidth a traffic type receives is based on the total number of shares available; for example, in the default configuration, the virtual machine traffic receives 100 shares of the 400 (50 + 50 + 50 + 50 + 100 + 50 + 50) shares available. The formula for this is as follows:

Shares Value / Total Available Shares = Percentage of Physical Network Bandwidth

Therefore, *100 / 400 = 25%.*

The amount of bandwidth available to vMotion would be calculated based on the 50 shares allocated to the vMotion traffic as follows:

50 / 400 = 12.5%

Using private VLANs

Private VLANs (**PVLANs**) are an extension of the VLAN standard. PVLANs can be configured on virtual distributed switches to isolate traffic between virtual machines in the same VLAN.

How to do it...

1. Identify the types of private VLANs available and the functionality of each.
2. Determine the use cases for the PVLANs and identify if the PVLANs can be used to satisfy design requirements.
3. Design the PVLANs to meet design requirements.

How it works...

A primary PVLAN is created on a vDSwitch, and secondary PVLANs are associated with the primary PVLAN. There are three types of secondary PVLANs: **Promiscuous**, **Community**, and **Isolated**. They are depicted in the following diagram:

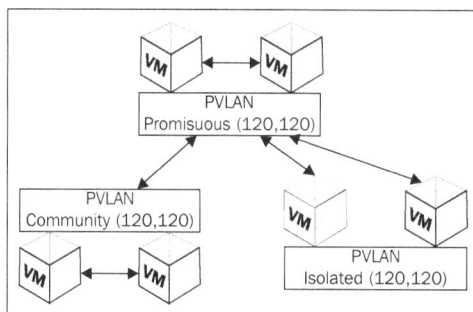

The virtual machine connections in a **Promiscuous PVLAN** can communicate with all the virtual machine connections in the same primary PVLAN. When a primary PVLAN is created, a Promiscuous PVLAN is created with the same PVLAN ID as the primary PVLAN.

Virtual machine connections in a **Community PVLAN** can communicate with other virtual machine connections in the same Community PVLAN and virtual machine connections in the Promiscuous PVLAN. Multiple Community PVLANs can be associated to a single primary PVLAN.

Virtual machine connections in an **Isolated PVLAN** can only communicate with virtual machine connections in the Promiscuous PVLAN. Only one Isolated PVLAN can exist per primary PVLAN.

Private VLANs are created by editing the settings of a vDSwitch as follows:

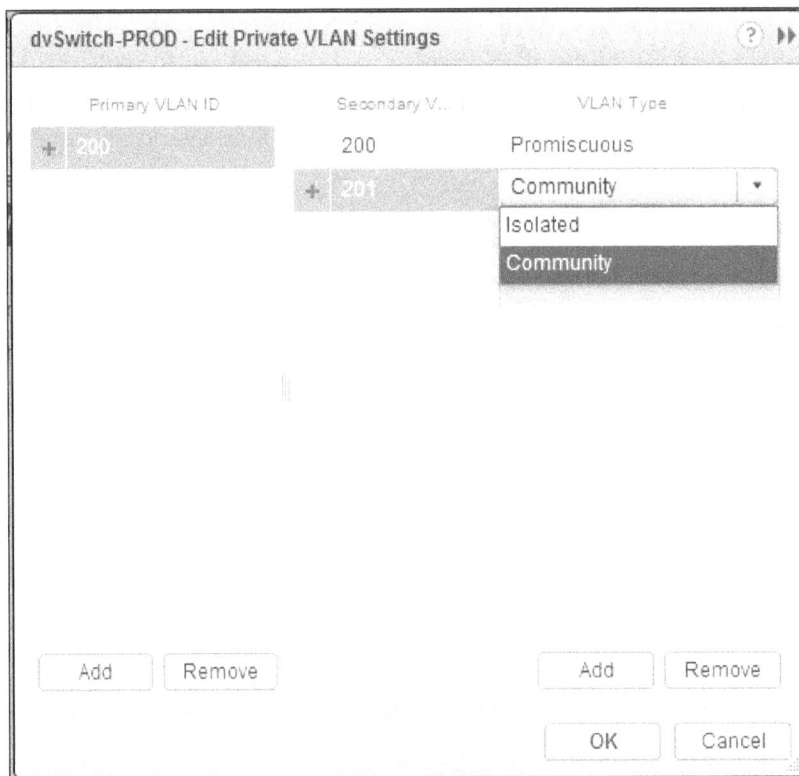

Once the PVLAN has been configured on the vDSwitch, a virtual machine network PortGroup is created with the PVLAN type and ID assigned as follows:

There's more...

In order for PVLAN traffic to be passed between ESXi hosts connected to a vDSwitch, the physical switch must be PVLAN aware and properly configured to support PVLANs. The process to configure PVLANs on a physical switch will vary from vendor to vendor. The following process shows the steps necessary to configure PVLANs on a Cisco IOS switch:

1. Enter the Cisco switch configuration mode:

   ```
   switch# configure terminal
   ```

2. Enable the PVLAN feature on the switch:

   ```
   switch(config)# feature private-vlan
   ```

3. Create the PVLAN on the switch, and set the PVLAN type:

   ```
   switch(config)# vlan <vlan-id>
   switch(config-vlan)# private-vlan primary
   ```

4. Associate the secondary PVLANs with a primary VLAN:

   ```
   switch(config-vlan)# private-vlan association <secondary pvlan>
   ```

5. The switch ports that are connected to the vDSwitch uplinks need to be configured to allow the PVLAN traffic:

   ```
   switch(config)# interface GigabitEthernet1/1
   switch(config-if)# switchport mode trunk
   switch(config-if)# switchport trunk allowed vlan <vlan/pvlan ids>
   ```

IP storage network design considerations

iSCSI, NFS, and Fiber Channel over Ethernet (FCoE) are IP-based storage protocols supported in a vSphere 5.x environment. This recipe covers the design considerations when designing the IP networks that will be used for storage traffic.

How to do it...

1. Identify the network connectivity and virtual switch configurations required for IP-connected storage.
2. Determine the best practices for providing connectivity for IP-connected storage.
3. Design the IP storage connectivity to meet design requirements.

How it works...

IP storage traffic should be separated from other IP traffic. This separation can be provided by either using physically separate hardware (network adapters and physical switches) or separate VLANs for IP storage traffic. The networks associated with IP storage should be directly connected and non-routable.

Multiple network paths to storage should be configured to provide redundancy and load balancing. Single points of failure should be minimized so that the loss of a single network path does not result in the loss of storage connectivity.

Software iSCSI, NFS, and Software FCoE each require a VMkernel interface to be created on a virtual switch. VMkernel interfaces used for iSCSI and FCoE must be bound to a single physical active adapter. Having more than one active adapter or a standby adapter is not supported with Software iSCSI or Software FCoE.

vSphere currently supports NFS v3 over TCP, and there is no multipathing available with this version of NFS. Using link aggregation will only provide failover and not load balancing. NFS will always use a single physical network path even if multiple VMkernels are configured. To manually load balance NFS traffic, create separate VMkernel ports connected to separate networks and mount separate NFS datastores.

The VMkernel port binding for Software iSCSI is configured in the properties of the Software iSCSI adapter. Only VMkernel ports that are compliant will be available for binding, as shown in the following screenshot:

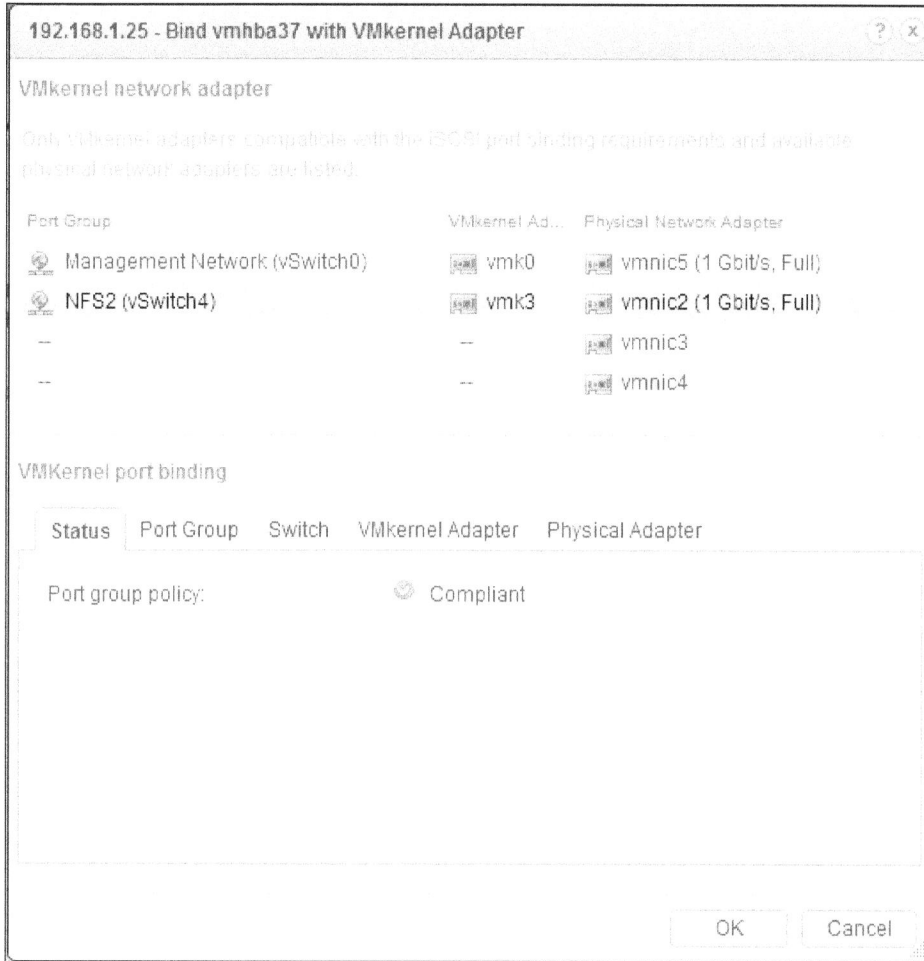

```
┌─────────────────────────────────────────────────────────────────────────┐
│ 192.168.1.25 - Bind vmhba37 with VMkernel Adapter              (?) (x)   │
├─────────────────────────────────────────────────────────────────────────┤
│ VMkernel network adapter                                                  │
│                                                                           │
│ Only VMkernel adapters compatible with the iSCSI port binding            │
│ requirements and available physical network adapters are listed.         │
│                                                                           │
│ Port Group                    VMkernel Ad...  Physical Network Adapter    │
│  🖳 Management Network (vSwitch0)  vmk0      vmnic5 (1 Gbit/s, Full)       │
│  🖳 NFS2 (vSwitch4)                vmk3      vmnic2 (1 Gbit/s, Full)       │
│  --                                --        vmnic3                        │
│  --                                --        vmnic4                        │
│                                                                           │
│ VMKernel port binding                                                     │
│                                                                           │
│   Status   Port Group   Switch   VMkernel Adapter   Physical Adapter     │
│                                                                           │
│   Port group policy:            ⊘ Compliant                              │
│                                                                           │
│                                                                           │
│                                                                           │
│                                                     [ OK ]   [ Cancel ]   │
└─────────────────────────────────────────────────────────────────────────┘
```

To enable the Software FCoE adapter, an NIC that supports FCoE offloads must be installed in the host. If a supported NIC is not installed, the ability to add the software FCoE adapter will not be available.

Physical network binding for FCoE is done when enabling a Software FCoE adapter. Compliant and supported physical adapters are available when adding the Software FCoE adapter. Separate FCoE adapters should be enabled and connected to each storage network fabric. A single ESXi host can support up to four software FCoE adapters. Each software FCoE adapter requires a dedicated VMkernel port bound to a dedicated physical adapter.

There's more...

Enabling **jumbo frames** on the network used for vMotion, iSCSI, or NFS can increase performance and throughput. With jumbo frames enabled, iSCSI or NFS packets can be transferred over the network in a single frame; there is no fragmentation. This decreases the amount of CPU overhead necessary to encapsulate and de-encapsulate IP storage packets.

Jumbo frames must be supported and enabled on the network from end to end; this includes the physical switches as well. In vSphere, jumbo frames are enabled either in the vSwitch configuration or on the vDSwitch uplinks by setting the value of **MTU** to 9000. Jumbo frames must also be enabled on VMkernel interfaces by setting the value of **MTU** for the PortGroup to 9000.

> Many physical switches may require a reboot after the MTU size has been changed. If you are using jumbo frames for this, it is a good idea to configure the maximum MTU on the switch during the initial install.

To enable jumbo frames, set the value of **MTU** on the vSwitch/vDSwitch uplinks to 9000 as shown in the following screenshot:

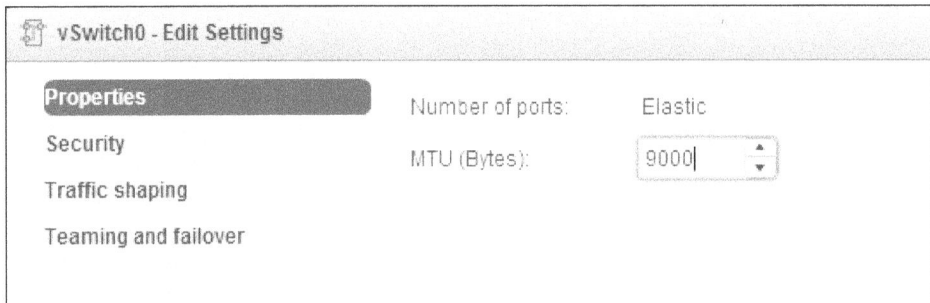

The **MTU** setting must also be changed to 9000 on a VMkernel interface on the vSwitch or vDSwitch as follows:

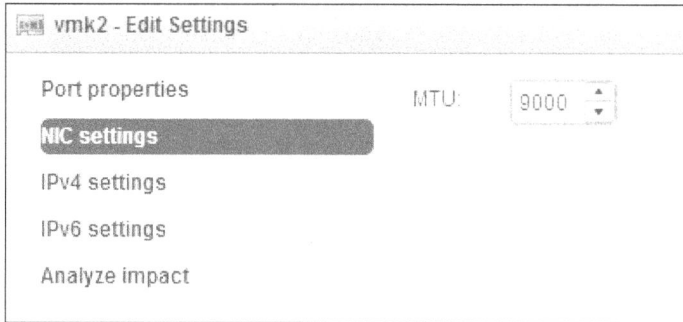

```
vmk2 - Edit Settings

Port properties                    MTU:    9000

NIC settings

IPv4 settings

IPv6 settings

Analyze impact
```

To enable jumbo frames on a Cisco switch, use the following command:

```
Switch(config)# system mtu jumbo 9000
```

The switch must be reloaded for the setting to take effect. The jumbo frames configuration can be tested from the ESXi shell using the vmkping command with the **data fragment** (**DF**) bit (-d) and size (-s) options set, as shown:

```
ESX1 # vmkping -d -s 8972 <IP_Address_of_IP_Storage_Array>
```

If jumbo frames is not configured correctly, vmkping will fail.

vMotion network design considerations

vMotion allows the running state of a virtual machine to be transferred from one ESXi host to another. The network traffic required for the migration uses the VMkernel interfaces that have been enabled for vMotion. vMotion connectivity between ESXi hosts is required when using **Distributed Resource Scheduler** (**DRS**) to balance the virtual machine load across hosts in a DRS-enabled cluster.

How to do it...

1. Identify vMotion network requirements.
2. Determine the best practices for configuring the network connectivity required to support vMotion.
3. Identify the benefits of keeping virtual machines together on the same host to minimize the network traffic that must transverse the physical uplinks.
4. Design the vMotion network connectivity to support design requirements.
5. Design DRS rules to support design requirements.

How it works...

vMotion requires, at a minimum, a single, active 1 Gb network adapter. A second standby adapter should be configured to provide redundancy for the vMotion network.

A vMotion migration can consume all available network bandwidth. If the vMotion network is shared with other network traffic, traffic shaping or NIOC should be enabled to prevent vMotion from impacting other virtual network traffic. If possible, vMotion should be configured on a separate physical network or separate VLAN.

vSphere 5 introduced the ability to configure multiple adapters for use with vMotion. **Multiple-NIC vMotion** allows for the bandwidth of multiple physical NICs to be leveraged by vMotion to speed up the migration of virtual machines between hosts:

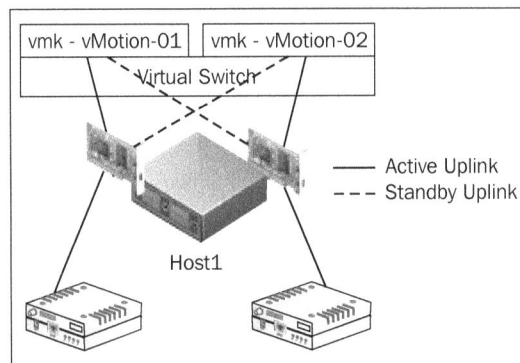

To configure Multiple-NIC vMotion, create multiple VMkernel interfaces with vMotion enabled. Configure each VMkernel interface to use a single Active adapter, and configure other available adapters as standby adapters. When a virtual machine is vMotioned, either manually or by DRS, all available links will be used for the vMotion traffic. More information on Multiple-NIC vMotion can be found in the VMware *Knowledge Base* article at http://kb.vmware.com/kb/2007467.

There's more...

Network communications between virtual machines that are connected to the same virtual switch on the same ESXi host will not use the physical network. All the network traffic between the virtual machines will remain on the host.

Keeping virtual machines that communicate with each other together on the same host will reduce the load on the physical network; for example, keeping a web frontend server, application server, and database server together on the same host will keep traffic between the servers internal to the host.

If the VMware DRS is configured on a vSphere Cluster, DRS rules can be configured on the cluster to keep virtual machines together on the same host.

In the following screenshot, a **Virtual Machine Affinity Rule** has been created to keep two virtual machines together on the same host:

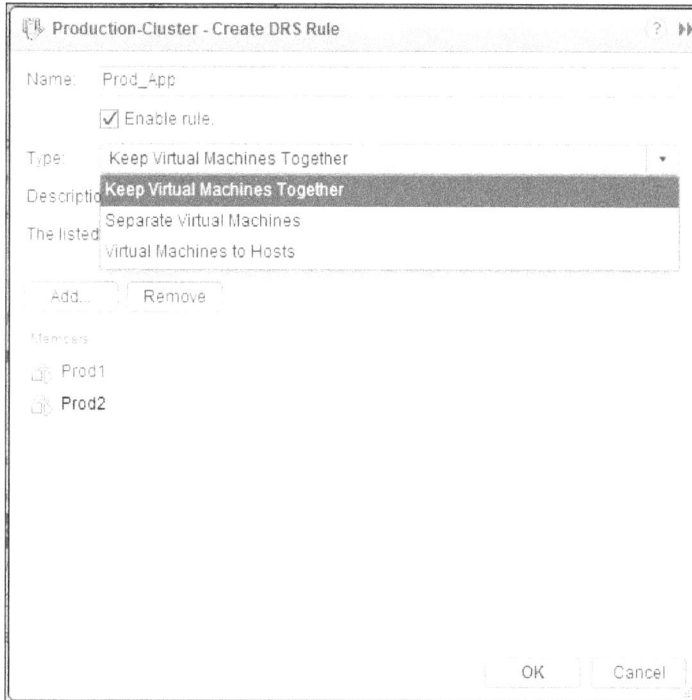

With DRS enabled, the virtual machines assigned to the DRS rule will be vMotioned to run on the same host.

Virtual machine anti-affinity rules (**Separate Virtual Machines**) can also be configured to ensure that virtual machines run on separate hosts. This can be used when service redundancy is provided by multiple virtual machines, such as with multiple virtual domain controllers. Keeping virtual machines separate will ensure that a host failure does not impact service redundancy.

7

The vSphere Compute Design

In this chapter, we will cover the following topics:

- ▶ Calculating CPU resource requirements
- ▶ Calculating memory resource requirements
- ▶ Scaling up or scaling out
- ▶ Determining the vCPU-to-core ratio
- ▶ Clustering compute resources
- ▶ Reserving HA resources to support failover
- ▶ Using Distributed Resource Scheduling to balance cluster resources
- ▶ Ensuring cluster vMotion compatibility

Introduction

This chapter covers logical compute design. **Compute** refers to the processor and memory resources required to support the virtual machines running in the vSphere environment. Calculating the required CPU and memory resources is an important part of the design process and ensures that the environment will be able to support the virtual machine workloads. Design decisions such as scaling up, scaling out, and clustering hosts are covered.

In a physical environment where a single operating system or a single application is installed on a dedicated physical hardware, compute utilization usually averages 10 to 20 percent of the available resources. A majority of the memory and CPU resources are idle and wasted. In a virtual environment, the resources available are utilized by multiple operating systems and applications. It is not uncommon to see a usage of 65 to 80 percent of the available resources.

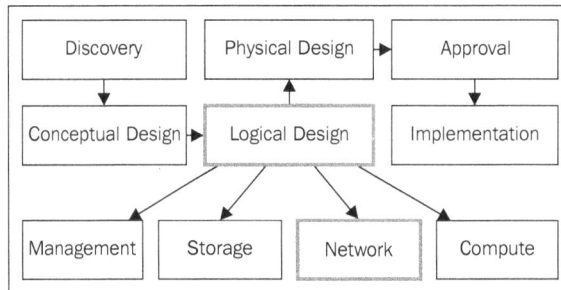

This chapter takes a look at the clustering hosts' resources in order to take advantage of the advanced VMware features: VMware **High Availability** (**HA**) and VMware **Distributed Resource Scheduler** (**DRS**). Reserving resources for failover and providing vMotion compatibility are also covered.

Calculating CPU resource requirements

There are several factors that must be considered when calculating CPU resources requirements, such as the amount of CPU resources required to support the current workloads, the amount of CPU resources required to support future growth, and the maximum CPU utilization threshold.

The following discovery information from *Chapter 3*, *The Design Factors*, will be used to calculate the CPU requirements:

- Currently, there are 100 physical servers, each hosting a single application. Each application services 10 customers.

- The business expects to add 50 new customers over the next year.

- Support growth over the next five years.

- Each application server is configured with two dual-core 2.7 GHz processors. The peak usage of a single application server is approximately 10 percent of the total or approximately 1 GHz.

How to do it...

1. Determine the amount of CPU resources required to support the current workloads:

   Number of Workloads x CPU Speed in MHz or GHz = Current CPU Resources Required

2. Determine the maximum utilization threshold. This is the maximum percentage of available resources that should be consumed.

3. Determine the amount of growth in CPU resources that the environment should support.

4. Calculate the amount of CPU resources required:

   Current Workload CPU Resources + Future Growth + Maximum Utilization Threshold = Total CPU Resources Required

How it works...

Calculating the required CPU resources necessary to support the current workloads is straightforward using the following formula:

Number of Workloads x CPU Speed in MHz or GHz = Current CPU Resources Required

100 x 1 GHz = 100 GHz

In order to determine the total CPU resources required, the amount required to support future growth must also be calculated. The amount of CPU resources required for future growth will be determined by the design requirements. Based on the requirements identified in *Chapter 3, The Design Factors*, the environment should be designed to support a growth of 25 additional virtual machines over the next five years.

A **maximum utilization threshold** must also be determined and accounted for in CPU resource requirements. This threshold determines the maximum percentage of total CPU resources that will be consumed. It is unlikely that the environment would be configured to consume 100 percent of the CPU resources available. If the maximum utilization threshold is 75 percent, an additional 25 percent of CPU resources will be added to calculate the total CPU resources required:

Current CPU Resources Required + Future Growth = Total CPU Resources Required

100 GHz + (25 x 1 GHz) = 125 GHz

When the maximum utilization threshold is 75%, the calculation will be as follows:

*125 GHz * (100/75) = ~167 GHz*

The environment must be designed to support the 167 GHz of CPU resources that are in turn required to support the current workloads, future workloads, and provide for a maximum utilization threshold of 75 percent.

Calculating memory resource requirements

There are several factors that must be considered when calculating memory requirements; these factors include the amount of memory required to support the current workloads, the amount of memory required to support future growth, the amount of memory required for virtual machine memory overhead, and the maximum memory utilization threshold.

As with CPU requirements, the discovery information from *Chapter 3*, *The Design Factors*, will also be used to calculate the memory requirements:

> ▸ Currently, there are 100 physical servers, each hosting a single application. Each application services 10 customers.

> ▸ The business expects to add 50 new customers over the next year.

> ▸ Support growth over the next five years.

> ▸ Each application server is configured with 8 GB of memory. The peak usage of a single application server is approximately 65 percent or around 5.2 GB.

How to do it...

1. Determine the amount of memory resources required to support the current workloads:

   Number of Workloads X Memory Usage = Current Memory Required

2. Determine the memory overhead required.

3. Determine the maximum utilization threshold. This is the maximum percentage of available resources that should be consumed.

4. Determine the amount of growth in the memory resources that the environment should support.

5. Determine any memory resource savings that may be realized from memory sharing (for example, **Transparent Page Sharing** (**TPS**)).

6. Calculate the amount of memory resources required:

   Current Workload Memory Usage + Memory Overhead + Future Growth + Maximum Utilization Threshold - TPS Savings = Total Memory Resources Required

How it works...

To calculate the amount of memory required to support the current workloads, the following formula is used:

Number of Workloads x Memory Usage = Current Memory Required

100 x 5.2 GB = 520 GB

The memory overhead of a virtual machine must also be accounted for when calculating memory requirements. The amount of memory required for an overhead depends on the configuration of the virtual machine. The number of vCPUs allocated to the virtual machine, the amount of memory allocated to the virtual machine, and the virtual hardware configured for the virtual machine will have an impact on the amount of memory required for overhead:

Typically, the memory overhead required for a virtual machine is between 20 MB and 150 MB. Memory overhead estimations based on the amount of RAM and the number of vCPUs can be found in the vSphere 5.1 documentation at `http://pubs.vmware.com/vsphere-51/index.jsp?topic=%2Fcom.vmware.vsphere.resmgmt.doc%2FGUID-B42C72C1-F8D5-40DC-93D1-FB31849B1114.html` and for vSphere 5.5 at `http://pubs.vmware.com/vsphere-55/index.jsp?topic=%2Fcom.vmware.vsphere.resmgmt.doc%2FGUID-B42C72C1-F8D5-40DC-93D1-FB31849B1114.html`.

This may seem like a small amount of memory, but over dozens or even hundreds of virtual machines, it can have a significant impact on the amount of total memory required:

(Number of Workloads x Memory Usage) + (Number of Workloads x Memory Overhead) = Current Memory Required

(100 x 5.2 GB) + (100 x 50 MB) = 525 GB

To calculate the total memory required, future growth must be considered. When memory is calculated for growth, the memory overhead required to support the additional virtual machines must also considered.

The maximum utilization threshold must also be determined for memory resources. This threshold defines what is the maximum percentage of the total memory resources that will be consumed. If the maximum utilization threshold is 75 percent, an additional 25 percent of memory resources will need to be added in order to calculate the total memory resources required:

*Current Memory Required + Future Growth * (100/Maximum Threshold%) = Total Memory Resources Required*

*525 GB + [(25 x 5.2 GB) + (25 x 50 MB)] * (100/75) = ~875 GB*

875 GB of memory is required to support the current workloads, future growth, and a maximum utilization threshold of 75 percent.

There's more...

Transparent Page Sharing (**TPS**) is a memory sharing mechanism used by ESXi that allows virtual machine memory content that is same to be shared between the virtual machines on the same host by eliminating the redundant copies of memory pages.

The amount of memory saved by memory sharing depends on workload characteristics. Many nearly identical virtual machines may provide substantial resource savings due to memory sharing, while a more diverse workload will result in little, if any, gains from TPS.

When virtual machine workloads are similar, running the same guest operating system and the same or similar applications, a percentage of the memory used by the virtual machines will be the same:

Total Memory Resources Required – Percentage of TPS Savings = Total Memory Resources Required

875 GB – 25% = ~657 GB

If savings associated with TPS are applied, the total amount of memory required is approximately 657 GB. If the design required that the memory should not be overcommitted or reserved for each virtual machine, any potential savings for TPS should not be applied.

In order to take advantage of TPS, large memory pages would need to be disabled on the ESXi hosts. This is done by setting `Mem.AllocGuestLargePage` to `0`. This configuration must be done on each host. Disabling large pages will increase sharing and decrease the amount of physical memory required, but it can have a performance impact, especially with memory-intensive workloads.

Scaling up or scaling out

Once the total CPU and memory resource requirements have been calculated, the amount of resources per host must be determined. Host resources can be designed based on two resource-scaling methodologies, **scaling up** or **scaling out**.

When scaling up, fewer, larger hosts are used to satisfy the resource requirements. More virtual machines run on a single host; because of this, more virtual machines are also affected by a host failure.

When scaling out, many smaller hosts are used to satisfy the resource requirements. Fewer virtual machines run on a single host, and fewer virtual machines will be affected by a host failure.

How to do it...

1. Determine whether the host in the environment should scale up or scale out.

2. Determine the number of virtual machine workloads per host.

3. Based on the number of virtual machines per host, calculate the number of hosts required. This should also include the number of hosts required to support growth and failover:

   (Number of Workloads / Number of Workloads per Host) + (Number of Future Workloads / Number of Workloads per Host) + Number of Failover Hosts = Number of Physical Hosts Required

4. Using the identified CPU requirements, calculate the CPU resources required per host:

   Total CPU Resources Required / (Number of Physical Hosts Required - Failover Hosts) = CPU Resources per Host

5. Using the identified memory requirements, calculate the memory resources required per host:

   Total Memory Resources Required / (Number of Physical Hosts Required - Failover Hosts) = Memory Resources per Host

How it works...

Many CPU and memory resources were calculated in the earlier recipes in this chapter and are stated as follows:

▸ The total number of CPU resources required is 167 GHz

▸ The total number of memory resources required, taking into account a 25 percent savings for Transparent Page Sharing, is 657 GB

Based on the design factors, the determination can be made on whether a host should be designed to scale up or scale out. In this case, the following design information provides what is needed to size the individual host resources:

- Currently, there are 100 physical servers, each hosting a single application. Each application services 10 customers.

- No more than 20 application servers or 200 customers should be affected by a hardware failure.

- The business expects to add 50 new customers over the next year.

- Support growth over the next five years.

Based on the requirements, the total number of hosts required to support the current workloads, the future workloads, and the redundancy requirements can be calculated:

Total Hosts Required = (100 physical servers / 20 virtual servers per host) + [((50 new customers x 5 years) / 10) / 20] + 2 failover hosts = 8.25 = 9 Physical Hosts Required

Use the following to determine the number of CPU resources required per host (the failover hosts are not included here because these resources are effectively reserved for failover):

167 GHz / 7 = 23.8 GHz CPU per Host

Use the following to determine the number of memory resources required per host (as with CPU resources, the failover hosts are not included in the calculation):

657 GB / 7 = ~94 GB Memory per Host

Each physical host will need to be sized to support 20 virtual machines and will require 23.8 GHz of CPU resources and 94 GB of memory resources.

There's more...

The requirements from *Chapter 3*, *The Design Factors*, are very specific about the maximum number of virtual machines that can be run on a host. This simplifies the scale-up or scale-out design decision. The following are a couple of other possible design requirements to work through in order to demonstrate the impact that scaling up and scaling out will have on resources.

- What if a requirement was to virtualize the environment using three hosts? What resources would be required for each host? If there are 100 virtual machines, how many will be impacted during a host hardware failure?

- What if the requirement was that each host should be configured with resources to support no more than 10 virtual machines? How will that change the number of resources required for each host? If there are 100 virtual machines, how many will be impacted during a host hardware failure?

Determining the vCPU-to-core ratio

The number of virtual machine vCPUs allocated compared to the number of physical CPU cores available is the **vCPU-to-core** ratio. Determining this ratio will depend on the CPU utilization of the workloads.

If workloads are CPU-intensive, the vCPU-to-core ratio will need to be smaller; if workloads are not CPU-intensive, the vCPU-to-core ratio can be larger. A typical vCPU-to-core ratio for server workloads is about 4:1—four vCPUs allocated for each available physical core. However, this can be much higher if workloads are not CPU-intensive.

A vCPU-to-core ratio that is too large can result in high CPU Ready times—the percentage of time that a virtual machine is ready but is unable to be scheduled to run on the physical CPU—which will have a negative impact on the virtual machine's performance.

How to do it...

1. Determine the number of vCPUs required:

    vCPUs per Workload x Number of Workloads Per Host = Number of vCPUs Required

2. Determine the vCPU-to-core ratio based on the CPU utilization of the workloads. If the workloads are CPU-intensive, the vCPU-to-CPU-core ratio will be lower; for less CPU-intensive workloads, the ratio will be higher. The ratio of 4:1 is generally a good starting point for server workloads.

3. Calculate the number of CPU cores required to support the vCPU-to-CPU-core ratio:

    Number of vCPUs x vCPU-to-core ratio = Number of Cores Required

How it works...

The vCPU-to-core ratio is calculated based on the number of vCPUs allocated and the number of physical CPU cores available. For example, if two vCPUs are allocated to each virtual machine:

2 vCPUs allocated to each virtual machine x 20 virtual machines = 40 vCPUs

In a design with 40 vCPUs that requires a 4:1 vCPU-to-core ratio, a minimum of 10 physical cores would be required.

If dual 8-core processors are used, the vCPU-to-core ratio can be calculated as follows:

2 x 8 Cores = 16 Total Cores

40 vCPUs and physical 16 Cores = 2.5 vCPUs to each physical core, or a 2.5:1 vCPU-to-core Ratio

Clustering compute resources

A **vSphere cluster** is a group of ESXi hosts. The CPU, memory, storage, and network resources of each host are combined to form a logical set of cluster resources. A vSphere cluster is required to facilitate the use of features such as vSphere HA, vSphere DRS, and Fault Tolerance.

A single vSphere 5.x cluster can contain up to 32 hosts. For vSphere features such as vSphere HA and DRS to work correctly, the configurations must be consistent across all hosts in the cluster. The consistency of shared storage and network configurations is a necessity.

How to do it...

1. Using the vSphere Web Client of vSphere Client, create a new vSphere cluster.
2. Enable vSphere High Availability on the cluster.
3. Enable vSphere Distributed Resource Scheduling on the cluster.

How it works...

A new cluster is created using either the vSphere Web Client or vSphere Client. Right-click on the datacenter object in which you want the cluster to be created and select **New Cluster**. The **New Cluster** dialog will open as shown in the following screenshot:

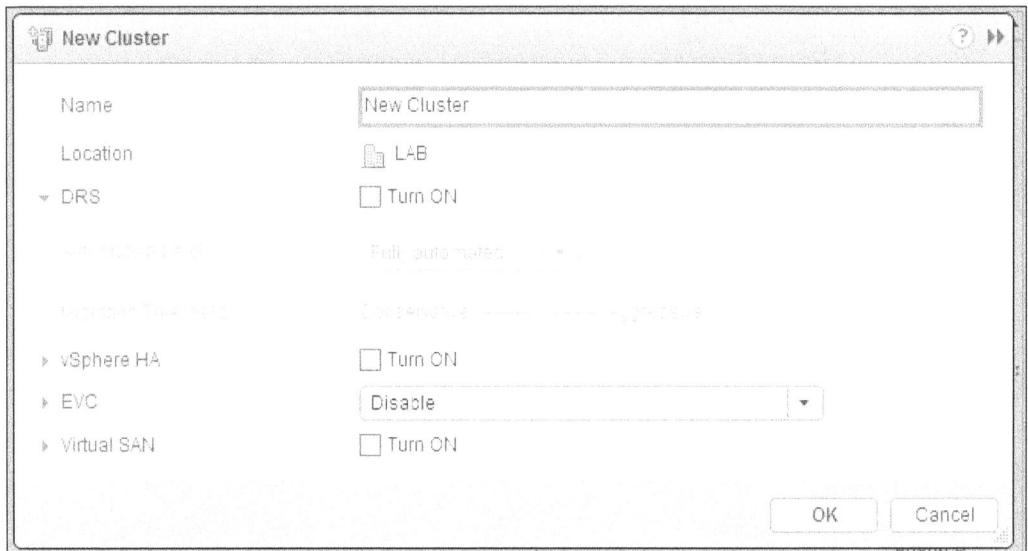

A name must be provided for the cluster. Other cluster options, such as enabling **DRS** and **vSphere HA** can be configured during the new cluster creation or can be configured at a later time by editing the properties of the cluster.

Once the cluster has been created, hosts can be added to the cluster. New hosts are added to the cluster using the **Add Host** wizard by right-clicking on the cluster and selecting **Add Host**. Existing hosts can be added to the cluster by dragging-and-dropping the host inventory object into the new cluster. The cluster's **Summary** tab displays the available cluster resources, the cluster resource usage, and details of vSphere DRS and vSphere HA configurations.

Hosts within a cluster should be configured with similar compute resources. In a cluster where the VMware DRS is enabled, processor compatibility is required. Checking for processor compatibility is covered later in this chapter.

Reserving HA resources to support failover

When vSphere High Availability (HA) has been enabled on a vSphere cluster, the virtual machines running on the cluster are protected from a host hardware failure or virtual machine guest operating system crash.

In the event that a host suffers a hardware failure or if ESXi crashes, the virtual machines are restarted on the surviving hosts in the cluster. Resources must be reserved in the cluster to guarantee that the necessary resources are available to restart the virtual machines.

How to do it...

1. Edit the settings of the vSphere cluster to enable High Availability.
2. Enable the HA Admission Control policy.
3. Select the HA Admission Control policy that should be applied to the cluster.
4. Define the failover settings required based on the HA Admission Control policy selected.

How it works...

VMware HA Admission Control ensures that enough physical resources are available to meet the CPU and memory reservation requirements needed to restart the virtual machines on surviving hosts, in case there is a host failure:

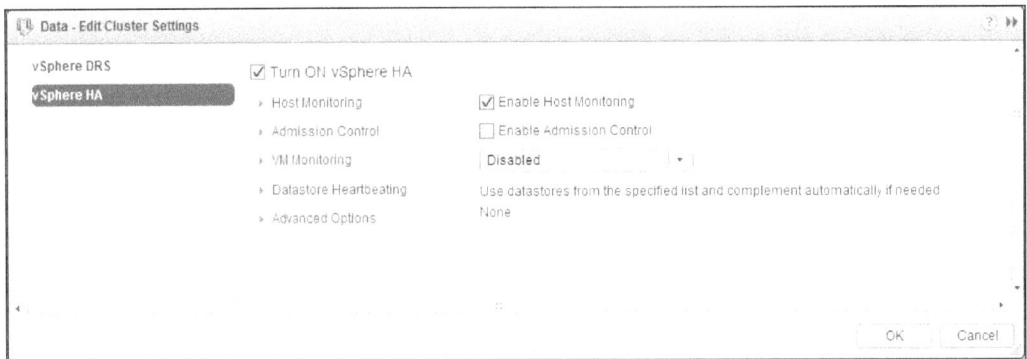

When HA Admission Control is enabled, virtual machines cannot be powered on if there are insufficient resources to meet the reservation requirements for the virtual machines protected in the HA cluster. The resource requirements are calculated based on the HA Admission Control policy selected.

In vSphere 5.x, there are three HA admission control policies:

- ▸ **Define failover capacity by static number of hosts**
- ▸ **Define failover capacity by reserving a percentage of the cluster resources**
- ▸ **Use dedicated failover hosts**

The **Define failover capacity by static number of hosts** policy (for vSphere client: **Host failures cluster tolerates**) reserves failover resources based on the slot size. The **slot size** is determined by the largest CPU and memory reservation for a virtual machine that has been powered on. The number of slots available in the cluster and the number of slots to be reserved based on the failover capacity selection are calculated by HA.

A single virtual machine with a large memory or CPU reservation will have an impact on the number of slots available. The value of **Fixed slot size** configured using the vSphere Web Client defines the amount of CPU and memory resources that make up a slot. In the versions of vSphere prior to 5.1, the slot size could be configured with the vSphere Client by setting the HA advanced options as `das.slotCPUInMHz` for CPU resources and as `das.slotMeminMB` for memory resources.

Using the **Define failover capacity by reserving a percentage of the cluster resources** policy (for vSphere Client: **Percentage of cluster resources reserved as failover spare capacity**) allows a percentage of the memory and CPU resources to be reserved to accommodate a host failure. This reservation is distributed across all hosts in the cluster. To guarantee resource availability in the event of a host failure, the percentage should be set to reserve the CPU and memory resources equal to a single host in a cluster; for example, for a 5-host cluster, 20 percent of cluster resources should be reserved. This will guarantee that enough resources are available to support a single host failure.

The **Use dedicated failover hosts** policy (for vSphere Client: **Specify failover hosts**) reserves a configured host to be available for failover. The hosts specified as failover hosts will not provide resources to virtual machines during normal operations. The host is a hot spare and virtual machines will only be started on the hosts.

If HA Admission Control is disabled, virtual machines can be powered on even if there are not enough resources available to ensure failover capacity. If surviving hosts are not able to provide the resources with reservations necessary to start virtual machines, the virtual machines will not be restarted when a host fails.

Using distributed resource scheduling to balance cluster resources

The vSphere DRS determines the initial placement and balances resources across available host resources in a vSphere cluster. Virtual machine resources can be guaranteed or limited. Rules can be applied to keep virtual machines together on the same host or to ensure that virtual machines run on separate hosts.

How to do it...

1. Edit the settings of the vSphere cluster to enable vSphere DRS.

2. Select a value for the DRS **Automation Level** that should be applied to the DRS-enabled cluster.

3. Select a value for **Migration Threshold** that should be applied to the DRS-enabled cluster.

How it works...

vSphere DRS can be enabled when creating a new vSphere cluster or by editing the settings of an existing cluster:

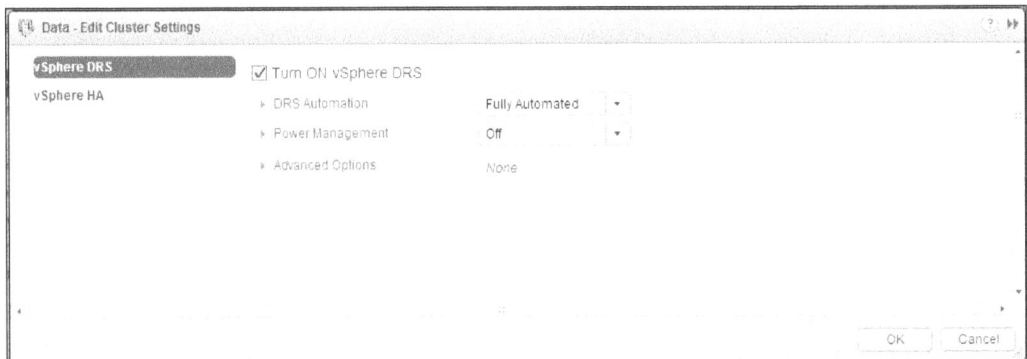

When DRS is enabled, the DRS **Automation Level** and **Migration Threshold** is set to determine how DRS will place and migrate virtual machines between hosts in the cluster in order to balance the resources across all hosts in the cluster.

If **Automation Level** is set to **Manual**, vCenter will make suggestions for initial virtual machine placement and virtual machine migrations. When a virtual machine is powered on, DRS makes a suggestion for the initial placement of the virtual machine based on the balance of cluster resources, but this must be acknowledged by or can be changed by the administrator. Migrations will not be performed unless they are acknowledged by an administrator.

Setting **Automation Level** to **Partially Automated** will make vCenter automatically select a cluster host to place the virtual machine at power-on, but it will only make recommendations for virtual machine migrations. Migrations are not performed unless acknowledged by an administrator.

When **Automation Level** is set to **Fully Automated**, it allows vCenter to automatically determine the initial placement of virtual machines. This setting also causes vCenter to automatically migrate virtual machines between the hosts in the cluster in order to balance resource usage across all cluster hosts. When **Automation Level** is set to **Fully Automated**, virtual machines will also be automatically migrated to other hosts in the cluster when a host is placed in the maintenance mode.

> The default DRS migration threshold will typically provide the best balance for most clusters. If cluster resources are not balanced or if too many DRS migrations are being invoked, the migration threshold can be adjusted to be either more conservative or more aggressive.

Migration Threshold determines how the cluster will be balanced when **Automation Level** is set to **Fully Automated** or how DRS recommendations will be generated when **Automation Level** is set to **Manual** or **Partially Automated**.

A conservative migration threshold setting will only cause virtual machines to migrate if the migration will result in a significant improvement in the balance of resources. Setting the migration threshold to be more aggressive will cause virtual machines to migrate if any benefit can be realized from the migration. Setting the migration threshold to be too aggressive can result in unnecessary virtual machine migrations or virtual machines constantly migrating in an attempt to aggressively balance the resources.

Ensuring cluster vMotion compatibility

vMotion provides for running virtual machines to be migrated between vSphere hosts. In order to facilitate live vMotion, the processors between hosts must contain the same CPU features and present the same instruction sets. **Enhanced vMotion Compatibility** (**EVC**) masks compatibility issues between the hosts in a cluster.

> Enabling EVC on a cluster ensures that hosts added to the cluster in the future will not have vMotion compatibility issues.

Processors must be from the same manufacturer; EVC does not provide vMotion compatibility between Intel and AMD processors. EVC is not required to support HA across different processor types and only support live vMotion between hosts.

How to do it...

1. Edit the settings of the vSphere cluster.
2. Change the value of **EVC Mode** to **Enable EVC** and select an EVC mode baseline.

How it works...

The EVC mode is enabled on the cluster when the cluster is created or by editing the **Properties** of the cluster. The EVC baseline is selected based on the processor manufacturer (EVC for AMD hosts or EVC for Intel hosts). The selected baseline compatibility is validated against all hosts in the cluster.

The following screenshot shows the EVC mode enabled for Intel hosts and the mode set to **Intel "Sandy Bridge" Generation**:

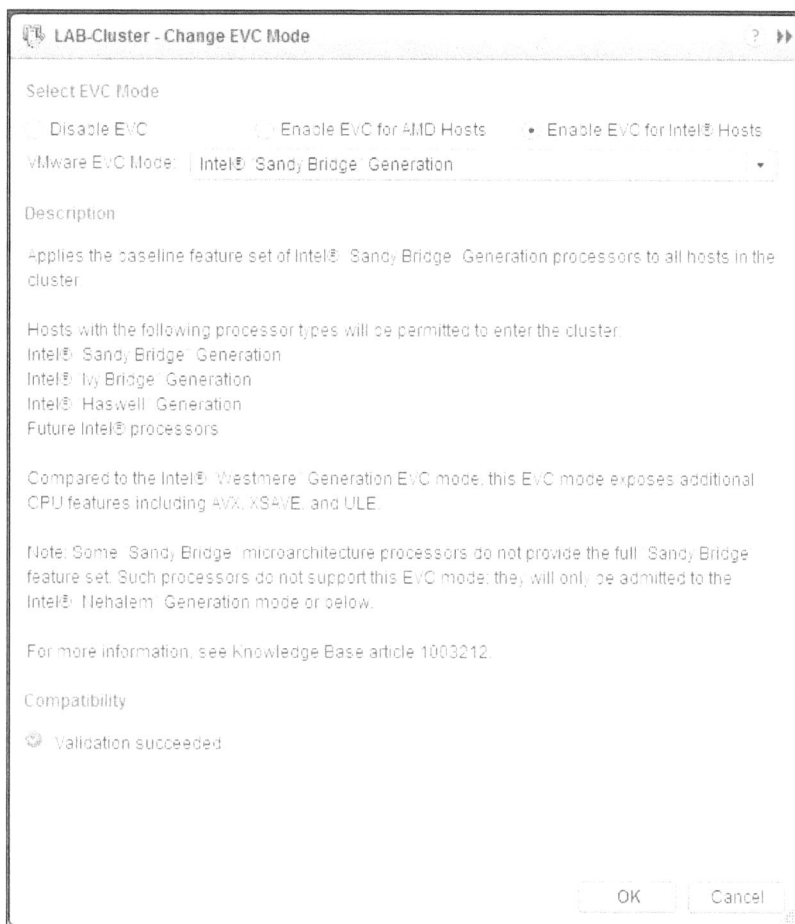

The EVC baseline configuration and the processor supported for each EVC baseline can be found on the VMware Knowledge Base at `http://kb.vmware.com/kb/1003212`.

8

The vSphere Physical Design

In this chapter, we will cover the following topics:

- ▶ Using the VMware Hardware Compatibility List (HCL)
- ▶ Understanding the physical storage design
- ▶ Understanding the physical network design
- ▶ Creating the physical compute design
- ▶ Creating a custom ESXi image
- ▶ Best practices for ESXi host BIOS settings

Introduction

The vSphere physical design process (shown in the following diagram) includes choosing and configuring the physical hardware required to support the storage, network, and compute requirements:

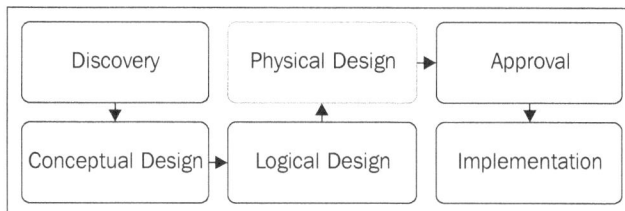

```
┌──────────────────────────────────────────────────────────┐
│  ┌──────────────┐   ┌──────────────┐   ┌──────────────┐   │
│  │  Discovery   │   │Physical Design│──▶│   Approval   │   │
│  └──────┬───────┘   └──────▲───────┘   └──────┬───────┘   │
│         │                  │                  │           │
│  ┌──────▼───────┐   ┌──────┴───────┐   ┌──────▼───────┐   │
│  │Conceptual Design│─▶│Logical Design│   │Implementation│  │
│  └──────────────┘   └──────────────┘   └──────────────┘   │
└──────────────────────────────────────────────────────────┘
```

During the physical design process, the hardware and configuration choices should map to the logical design and satisfy the functional and nonfunctional design requirements.

A design architect should answer the following questions about each design decision:

- ▸ Does the design meet the requirements of the logical design?
- ▸ Does the design satisfy the functional and nonfunctional requirements?
- ▸ Is the selected hardware supported?

There will often be more than one physical solution that will meet the design requirements.

This chapter contains recipes for verifying whether or not our hardware is supported by checking VMware's Hardware Compatibility List, the physical design of storage, network, and compute resources, creating a custom ESXi image, and best practices for BIOS settings on a server running ESXi.

Using the VMware Hardware Compatibility List (HCL)

VMware's **Hardware Compatibility List** (**HCL**) is a database of all tested and supported physical hardware. The physical hardware chosen to support the created design must be checked against the HCL to ensure that it will be supported. This includes storage devices, I/O devices, and servers. It is important to ensure not only that the hardware vendor and model is supported, but also the firmware version of the hardware.

Verifying supportability against the HCL is important not only for new designs, but also when upgrading a design from one version to another on vSphere. Legacy hardware is often removed from the HCL when new versions of vSphere are released.

How to do it...

To verify whether or not a certain hardware device is supported with the current version of vSphere, perform the following process:

1. Visit `http://www.vmware.com/go/hcl/`.
2. Select the type or category of device to determine its compatibility by selecting it using the **What are you looking for** dropdown. For example, if the compatibility of a Network Interface Card (NIC) is being determined, select **IO Devices**, as shown in the following screenshot:

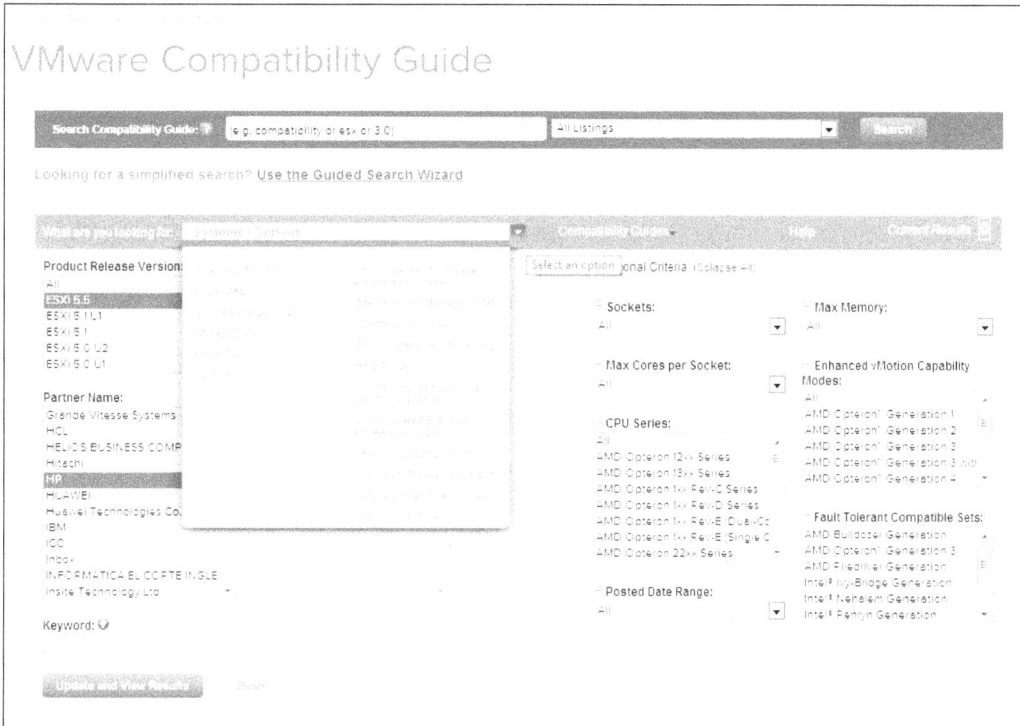

3. Select values for **Product Release Version**, **Brand Name**, and **IO Device Type**, as shown in the following screenshot:

4. Enter a value for **Keyword**, such as the model number. In this example, the search will be for NC364T, which is an HP quad port 1 Gb server adapter, as shown in the following screenshot:

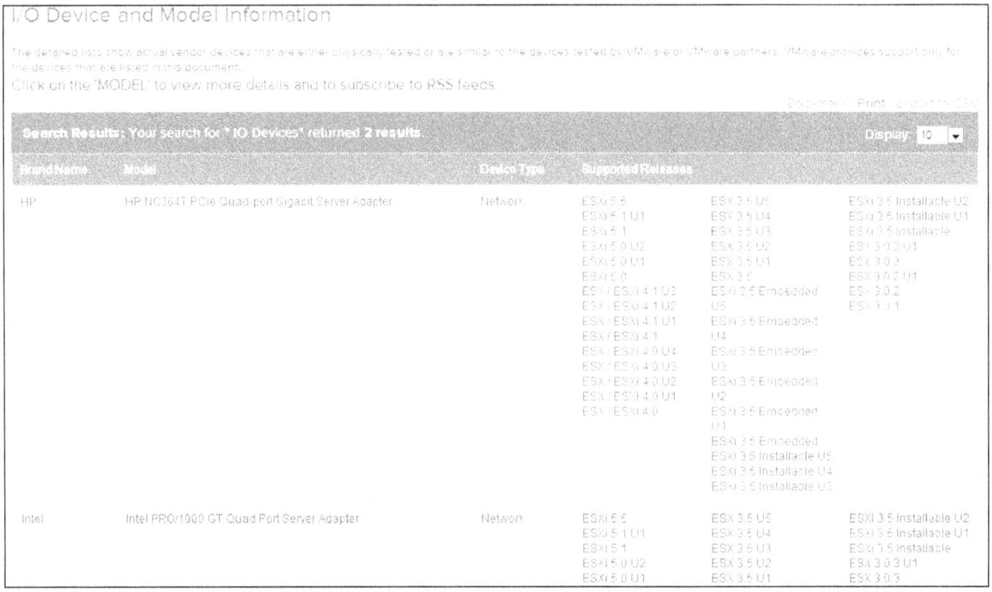

5. Clicking on the device model will display details about the device, the firmware versions that are supported, and the device driver used by ESXi, as shown in the following screenshot:

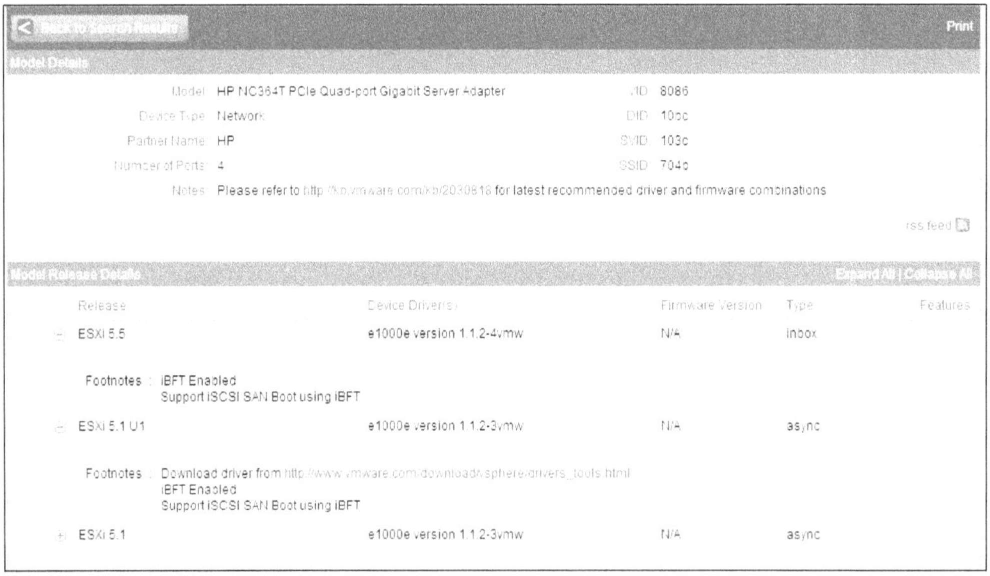

How it works...

The VMware HCL provides an easy-to-search online database of hardware that has been tested and is supported in a vSphere environment.

> Hardware that is not listed on VMware's Hardware Compatibility List may still work with vSphere. However, if the hardware is not listed on the HCL, it may cause issues with obtaining support from VMware in the event of issues with the environment. Only hardware found on the HCL should be used in vSphere production environments.

Selecting the hardware type, VMware product and version, hardware vendor, device type, and supported features allows a design architect to quickly view and select supported hardware. Details about the supported firmware or BIOS versions, the availability of native drivers, and the requirement for third-party drivers can also be quickly viewed for hardware information on the HCL.

There's more...

VMware also provides compatibility guides. The compatibility guides can be accessed through a menu on the HCL page located at `http://www.vmware.com/go/hcl`. These guides provide details about the features supported by a specific piece of support hardware and can be seen in the following screenshot:

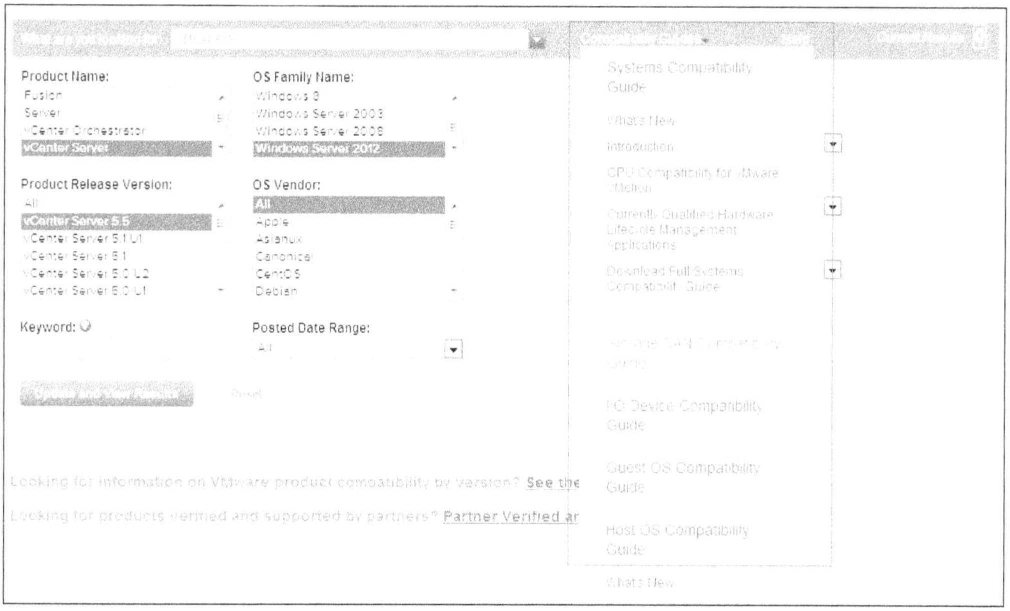

The following screenshot is an excerpt from the Storage/SAN Compatibility Guide showing the support details of the EMC VNX5300 array:

Another important guide to reference is VMware's *Product Interoperability Matrix*, located at `http://partnerweb.vmware.com/comp_guide2/sim/interop_matrix.php`. This guide provides interoperability information about vSphere products, databases, and host operating systems. If multiple VMware products will be used in the storage design, their interoperability must be checked against the matrix to determine which versions are compatible with which products.

For example, if the VMware **Site Recovery Manager** (**SRM**) is going to be used in a vSphere 5.1 design, the interoperability matrix is checked to determine which versions of SRM are compatible with that version of vSphere:

The VMware compatibility guides are also available from the **Product Interoperability Matrixes** page.

Understanding the physical storage design

Storage is the foundation of any vSphere design. Properly designed storage is key for vSphere features, such as **High Availability** (**HA**), **Distributed Resource Scheduling** (**DRS**), and **Fault Tolerance** (**FT**), to operate correctly.

How to do it...

Performance, capacity, availability, and recoverability are all factors that must be taken into account when determining the hardware and the configuration of the physical storage. The physical storage design requires the following steps:

1. Select a storage hardware that satisfies the logical storage design. This includes the storage array, storage host bus adapters, and any switching, fiber channel, or Ethernet that may be required to support storage connectivity.
2. Verify the compatibility of each storage hardware component using the VMware HCL.
3. Design the storage configuration to satisfy the design factors related to availability, recoverability, performance, and capacity.

How it works...

The physical storage design must meet the capacity and performance requirements defined by the logical storage design, and these requirements must be mapped back to the design factors.

The logical storage design identifies the capacity, IOPS, and throughput required to support the vSphere design. The design factors identify the functional requirements, such as availability and recoverability, and any constraints that may be placed on the physical design, such as using an array from a specific vendor or using a specific storage protocol.

The logical storage design specifications are as follows:

- Storage capacity: 16 TB
- Storage IOPS: 6250
- I/O profile: 8k
- I/O size: 90% Read / 10% Write
- Total storage throughput: 55 MB/s
- Number of virtual machines per datastore: 20
- Datastore size: 2.5 TB

The factors that influence the physical storage design include the following:

- Shared or local storage

- Block storage or file storage

- Array specifications, such as active/active or active/passive; the number of storage processors; and cache

- Storage protocol that uses Fiber Channel, iSCSI, NFS, or Fiber Channel over Ethernet (FCoE) as well as the type and number of disks and the RAID configuration

- Support for VMware integration: **vStorage APIs for Array Integration** (**VAAI**) and **vSphere APIs for Storage Awareness** (**VASA**)

- Support for advanced storage technologies: de-duplication, tiering, and flash-based cache

- **Recovery Point Objective** (**RPO**), which is the amount of data that will not be lost in the event of a disaster and the **Recovery Time Objective** (**RTO**), which is the amount of time it takes to recover the system and data in the event of a disaster

The chief considerations when choosing a storage platform are IOPS, throughput, and support for features such as VAAI, VASA, SRM and accelerated backups. Physical storage design should focus on both performance and capacity. The physical storage design must be able to meet the performance requirements of the design.

Meeting the design capacity requirements is typically easy to accomplish, but ensuring that the storage will meet the performance requirements takes a bit more work. The I/O profile of the workloads, number of IOPS required, types of disks used, and RAID level selected all have an impact on the storage performance. It is good practice to first design the storage to meet the performance requirements and then design to meet the capacity requirements.

Understanding the physical network design

Network connectivity must be provided for both virtual machine network connectivity and VMkernel connectivity. Physical switches, uplinks, virtual switches, and virtual PortGroups are all components of the physical network design.

How to do it...

Performance, capacity, availability, and recoverability are all factors that must be taken into account when determining the hardware and the configuration of the physical network. The following steps are necessary to successfully complete the physical network design:

1. Select the network hardware that satisfies the logical network design, including physical network switches and network interface cards.

2. Verify whether or not the network I/O device hardware, such as network interface cards and **converged network adapters** (**CNA**), is compatible and supported using the VMware HCL.

3. Design the physical network topology and virtual network configuration to satisfy the design factors related to availability, recoverability, performance, and capacity.

How it works...

The physical network design must satisfy the performance and availability requirements defined by the logical network design, which in turn must support the design factors. The logical network design identifies the capacity requirements and the design factors define the availability and recoverability requirements.

Besides providing virtual machine connectivity, many vSphere features, such as High Availability, vMotion, and Fault Tolerance, have specific virtual and physical network connectivity requirements that must be taken into account when designing the physical network. If IP-connected storage, iSCSI, or NFS is used, physical network connectivity for these must also be included as part of the physical network design.

The logical network design specifications are as follows:

▸ Total virtual machine throughput: 1000 Mbps

▸ Virtual machines per host: 20

▸ Virtual-machine throughput per host: 200 Mbps

▸ IP storage: iSCSI

▸ Storage throughput: 55 MB/s

▸ vMotion/DRS: Enabled

The factors that influence the physical network design include the following:

▸ Number and type of physical switches

▸ Topology of the existing physical network

▸ Using either physically or logically separated (such as VLANs) networks

▸ Number of physical uplinks per host

▸ Physical adapter type: 1 Gb or 10 Gb

▸ Teaming and link aggregation

▸ Network bandwidth and throughput

▸ Failover and failback policies.

▸ Quality of Service and traffic shaping

    ▸   Type of virtual switches to use: virtual standard switches or virtual distributed switches

    ▸   Networks required for VMkernels to support management, vMotion, Fault Tolerance, and IP-connected storage

In the following diagram of an example virtual- and physical-network design, the VLANs and virtual standard switches have been configured to distinguish traffic types; single points of failure have been minimized using multiple uplinks and failover policies have been configured to provide redundancy and performance:

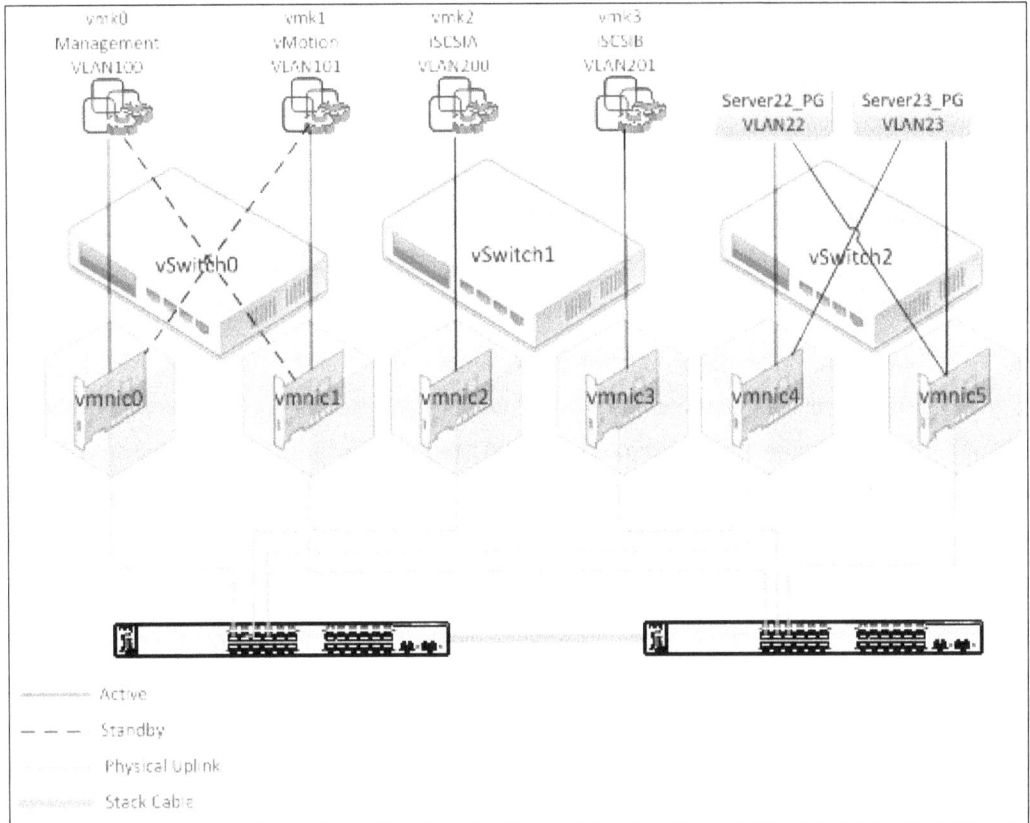

Creating the physical compute design

The physical compute design selects the CPU and memory resources to meet the requirements of the design. Besides the CPU and memory resources, the physical compute design also includes selecting the form factor to support the interface cards necessary to support the design.

How to do it...

As with other parts of the physical design, the performance, capacity, availability, and recoverability are all factors to consider in the physical compute design. The following steps can be performed to create the physical compute design:

1. Select server hardware that satisfies the logical compute design.

2. Verify the compatibility of each component of the compute hardware using the VMware HCL.

3. Configure compute resources to satisfy the design factors related to availability, recoverability, performance, and capacity.

How it works...

The logical compute design defines the capacity and performance requirements for CPU and memory resources.

The logical compute design specifications are as follows:

- ▸ Total CPU resources: 167 GHz

- ▸ Total memory resources (25% TPS savings): 657 GB

- ▸ Number of virtual machines per host: 20

- ▸ Number of hosts required (*N+2*): 9

- ▸ CPU resources per host: 23.8 GHz

- ▸ Memory resources per host: 94 GB

The hardware selected for the physical compute design must satisfy the resource requirements of the logical compute design. These resources include the CPU and memory resources. The physical hardware selected must also be able to support the network and storage connectivity resources defined in the logical network and storage design.

Along with the design requirements and constraints, the factors that influence the physical compute design include the following:

- ▸ The required CPU resources

- ▸ The required memory resources

- ▸ vCPU-to-CPU-core ratio

- ▸ Processor manufacturer and model

- ▸ Number of hosts required—scale up or scale out

- ▸ Host form factor: rack or blade

- ▸ The number of PCI slots

- ▸ The number and type of network uplinks
- ▸ The number and type of **Host Bus Adapters** (**HBA**)
- ▸ Power, space, and cooling requirements

An example of a physical design using HP DL380 rack servers is shown in the following diagram:

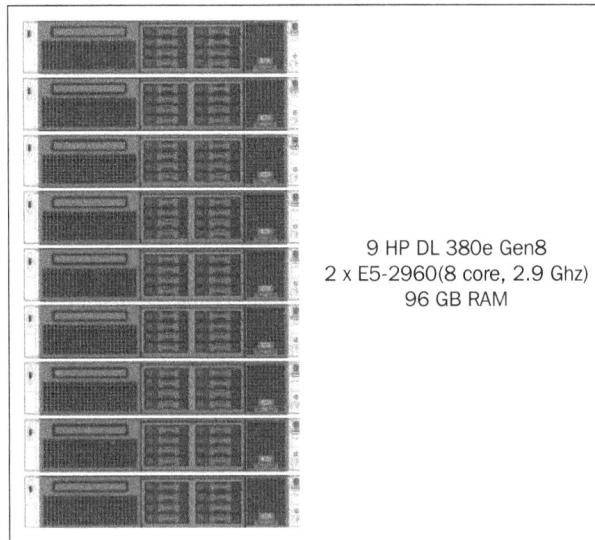

9 HP DL 380e Gen8
2 x E5-2960(8 core, 2.9 Ghz)
96 GB RAM

Each rack server has its own connectivity. The following diagram shows how a rack server is connected to the network:

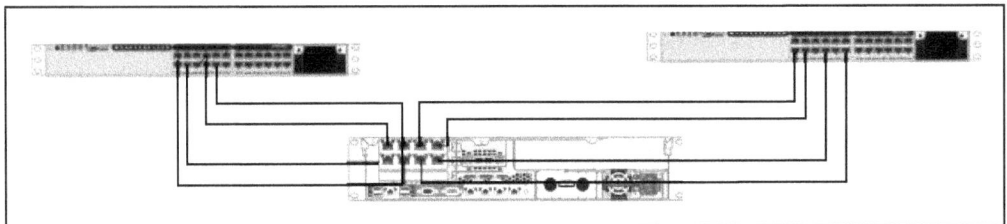

Another example of a physical design is using blade servers. This increases server density, while simplifying connectivity.

The following diagram is an example of a physical compute design using the Cisco UCS blade platform; the blades have been configured to support the logical requirements and multiple chassis have been chosen to eliminate single points of failure:

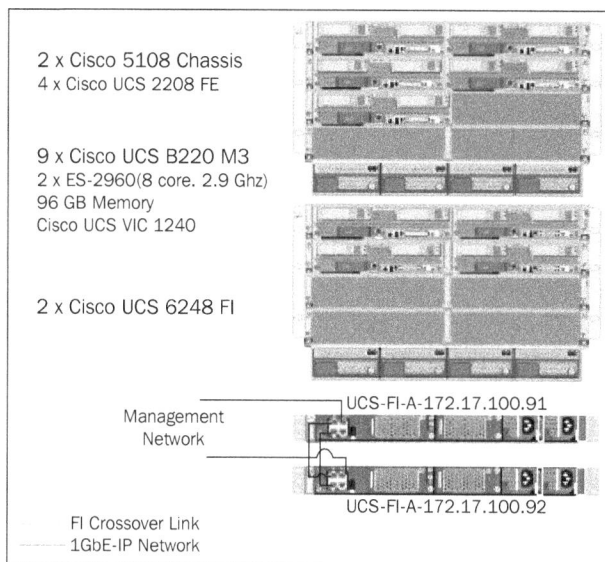

2 x Cisco 5108 Chassis
4 x Cisco UCS 2208 FE

9 x Cisco UCS B220 M3
2 x ES-2960(8 core. 2.9 Ghz)
96 GB Memory
Cisco UCS VIC 1240

2 x Cisco UCS 6248 FI

Management
Network

UCS-FI-A-172.17.100.91

UCS-FI-A-172.17.100.92

FI Crossover Link
1GbE-IP Network

The following diagram is the rear view of the Cisco UCS blade solution, showing the supporting components, including connectivity of the chassis to the Fabric Interconnects. The diagram also shows connectivity between the Fabric Interconnects and the network and storage. Multiple links to the chassis, network, and storage not only provide the capacity and performance required, but also eliminate single points of failure, as shown in the following diagram:

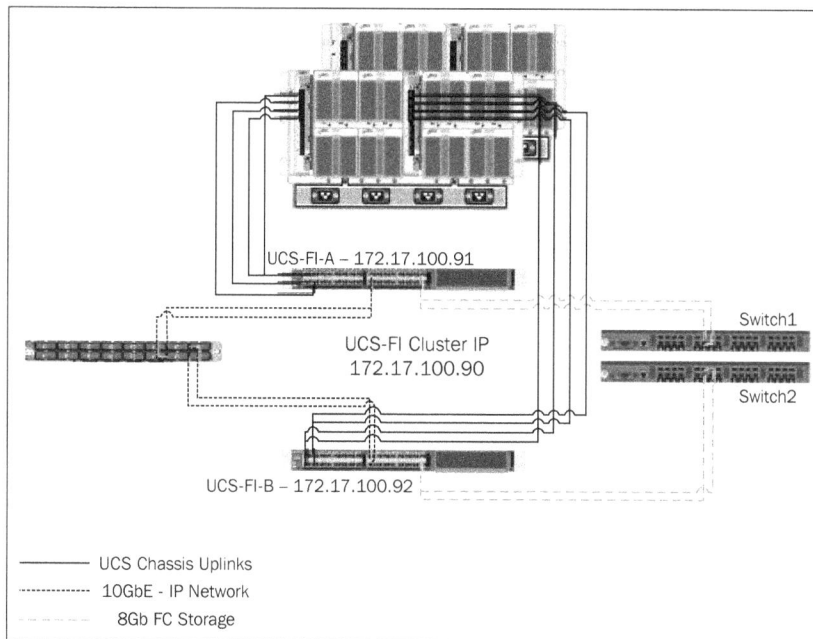

UCS-FI-A – 172.17.100.91

Switch1

UCS-FI Cluster IP
172.17.100.90

Switch2

UCS-FI-B – 172.17.100.92

UCS Chassis Uplinks
10GbE - IP Network
8Gb FC Storage

Creating a custom ESXi image

Drivers for some supported hardware devices are not included as part of the base ESXi image. These devices require a driver be installed before the hardware can be used in vSphere.

How to do it...

Third-party drivers are packaged as **vSphere Installation Bundles** (**VIBs**). A VIB file is similar to a ZIP archive in that it is a single file that includes an archive of the driver files, an XML descriptor file, and a signature file. VIB files have the `.vib` file extension.

The required drives can be installed after ESXi has been installed, using the `esxcli` command:

```
esxcli software vib install -v <path to vib package>
```

A custom ESXi image can also be created using the Image Builder tools included with PowerCLI. **PowerCLI** can be downloaded from `https://www.vmware.com/support/developer/PowerCLI/`. Custom ESXi images can be used when deploying hosts using VMware Auto Deploy or custom images can be exported to an ISO to be used for installation or upgrades. Perform the following steps to create a custom EXSi image:

1. Download **ESXi Offline Bundle** from the My VMware portal. The following screenshot displays the **ESXi Offline Bundle** download link on the My VMware portal:

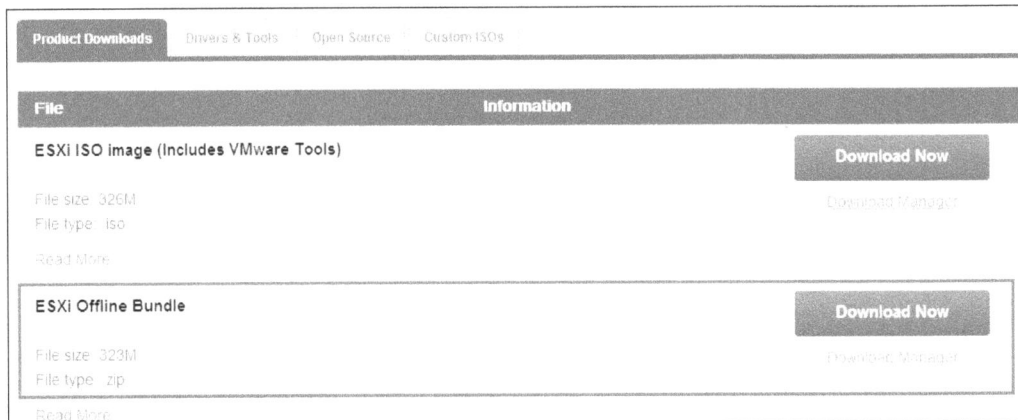

File	Information
ESXi ISO image (Includes VMware Tools)	Download Now
File size 326M	Download Manager
File type iso	
Read More	
ESXi Offline Bundle	Download Now
File size 323M	Download Manager
File type zip	
Read More	

Product Downloads Drivers & Tools Open Source Custom ISOs

2. Download the required third-party VIBs. This example uses the drivers of QLogic FC-FCoE downloaded from the My VMware portal, as shown in the following screenshot:

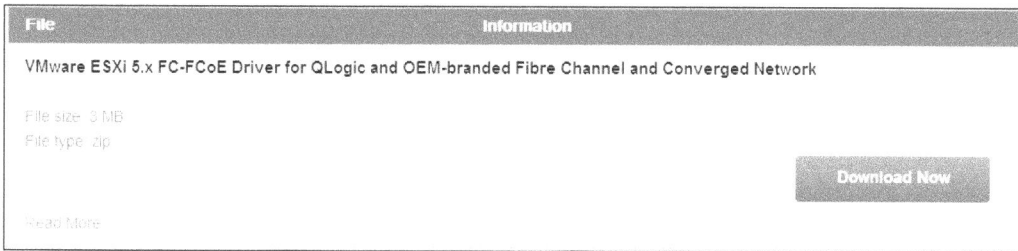

File	Information
VMware ESXi 5.x FC-FCoE Driver for QLogic and OEM-branded Fibre Channel and Converged Network	

File size: 3 MB
File type: zip

Download Now

Read More

3. Use Image Builder PowerCLI to add the **ESXi Offline Bundle** and third-party VIBs as software depots, as follows:

```
Add-EsxSoftwareDepot <pathtoESXiOfflineBundel.zip>

Add-EsxSoftwareDepot <pathto3rdPartyVIB.zip>
```

4. The following screenshot illustrates adding the **Offline ESXi Bundle** and third-party software bundles using the `Add-EsxSoftwareDepot` Image Builder PowerCLI command:

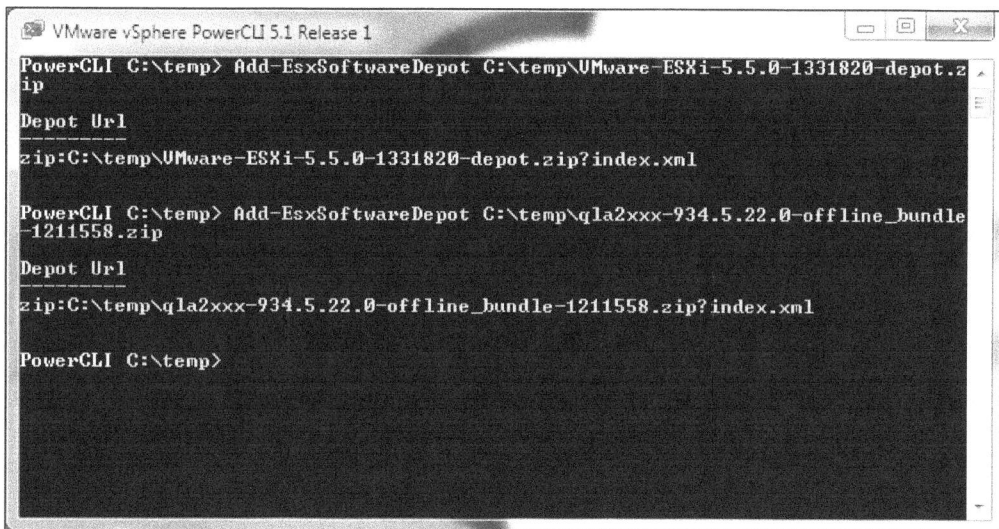

```
VMware vSphere PowerCLI 5.1 Release 1

PowerCLI C:\temp> Add-EsxSoftwareDepot C:\temp\VMware-ESXi-5.5.0-1331820-depot.z
ip

Depot Url
--------
zip:C:\temp\VMware-ESXi-5.5.0-1331820-depot.zip?index.xml

PowerCLI C:\temp> Add-EsxSoftwareDepot C:\temp\qla2xxx-934.5.22.0-offline_bundle
-1211558.zip

Depot Url
--------
zip:C:\temp\qla2xxx-934.5.22.0-offline_bundle-1211558.zip?index.xml

PowerCLI C:\temp>
```

5. List the available software packages to locate the Qlogic drivers and note the package names:

```
Get-EsxSoftwarePackage | where {$_.Vendor -eq "Qlogic"}
```

The following screenshot illustrates the use of the `Get-EsxSoftwarePackage` PowerCLI command to locate the package name of the third-party package that will be added to the new ESXi image:

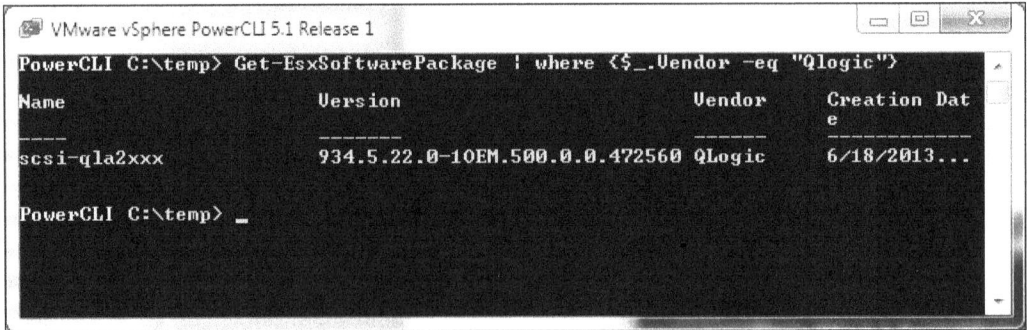

6. List the available image profiles, using the following command:

```
Get-EsxImageProfile
```

The following screenshot illustrates the output of the `Get-EsxImageProfile` PowerCLI command that lists the available profiles:

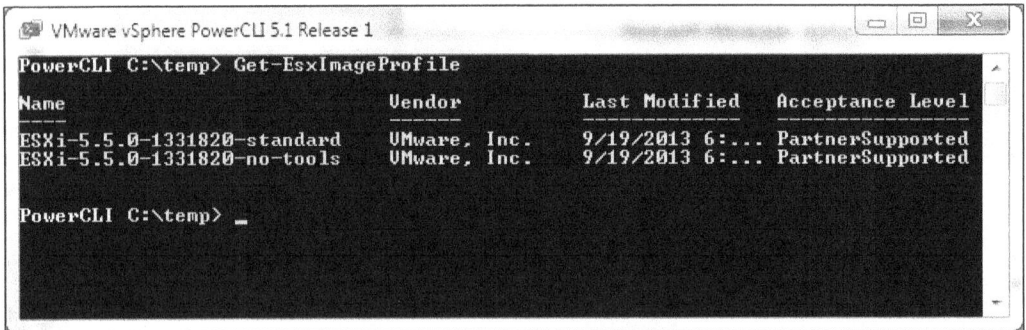

7. Create a clone of an image profile to apply customizations to. The clone will allow the profile to be manipulated without making changes to the original profile:

```
New-EsxImageProfile -CloneProfile <ProfiletoClone> -Name
<CustomProfileName> -Vendor Custom -AcceptanceLevel
PartnerSupported
```

The following screenshot illustrates the output of the `New-EsxImageProfile` PowerCLI command that creates a clone of an existing profile:

```
VMware vSphere PowerCLI 5.1 Release 1
PowerCLI C:\temp> New-EsxImageProfile -CloneProfile ESXi-5.5.0-1331820-standard
-Name Custom5.5-Qlogic -Vendor Custom -AcceptanceLevel PartnerSupported

Name                          Vendor          Last Modified     Acceptance Level
----                          ------          -------------     ----------------
Custom5.5-Qlogic              Custom          9/19/2013 6:...   PartnerSupported

PowerCLI C:\temp>
```

8. Add the software packages to the cloned image profile; this step is repeated for each package to be added to the new image profile:

```
Add-EsxSoftwarePackage -ImageProfile <CustomProfileName>
-SoftwarePackage <SoftwarePackagetoAdd>
```

The following screenshot displays the output of the `Add-EsxSoftwarePackage` PowerCLI command when the third-party software package is added to the new ESXi image:

```
VMware vSphere PowerCLI 5.1 Release 1
PowerCLI C:\temp> Add-EsxSoftwarePackage -ImageProfile Custom5.5-Qlogic -Softwar
ePackage scsi-qla2xxx

Name                          Vendor          Last Modified     Acceptance Level
----                          ------          -------------     ----------------
Custom5.5-Qlogic              Custom          10/6/2013 8:...   PartnerSupported

PowerCLI C:\temp>
```

9. Create an ISO from the cloned image profile using the following command; the ISO will include the additional software packages:

```
Export-EsxImageProfile -ImageProfile <CustomProfileName>
-ExportToIso -filepath <Pathtonew.iso>
```

The following screenshot shows the `Export-EsxImageProfile` PowerCLI command. There will be no message output from the command if it completes successfully, but the ESXi image ISO will be created and made available in the provided path:

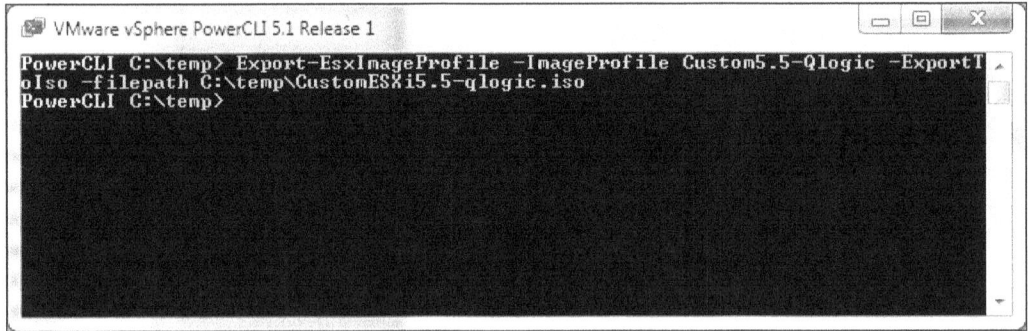

```
VMware vSphere PowerCLI 5.1 Release 1                                    □ ▣ ✕
PowerCLI C:\temp> Export-EsxImageProfile -ImageProfile Custom5.5-Qlogic -ExportT
oIso -filepath C:\temp\CustomESXi5.5-qlogic.iso
PowerCLI C:\temp>
```

The new ISO image includes the third-party VIBs and can be used to install ESXi.

How it works...

The Image Builder PowerCLI commands are used to create a custom image from the ESXi Offline Bundle and the vendor-provided bundle. In order to maintain the smallest footprint possible, not all supported hardware drivers are included with the native ESXi installation package.

The ESXi Offline Bundle contains two profiles: one that includes VMware tools—the standard profile—and one without VMware tools—the no-tools profile. A clone of the profile is created and the vendor software is added to it. When all of the necessary software have been added to the profile, it is exported to an ISO image that can be used to deploy ESXi hosts.

Custom image profiles created using the Image Builder PowerCLI commands are also used when using Auto Deploy to deploy stateless or stateful hosts. The procedure for creating a custom image profile to be used by Auto Deploy is the same, with the exception of the profile being exported to the custom ISO.

There's more...

Custom ESXi ISOs are also provided by manufacturers. Cisco, HP, Hitachi, Fujitsu, and other hardware manufacturers provide these custom ESXi ISO images, which can be downloaded from the My VMware portal using the **Custom ISOs** tab, as illustrated in the following screenshot:

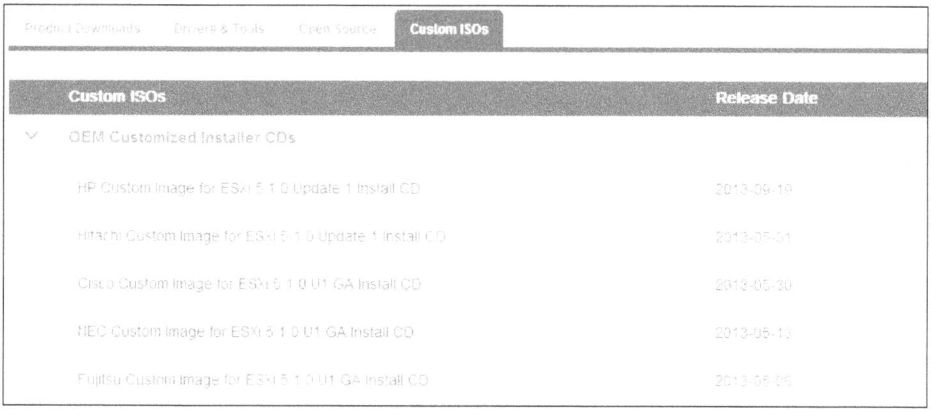

These custom ISOs are preconfigured to include the drivers necessary for manufacturer-specific hardware.

Best practices for ESXi host BIOS settings

The BIOS settings will vary depending on the hardware manufacturer and the BIOS version. Supported BIOS versions should be verified on the VMware HCL for the hardware selected.

The following screenshot shows the HCL details of a Dell PowerEdge R620 with the supported BIOS versions:

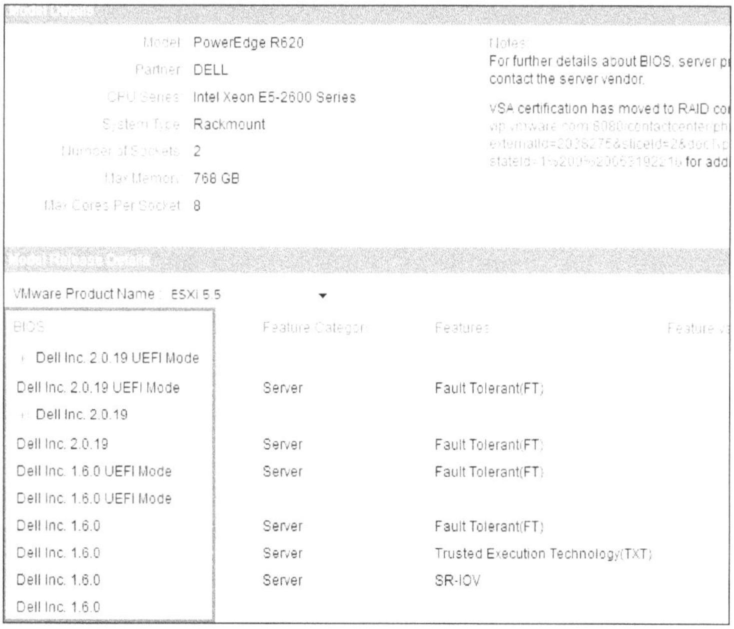

If the hardware is supported, but the running BIOS version is not supported, the BIOS should be upgraded to a supported version.

How to do it...

The BIOS settings will vary depending on the hardware manufacturer and the BIOS version. The settings available along with the layout and access will vary depending on BIOS manufacturer and BIOS version. The following screenshot is an example of a BIOS setup utility:

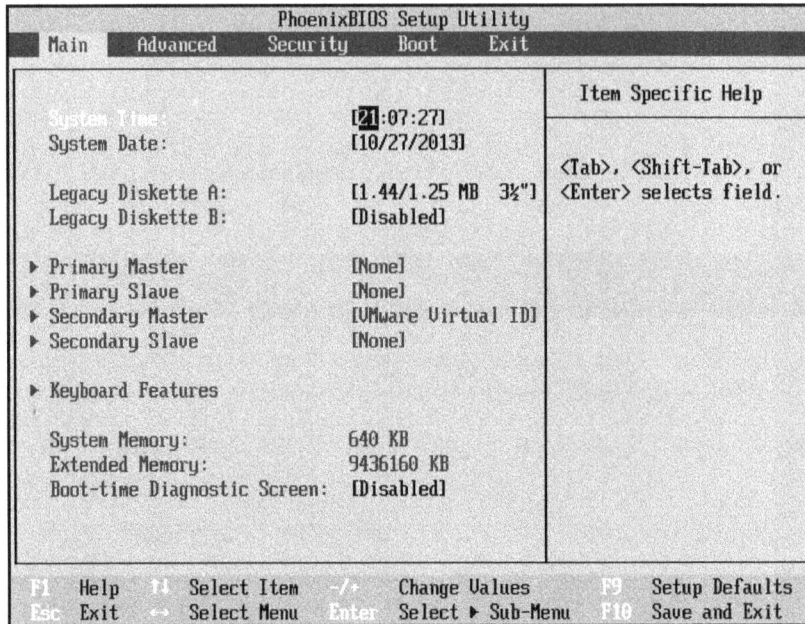

```
                        PhoenixBIOS Setup Utility
    Main     Advanced    Security    Boot    Exit

  ┌──────────────────────────────────────────────┬──────────────────────────┐
  │                                              │   Item Specific Help     │
  │  System Time:          [21:07:27]            │                          │
  │  System Date:          [10/27/2013]          │                          │
  │                                              │ <Tab>, <Shift-Tab>, or   │
  │  Legacy Diskette A:    [1.44/1.25 MB  3½"]   │ <Enter> selects field.   │
  │  Legacy Diskette B:    [Disabled]            │                          │
  │                                              │                          │
  │ ▶ Primary Master       [None]                │                          │
  │ ▶ Primary Slave        [None]                │                          │
  │ ▶ Secondary Master     [VMware Virtual ID]   │                          │
  │ ▶ Secondary Slave      [None]                │                          │
  │                                              │                          │
  │ ▶ Keyboard Features                          │                          │
  │                                              │                          │
  │   System Memory:        640 KB               │                          │
  │   Extended Memory:      9436160 KB           │                          │
  │   Boot-time Diagnostic Screen:  [Disabled]   │                          │
  │                                              │                          │
  └──────────────────────────────────────────────┴──────────────────────────┘
   F1   Help    ↑↓  Select Item   -/+    Change Values    F9   Setup Defaults
   Esc  Exit    ↔   Select Menu   Enter  Select ▶ Sub-Menu F10  Save and Exit
```

The following settings are provided as a guideline for optimizing the BIOS for an ESXi installation. Ask the hardware vendor for recommendations on settings specific to the hardware and BIOS versions:

1. Enable Intel VTx or AMD-V.

2. Enable Intel **Extended Page Tables** (**EPT**) or AMD **Rapid Virtualization Indexing** (**RVI**).

3. Disable node interleaving if the system supports **non-uniform memory architecture** (**NUMA**).

4. Enable Turbo Boost if the processor supports it.

5. Enable **Hyper-Threading** (**HT**) if supported by the processor.

6. Set Intel **Execute Disable** (**XD**) or AMD **No Execute** (**NX**) to **Yes**.

7. Set power-saving features to **OS Control Mode**.

8. Enable the C1E halt state.

9. Disable any unnecessary hardware or features (floppy controllers, serial ports, USB controllers, and so on).

How it works...

Intel VTx, **Intel EPT**, **AMD-V**, and **AMD RVI** are hardware-based virtualization technologies that provide extensions to perform tasks normally handled by software to improve resource usage and enhance virtual-machine performance. Enabling Intel VTx or AMD-V is required if the host will be running 64-bit guests.

> If the design calls for disabling Large Memory Pages in order to realize the advantages of **Transparent Page Sharing** (**TPS**) at times other than when there is memory contention, the Intel EPT or AMD RVI must be disabled. Enabling EPT or RVI will enforce large pages, even if they have been disabled in ESXi.

If the system is NUMA-capable, the option to enable node interleaving, which will disable NUMA, may be available. Enabling NUMA, by disabling node interleaving, will provide the best performance. This ensures that memory accessed by a processor is local to that processor or in the same NUMA node as that processor.

Enabling Turbo Boost will increase efficiency by balancing CPU workloads over unused cores.

Intel Hyper-Threading allows multiple threads to run on each core. When HT is enabled, the number of logical processors available is doubled. Each core is able to accept two concurrent threads of instructions.

Setting the power-saving features to **OS Control Mode** will allow ESXi to manage power saving on the host. If **OS Control Mode** is not available or supported, power-saving features should be disabled. Enabling the C1E halt state increases power savings.

9
The Virtual Machine Design

In this chapter, we will cover the following topics:

- ▶ Right-sizing virtual machines
- ▶ Enabling CPU Hot Add and Memory Hot Plug
- ▶ Creating virtual machine templates
- ▶ Using vApps to organize virtualized applications
- ▶ Using VM affinity and anti-affinity rules
- ▶ Converting physical servers with vCenter Converter Standalone

Introduction

Virtual machine design is just as important as physical hardware design and should be part of the physical design process. Correctly designing and configuring virtual machines with proper resource allocation will help increase consolidation in the virtual environment and ensure that a virtual machine has access to the resources that it requires to run the workloads efficiently.

A few questions that should be answered as part of the virtual machine design are as follows:

- ▶ What resources will be assigned to individual virtual machines?
- ▶ How will new virtual machines be deployed?
- ▶ How will multiple virtual machines supporting an application be grouped based on dependencies?
- ▶ How will virtual machines be placed on host resources to ensure the efficient use of resources and ensure availability?
- ▶ How will physical servers be converted to virtual machines?

This chapter will cover right-sizing virtual machines to ensure that they have the resources they require without over-allocating resources. The chapter will cover how to create a virtual machine template and quickly deploy a virtual machine.

Configuring the ability to add CPU and memory resources without taking the virtual machine out of production will also be covered, along with how to group virtual machines into applications or vApps. We'll also discuss using affinity and anti-affinity rules on a DRS cluster to reduce the demand on a physical network or to provide application availability in the event of a host failure. Finally, the chapter will demonstrate how to convert a physical server to a virtual machine.

Right-sizing virtual machines

Right-sizing a virtual machine means allocating the correct amount of CPU, memory, and storage resources required to support a virtual machine's workload. Optimal performance of the virtual machine and efficient use of the underlying hardware are both obtained through right-sizing virtual machine resources.

In a physical server environment, it is difficult to add resources. Because of this, physical servers are often configured with more resources than actually required in order to ensure there are sufficient resources available if the need for resources increases. Typically, physical servers only use a small percentage of the resources available to them; this means that a great deal of resources are constantly kept idle or wasted. Adding resources to a physical server also typically requires the server to be powered off and possibly even removed from the rack, which takes even more time and impacts production.

In a virtual environment, it becomes much easier to add CPU, memory, and disk resources to a virtual machine. This eliminates the need to over-allocate resources. Virtual machines are configured with the resources they require, and more resources can be added as the demand increases. If a virtual machine has been configured to use CPU Hot Add and Memory Hot Plug, additional resources can be added without taking the virtual machine out of production.

How to do it...

Perform the following steps for right-sizing virtual machines:

1. Determine the CPU, memory, and storage resources required by the virtual machine.

    > When sizing virtual machine resources, start with the minimum requirements and add additional resources to the virtual machine as needed.

2. Adjust the virtual machine CPU, memory, and storage resource allocation to meet the requirements of the workload without over-allocating.

How it works...

Tools such as VMware Capacity Planner or Windows Perfmon can be used to determine the actual resources required by an application running on a physical server. Resources used by a virtual machine can be examined using the vSphere Client program. From the **Summary** tab on the summary page of a virtual machine, it is easy to determine what CPU, memory, and disk resources have been allocated to the virtual machine along with the current usage of each of these resources, as shown in the following screenshot:

Performance charts can also be used to provide information about CPU and memory usage over time. The real-time advanced memory performance chart shown in the following screenshot shows the memory metrics of the Win7Client virtual machine:

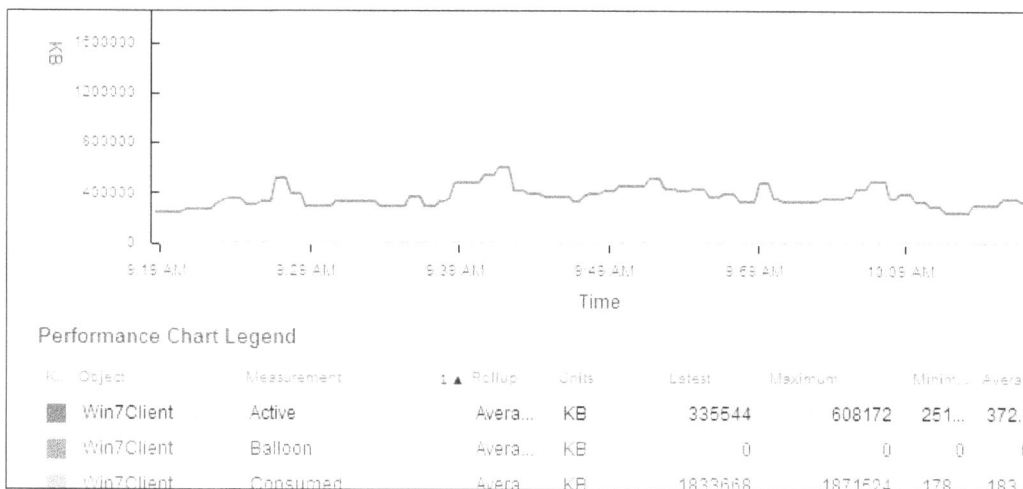

The chart options can be adjusted to show metrics for the last day, week, month, or even the last year. These metrics can be used to determine if a virtual machine has been allocated more memory than required.

Once the resource requirements have been identified, the virtual machine resources can be modified or right-sized to ensure that a virtual machine has not been allocated more resources than required for the workload running on it.

vCenter Operations Manager (**vCOPs**) is a separate VMware product that can be used to monitor the resources used by a virtual machine and has capacity planning and efficiency monitoring specific to right-sizing virtual machines. More information on vCOPs can be found at `http://www.vmware.com/products/vcenter-operations-management/`.

Enabling CPU Hot Add and Memory Hot Plug

Adding CPU and memory resources to a virtual machine is a simple process. The process to add resources to a virtual machine is to power down the virtual machine, increase the number of vCPUs or amount of memory, and power on the virtual machine again.

In vSphere 4.0, two new features, **CPU Hot Add** and **Memory Hot Plug**, were introduced to allow for virtual machine vCPUs and virtual machine memory to be increased without requiring for the virtual machine to be powered off. CPU Hot Add and Memory Hot Plug must first be enabled on the virtual machine, which does require it to be powered off. Once enabled, however, CPU and memory resources may be added dynamically; powering off the virtual machine is not necessary.

How to do it...

Perform the following steps to enable vCPU Hot Add and Memory Hot Plug for virtual machines:

1. Check the VMware *Guest OS Compatibility Guide* that can be found at `http://partnerweb.vmware.com/comp_guide2/pdf/VMware_GOS_Compatibility_Guide.pdf` to identify if vCPU and memory hot-adding is supported for the virtual machine guest operating system. The following screenshot is from the VMware *Guest OS Compatibility Guide* and shows the **Hot Add Memory** and **Hot Add vCPU** support for Windows Server 2008 Datacenter Edition R2 with Service Pack 1 on ESXi 5.x:

ESXi5.5 [1], 5.1 U1 [1], 5.1 [1], 5.0 U3 [1], 5.0 U2 [1], 5.0 U1 [1], 5.0 2.3.1	Guest OS Customization, e1000, Enhanced VMXNET, VMXNET 3 (Recommended), IDE, LSI Logic, LSI Logic SAS, VMware Paravirtual, Hot Add Memory, Hot Add vCPU, SMP, Tools Available on Media

2. To configure CPU Hot Add or Memory Hot Plug for a virtual machine, it must be powered off first.

3. To enable CPU Hot Add on the virtual machine, edit the virtual machine settings and expand the **CPU** settings. Select the **Enable CPU Hot Add** checkbox as shown in the following screenshot:

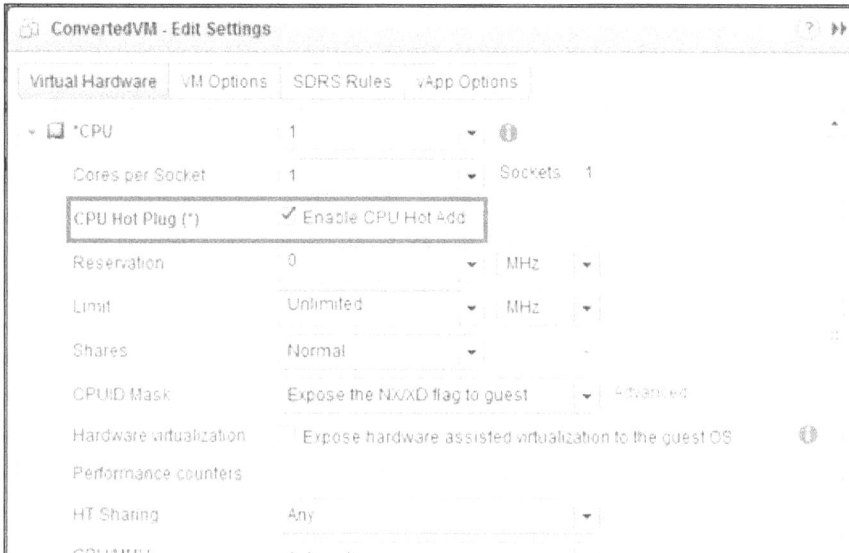

4. To enable Memory Hot Plug, expand the **Memory** settings and select the **Enable** checkbox for **Memory Hot Plug (*)** as shown in the following screenshot:

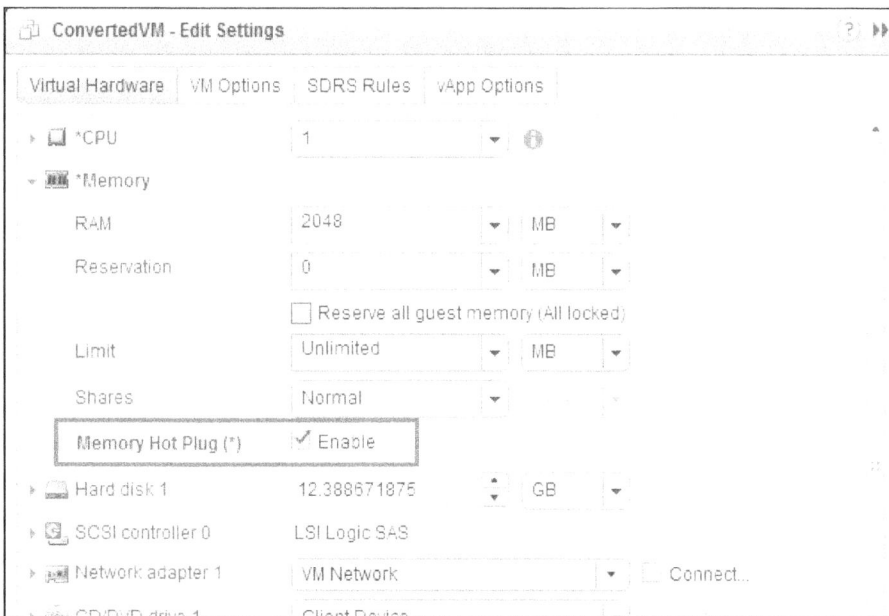

5. Once CPU Hot Add and Memory Hot Plug have been enabled for a virtual machine, the virtual machine can be powered back on.

6. vCPUs or memory can now be added to the running virtual machine without having to shut it down.

How it works...

Once CPU Hot Add and Memory Hot Plug have been enabled on a virtual machine, it will not be necessary to power off the virtual machine to add additional vCPUs or additional memory.

> Though vCPUs and memory can be added while the virtual machine is running, once Hot Add / Hot Plug has been enabled, some operating systems may require for the guest to be rebooted before the added vCPUs or memory is recognized by the operating system.

Enabling the **CPU Hot Add** and **Memory Hot Plug** features does increase the virtual machine overhead reservation slightly. Also, remember that when a virtual machine's memory is increased, the virtual machine swap file (`.vswp`) also increases to the size of the allocated memory (minus any memory reservations). The swap file grows automatically when the virtual machine's memory is increased.

> CPU resources do not have to be added in "twos". If a virtual machine requires the resources associated with three CPUs, three vCPUs can be assigned to the virtual machine. It is also not necessary to allocate virtual machine memory in GB increments; a virtual machine can be allocated 1,256 MB of memory if that is what is necessary to meet resource requirements.

With CPU Hot Add and Memory Hot Plug enabled, the removal of vCPUs and memory from a virtual machine will, more than likely, still require that the virtual machine be powered off or the operating system be rebooted before the resources are removed or before the removal of resources is recognized by the guest operating system.

Creating virtual machine templates

Virtual machines can be deployed quickly from prebuilt templates. Virtual machine templates are configured with minimum CPU, memory, and storage resources. The guest operating system and any prerequisite applications are installed in the template. Instead of taking hours (or even days in some cases) to install the operating system and prepare the server, once a template has been created, a new virtual machine can be deployed within minutes. Virtual machine templates not only allow for quick deployment but also help maintain consistency across virtual machines deployed in the environment.

How to do it...

The following steps are required to create a virtual machine template:

1. Create a virtual machine; configure the vCPU, memory, and storage resources; install the guest operating system; install the required applications; and apply any application or operating system updates or patches.

2. The virtual machine can be cloned to a template using the **Clone to Template** wizard as shown in the following screenshot:

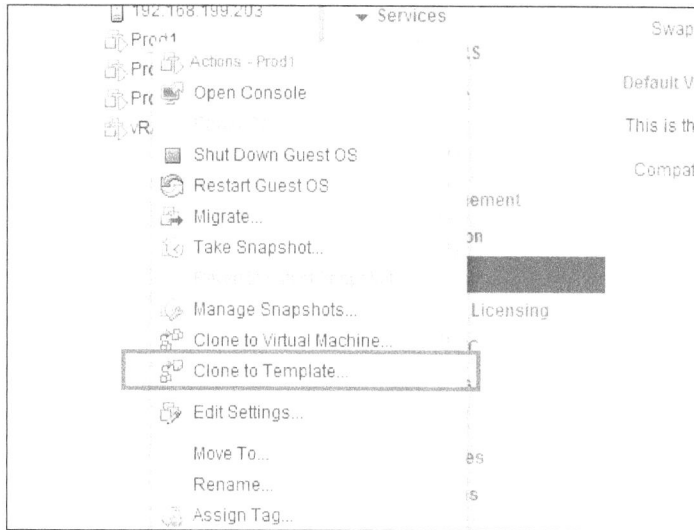

3. The virtual machine can also be converted to a template using the **Convert to Template** wizard as shown in the following screenshot:

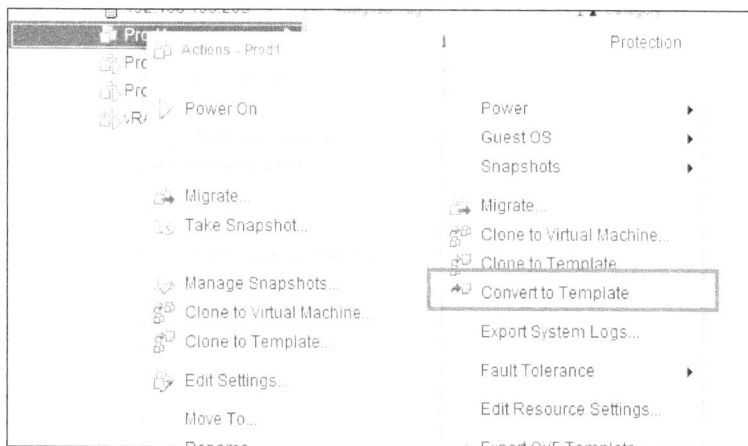

4. Once the virtual machine template has been created, new virtual machines can be deployed from the template using the **Deploy VM from this Template** wizard as shown in the following screenshot:

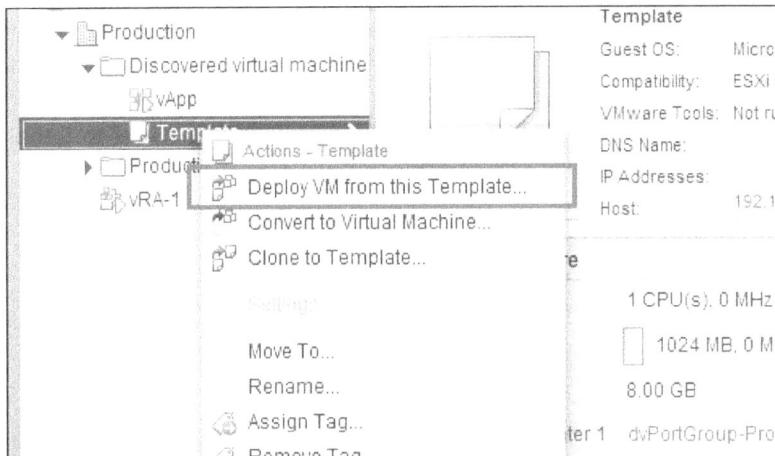

How it works...

When cloning a virtual machine to a template, the **Clone to Template** wizard allows the administrator to choose the datacenter, cluster, and storage to create the new virtual machine template. Cloning a virtual machine to a template can be done while the source virtual machine is powered on.

When a virtual machine is converted to a template, the virtual machine is converted locally; the template will have the same inventory properties (datacenter, cluster, and storage) as the virtual machine that has been converted. The virtual machine configuration file (.vmx) is changed to a template configuration file (.vmtx) when a virtual machine is converted. The virtual machine needs to be powered off in order to be converted to a virtual machine template.

The following screenshot shows the virtual machine template files on a datastore (the virtual machine template configuration file has been boxed in red):

The virtual machine template file is similar to the `.vmx` file and contains configuration information about the virtual hardware presented to the virtual machine or template.

There's more...

A guest customization specification can be applied to a virtual machine that is being deployed from a template. The customization specification allows settings unique to the deployed virtual machine to be applied during the deployment process. These custom specifications include information such as the computer's name, licensing, IP address, and domain membership. The **New VM Guest Customization Spec** wizard is displayed in the following screenshot:

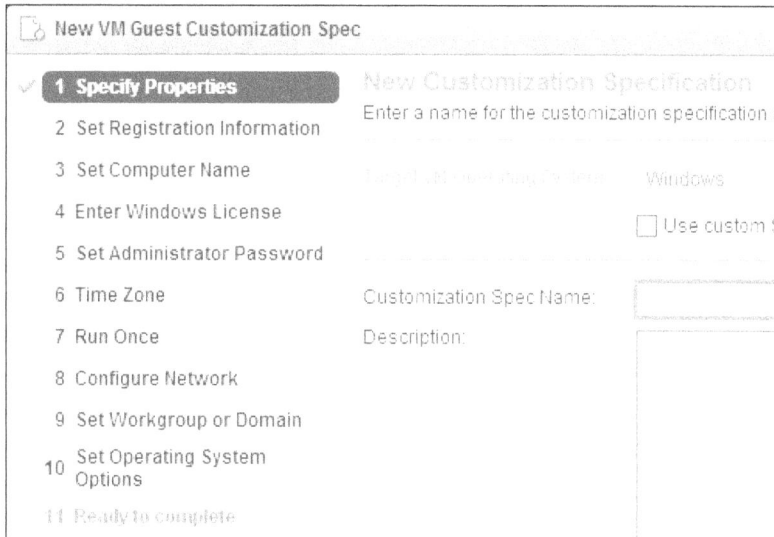

The customization specification can be saved so it can be applied to future virtual machines deployed from templates. Guest customization specifications can also be applied when cloning a virtual machine.

Using vApps to organize virtualized applications

vApps can be used to group individual virtual machines with interdependencies into a single application. A common use case for this would be a multitier web application that requires a web server frontend, an application server, and the supporting database server. The application can then be managed as a single inventory object.

How to do it...

The following steps are to be performed for using vApps to organize virtual machine workloads:

1. Create a new vApp by launching the **New vApp** wizard as shown in the following screenshot:

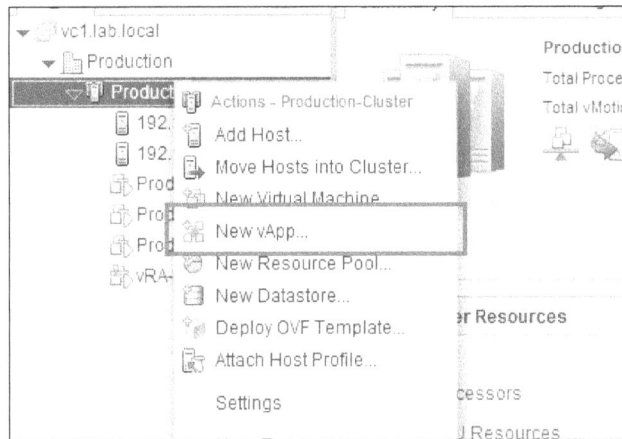

2. The method for creating the vApp (either creating a new vApp or cloning an existing vApp), the vApp name, the folder location, and the resource allocation settings are configured in the **New vApp** wizard as shown in the following screenshot:

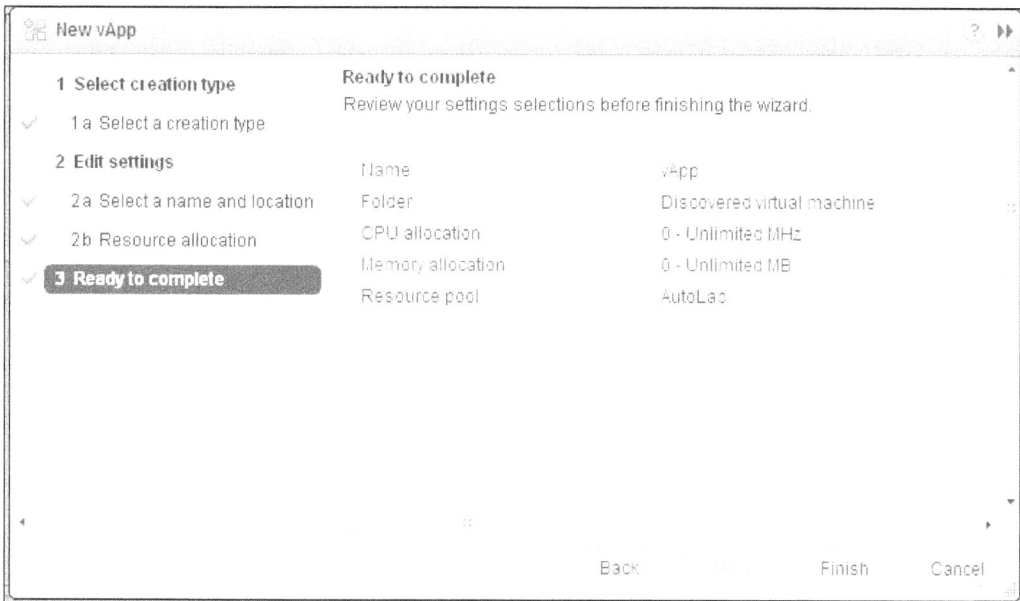

3. Once the vApp has been created, you can add virtual machines to the new vApp by dragging them into the vApp. The following screenshot shows a vApp containing the **Prod1** and **Prod2** virtual machines:

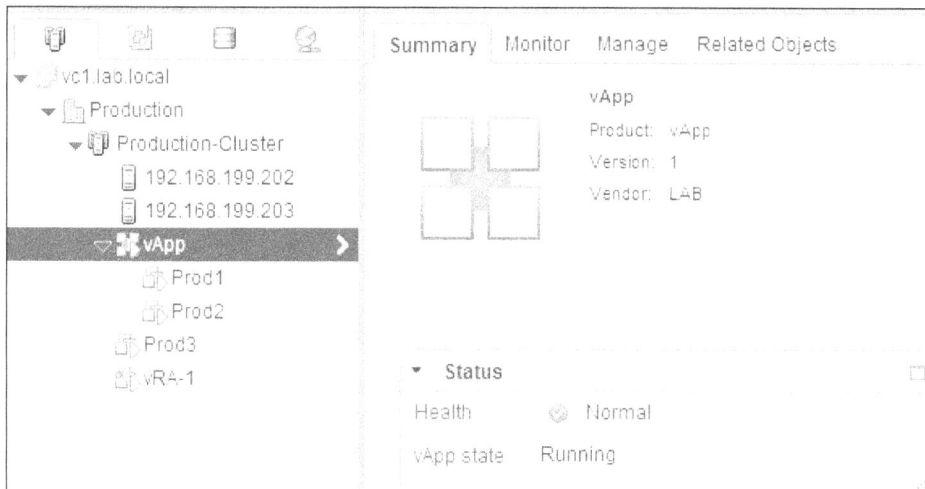

4. The settings of the vApp can be edited. In the following screenshot, **Start order** is configured to start virtual machines in the vApp in a specific order. **Start order** ensures that virtual machines are started in order of their dependency when the vApp is powered on:

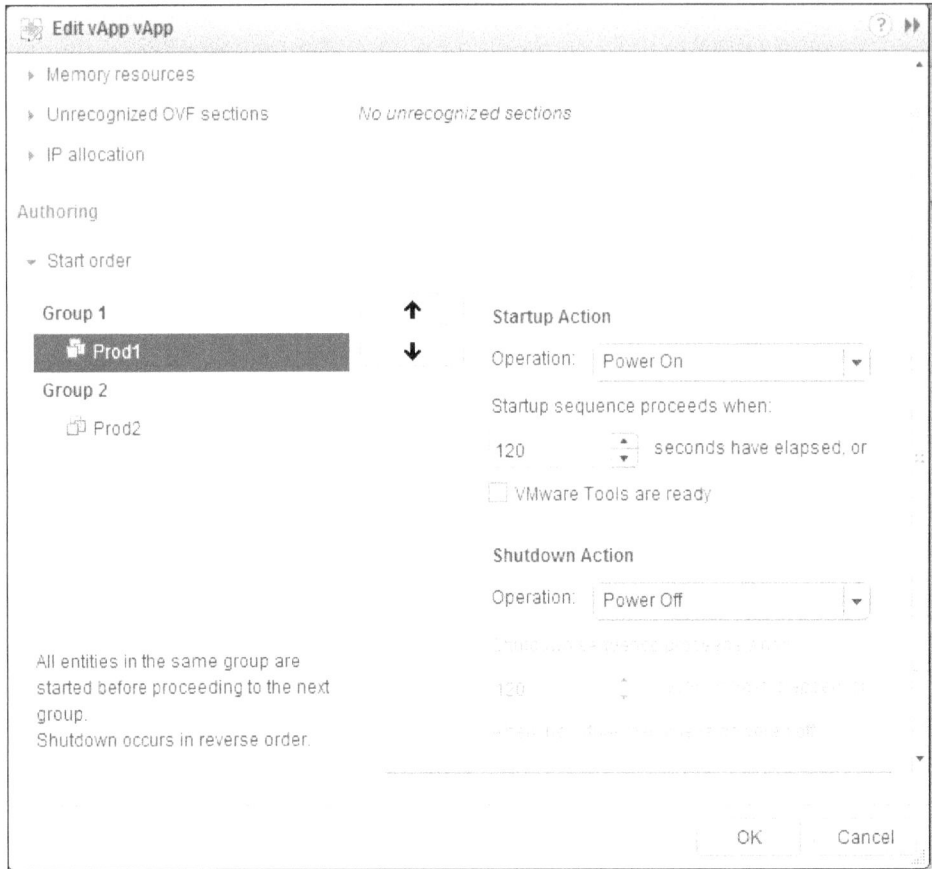

How it works...

A **vApp** is a container of virtual machines that support an application. Once placed in a vApp, startup and shutdown can be configured based on application dependencies, resources can be reserved or limited, and the entire vApp can be exported in the OVA or OVF format. A vApp can also be cloned to duplicate the application.

Using VM affinity and anti-affinity rules

When virtual machines are powered on in a DRS cluster, vCenter determines where the virtual machines should be placed in order to balance resource usage across the cluster. The DRS scheduler runs periodically to migrate virtual machines using vMotion, to maintain a balance of resource usage across the cluster. Affinity or anti-affinity rules can be used to control where VMs are placed within a cluster. Affinity rules keep VMs on the same physical host, reducing the load on the physical network by keeping traffic between them from leaving the host. Anti-affinity rules keep VMs separated on different physical hosts, ensuring higher availability.

One case of an affinity rule would be to keep all of the virtual machines supporting an application on the same host. This would ensure that network communications between the virtual machines supporting the application do not traverse the physical network.

An example use case of an anti-affinity rule would be to keep multiple virtual Active Directory domain controllers running on separate hosts to ensure that all of the domain controllers are not affected by a host failure.

How to do it...

The following steps are required for using VM affinity and anti-affinity rules:

1. DRS rules are created on the **Settings** page of a DRS-enabled cluster, as shown in the following screenshot:

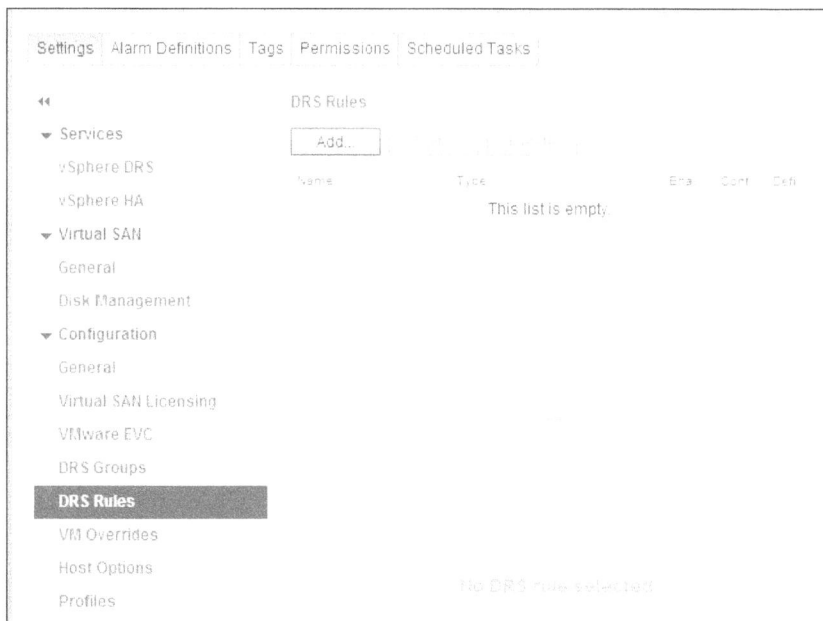

2. DRS rules can be created for three purposes: to **Keep Virtual Machines Together** on the same host, to **Separate Virtual Machines** across different hosts, or to assign **Virtual Machines to Hosts**, as shown in the following screenshot:

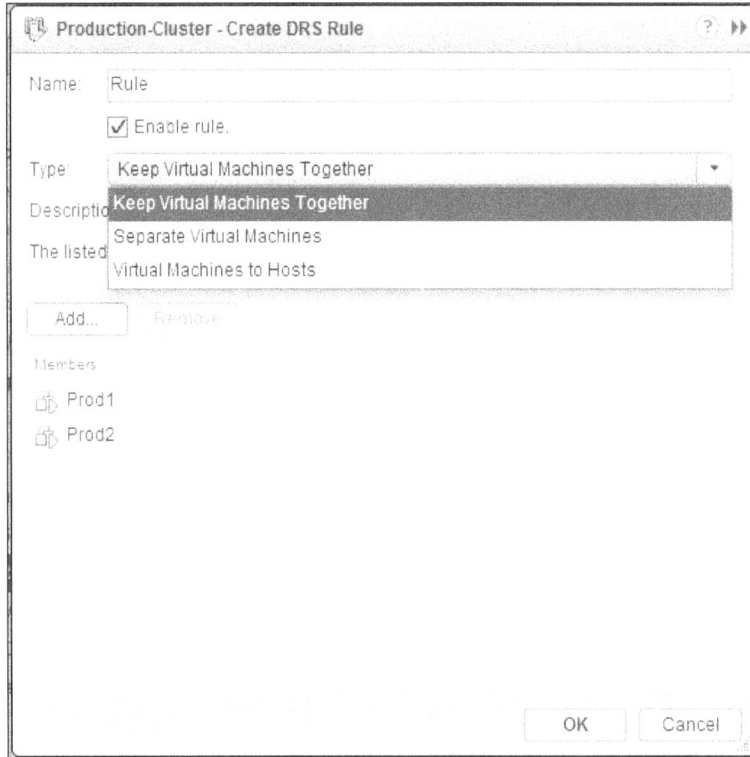

How it works...

With the DRS rules configured, the distributed resource scheduler will apply the rules when determining the placement of virtual machines when they are powered on or when migrating virtual machines to other hosts in order to balance the cluster resource usage.

When an affinity rule has been configured to keep several virtual machines together, if DRS migrates one of the virtual machines in the rule, all the virtual machines configured will also be migrated to the new host. When an anti-affinity rule has been configured to keep virtual machines separated, DRS will not migrate a virtual machine to a host running another virtual machine configured in the rule.

Virtual Machine to Hosts rules can be created while keeping virtual machines on specific hosts or groups of hosts. These types of DRS rules are useful for keeping management virtual machines, such as vCenter Server, on specific hosts to make these virtual machines easier to find in the event of a failure.

Converting physical servers with vCenter Converter Standalone

There are two methods for virtualizing workloads running on physical servers. The workloads can be migrated into the virtual environment by creating new virtual machines, loading a guest operating system, installing applications, and migrating the application data to the new virtual machines; or, physical servers can directly be converted to virtual machines using VMware **vCenter Converter Standalone**.

How to do it...

The following steps are required for using VMware vCenter Converter Standalone:

1. Download VMware Converter from `http://www.vmware.com/web/vmware/downloads`.

   VMware Converter can be installed either as a local installation or as a client-server installation. More information on installing VMware Converter is available in the VMware vCenter Converter Standalone guide found at `http://www.vmware.com/support/pubs/converter_pubs.html`.

   > The local installation is used to convert the physical machine that the converter is installed on.
   >
   > When installed using the client-server installation, the local machine becomes a server that can be managed remotely using the Converter Standalone client to convert physical servers.

2. Once VMware Converter has been installed, the VMware vCenter Converter Standalone client is used to connect to the Converter server, either local or installed on a remote machine. The **VMware vCenter Converter Standalone** login dialog is shown in the following screenshot:

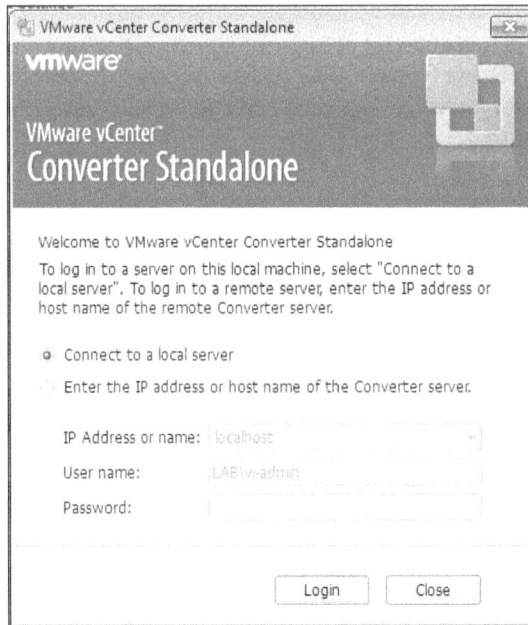

3. To convert a machine, select **Convert machine** to start the conversion wizard as shown in the following screenshot:

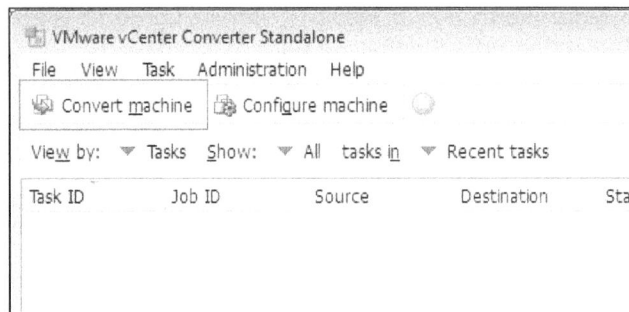

4. The first step of the conversion is to select the **Source System** type. This is the type of system that will be converted to the virtual environment. The source type can be **Powered-on machine** (physical or virtual), **VMware Infrastructure virtual machine**, **Backup image or third-party virtual machine**, or **Hyper-V Server**.

5. Once the source type has been selected, specify the powered-on virtual machine's information. This is the machine that will be converted and can either be the local machine or a remote machine. To convert a remote machine, the **IP address or name** field must be filled in along with administrator credentials and the **OS Family** field. If converting the local machine, the user running the converter must have administrator access to the local machine. The following screenshot shows a sample **Source System** configuration to convert a remote powered-on machine:

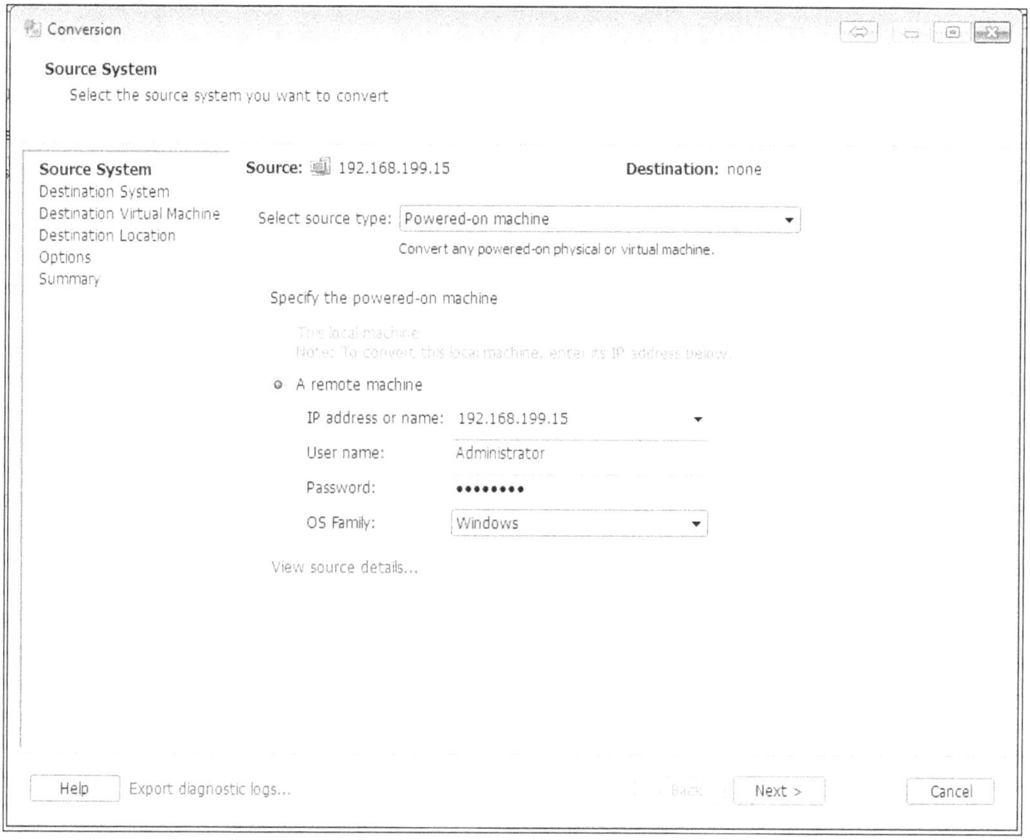

6. Once the source system information has been provided, the **Converter Standalone agent** will be installed on the source system. Once the conversion is finished, the agent can be uninstalled automatically or manually:

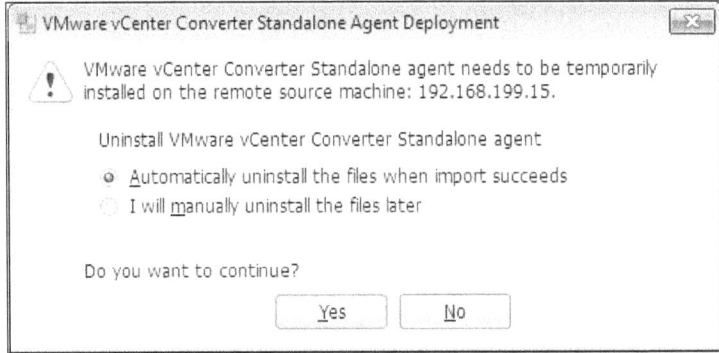

7. Once the **Converter Standalone agent** has been successfully installed, the destination system where the source system will be converted is configured. The destination type, the destination IP address, and the destination credentials are configured. The following screenshot shows the configuration of a vCenter Server as the **Destination System**:

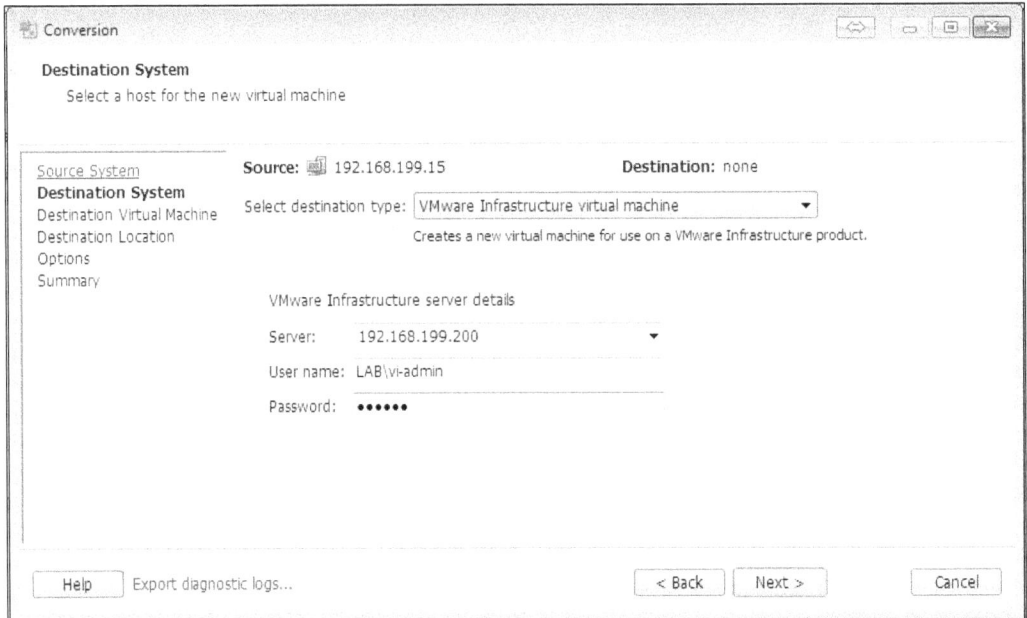

8. Information about the **Destination Virtual Machine**, such as the name and the virtual machine inventory placement, is then configured. The following screenshot shows the name and inventory placement for a physical-to-virtual conversion:

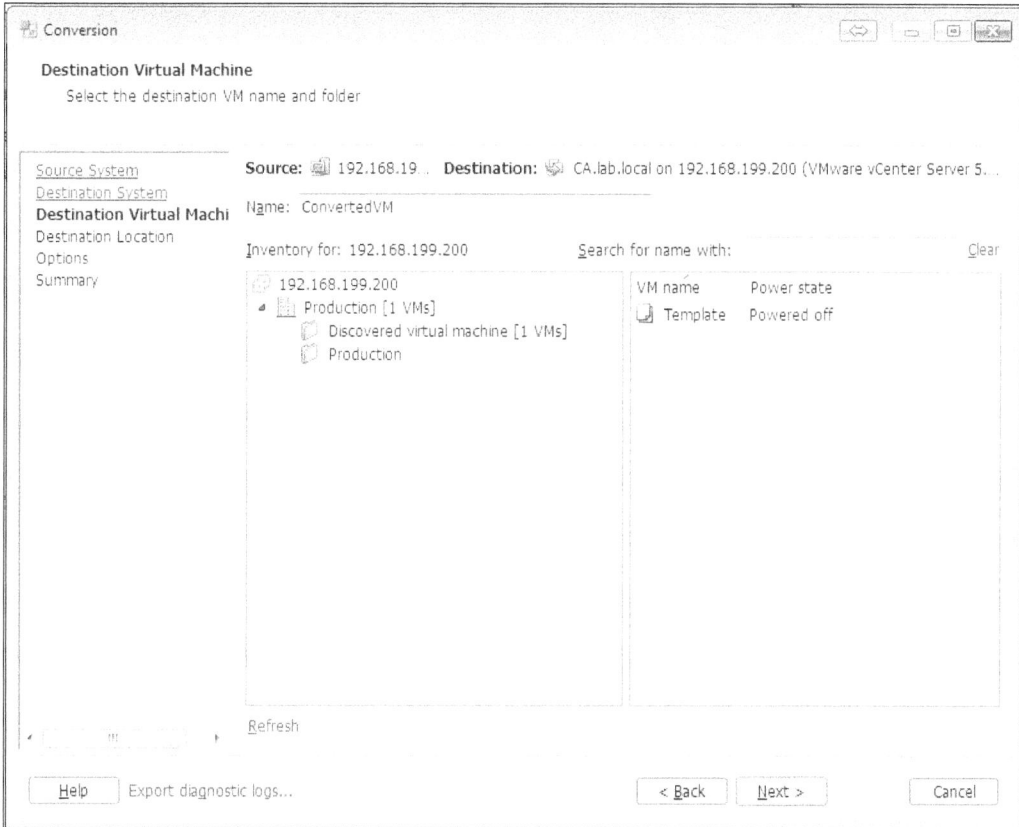

9. The **Destination Location** is then selected, as shown in the following screenshot. This location is the datacenter, cluster, or host that the converted machine will be deployed to. The datastore where the converted machine configuration file (.vmx) will reside and the virtual machine version to use is also configured here:

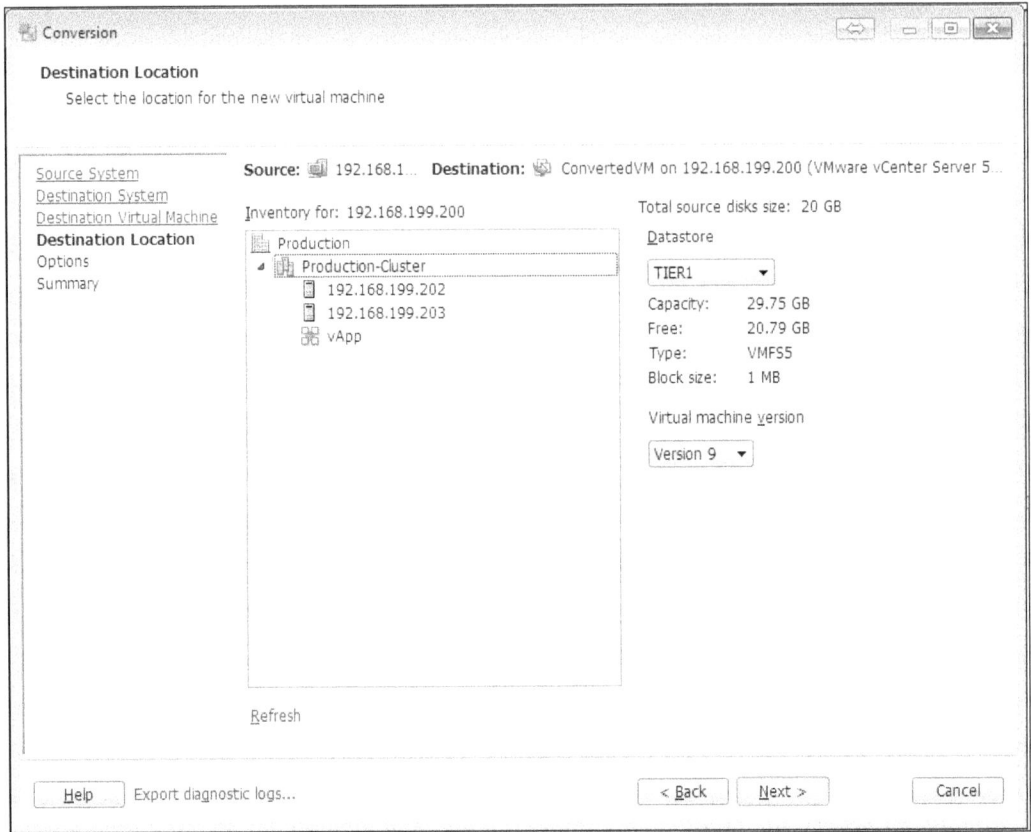

10. A number of options can be configured for the converted machine, including what virtual machine network to connect to, what datastore to deploy the converted disk to and in what format, and the device configuration. The following screenshot shows the **Options** configuration screen with the volume configuration for the machine that is being converted:

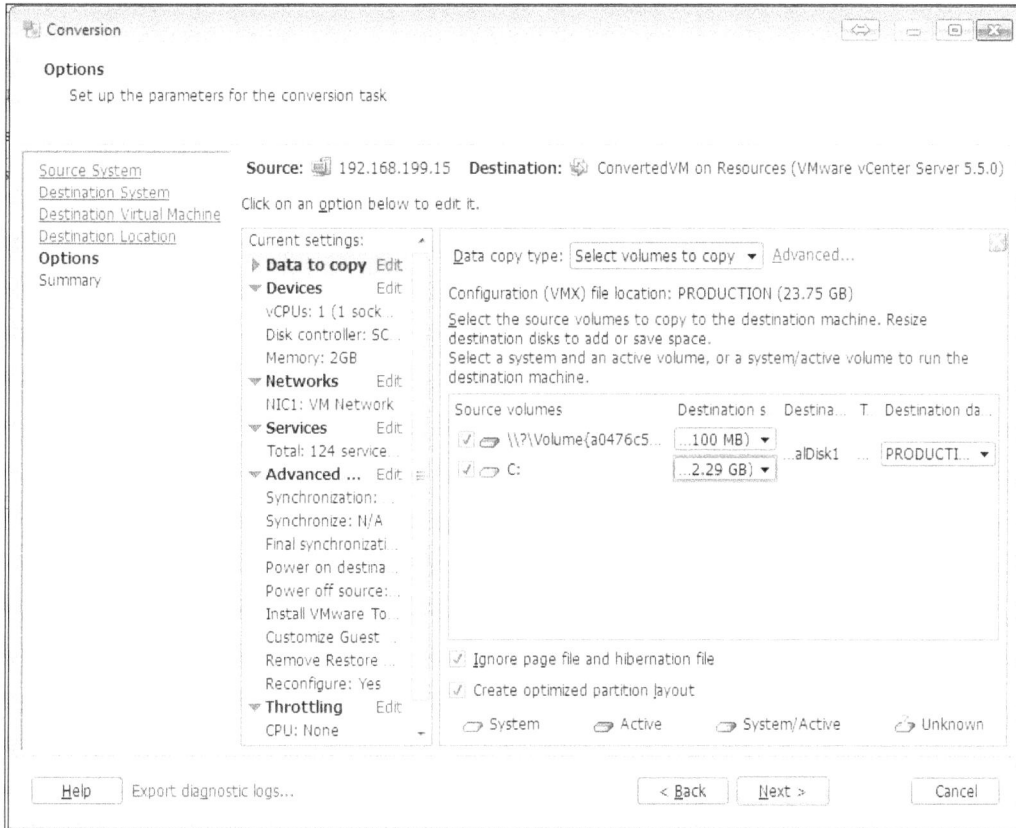

11. The **Summary** screen is displayed where the conversion options can be reviewed before starting the conversion process. An example **Summary** dialog is shown in the following screenshot:

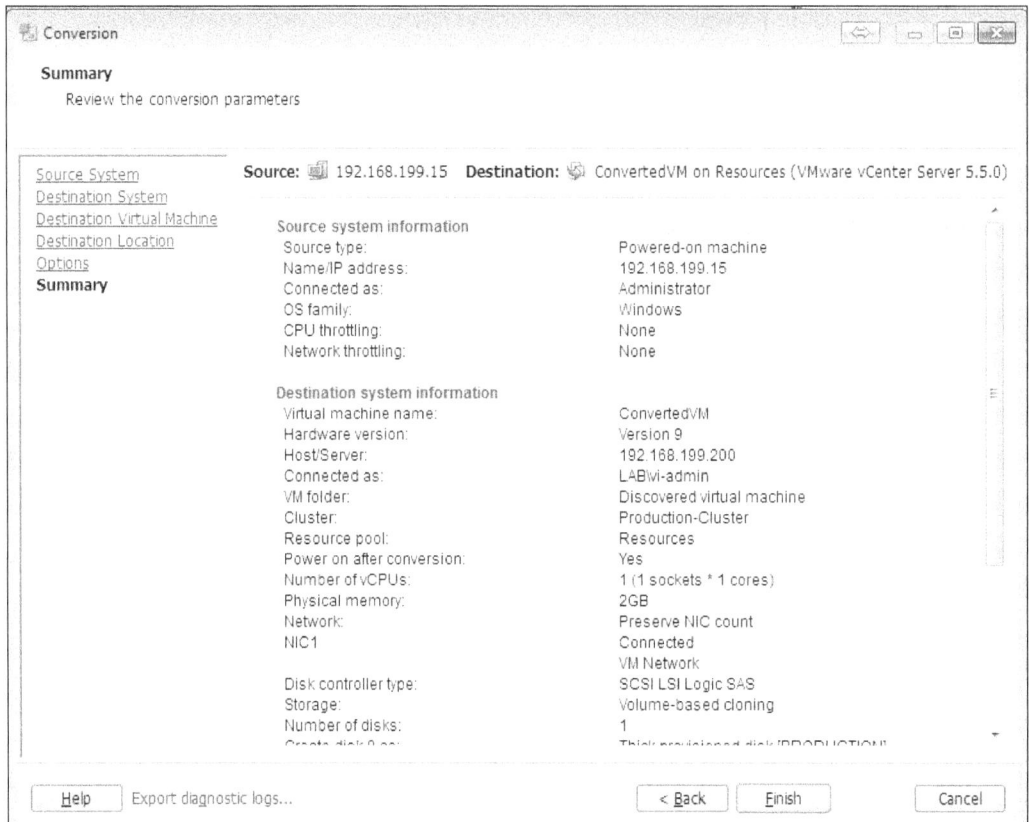

12. Once the conversion starts, the progress can be monitored in the **VMware vCenter Converter Standalone** client as shown in the following screenshot. The client allows for multiple conversions to be configured and run simultaneously:

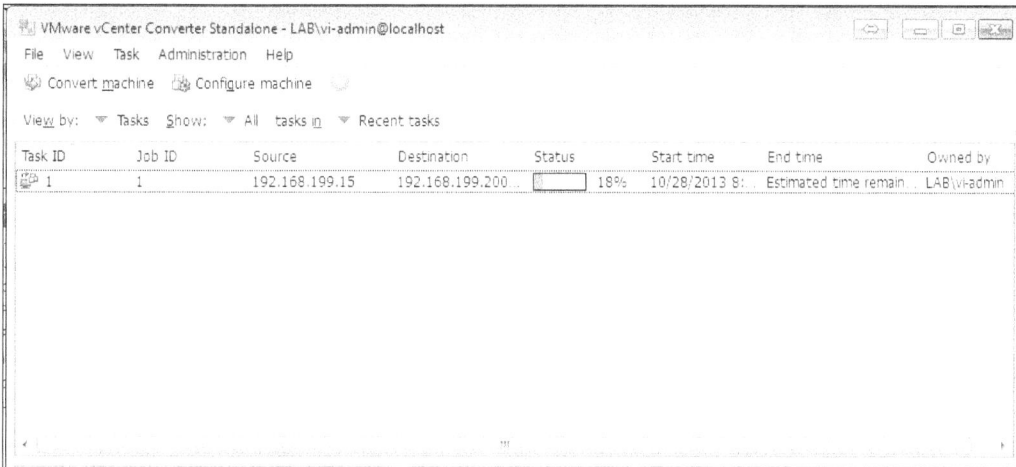

How it works...

When a physical server is converted using vCenter Converter Standalone, the physical server is cloned into the virtual environment. This creates a copy of the physical server as a virtual machine containing a duplicate of the operating system, applications, and data from the physical server.

When the physical server is converted, new virtual hardware is presented to the virtual machine. The physical hardware that was associated with the virtual machines is no longer present and references to it should be removed. In Windows, this is done using the Device Manager.

> During the physical-to-virtual conversion, the physical hardware is replaced with virtual hardware. During the conversion, references to the physical hardware and the associated drivers are not removed from the operating system. To remove non-present hardware from a Windows Server, set an environment variable devmgr_show_nonpresent_devices to 1. This will enable non-present devices to be visible in the Device Manager.

The conversion can be verified by booting the new virtual machine while it is disconnected from the virtual switch and checking that the operating system and applications were converted correctly. Once verified, the physical server can be powered off or removed from the network, and the newly converted virtual machine can be connected to the network.

The migration of servers and applications can be time consuming, and vCenter Converter Standalone provides a way to quickly convert physical servers to virtual machines.

10

Disaster Recovery and Business Continuity

In this chapter, we will cover the following topics:

- ► Backing up ESXi host configurations
- ► Configuring ESXi host logging
- ► Backing up virtual distributed switch configurations
- ► Deploying VMware Data Protection
- ► Using VMware Data Protection to back up virtual machines
- ► Replicating virtual machines with vSphere Replication
- ► Protecting the virtual datacenter with Site Recovery Manager

Introduction

The factors that influence the design of the backup and recovery of the virtual datacenter are **Recovery Point Objective** (**RPO**) and **Recovery Time Objective** (**RTO**). RPO defines the amount of data loss that is acceptable. RTO is the amount of time it should take to restore an application or service a workload after an outage.

The acceptable RPO and RTO should be defined for each workload. It is important to consider the application's dependencies when determining the RPO and RTO. Specifically, the RTO of an application will depend on the RTO of all of the application's dependencies. For example, if an application depends on a database server and the RTO of the database server is determined to be two hours, the RTO of the application itself cannot be less than two hours if the outage affects both the server running the application and the database server that supports the application.

vSphere provides many options that provide the continued operation of the virtual machines and the workloads they run in the event of an outage. These solutions do not replace the need for virtual machine backups.

The following are two different methods for backing up virtual machine workloads:

▸ Traditional backup using in-guest backup agents
▸ Agentless backup using the vSphere Storage APIs—Data Protection

The backup and recovery design should not only include virtual machines but also the backups of the virtual infrastructure configuration containing the management, network, and other configurations. This ensures that the virtual infrastructure can be restored after a failure within the infrastructure, such as a host failure or a vCenter failure.

Backing up vCenter and the supporting vCenter databases was covered in *Chapter 4, The vSphere Management Design*. This chapter will cover backing up some of the infrastructure components. This includes backing up the ESXi host and the virtual distributed switch configurations to ensure that the infrastructure can be restored in the event of an outage.

VMware provides several products to back up virtual machines and recover them in the event of a virtual machine or infrastructure failure. This chapter demonstrates many of these options including the deployment and basic configurations for the protection and recovery of virtual machines. The backup and recovery solution that will be selected will depend on the design factors.

Backing up ESXi host configurations

A full backup of an ESXi host is not necessary because the installation of ESXi is a quick and simple process. Host configurations should be backed up in order to quickly restore the configuration of a host in case ESXi needs to be reinstalled.

If hosts are deployed using Auto Deploy or the host configurations are stored in a host profile, the individual backups of host configurations may not be necessary but are a good way to ensure that a backup of the host configuration is available in case there is an issue with vCenter or a configured host profile.

How to do it...

The simplest way to back up ESXi host configurations is to use the `vicfg-cfgbackup` vCLI command as shown in the following steps:

1. Use the `vicfg-cfgbackup` vCLI command to create a backup of an ESXi host configuration:

   ```
   vicfg-cfgbackup –server <esxihostname> -s <pathtobackupfile>
   ```

2. Use the `vicfg-cfgbackup` vCLI command to restore an ESXi host configuration from a backup:

    ```
    vicfg-cfgbackup -server <esxihostname> -l <pathtobackupfile>
    ```

How it works...

The **vSphere Command-line Interface** (**vCLI**) can be downloaded from VMware at `http://www.vmware.com/support/developer/vcli/` and installed on a Windows PC or Linux workstation. vCLI is also included as part of the **vSphere Management Assistant** (**vMA**) found at `https://my.vmware.com/web/vmware/details?productId=352&downloadGroup=VMA550`, which can be deployed in the vSphere environment.

The ESXi backup is saved to the specified file. This file is not human-readable but contains the configuration information of the ESXi host and can be used to restore the configuration in the event that the host is lost and has to be reinstalled. The backup can also be used to return the host to a known good configuration if a configuration change is made that negatively impacts the host.

A configuration backup should be made before upgrading hosts or before making configuration changes to a host.

Restoring a host configuration using `vicfg-cfgbackup` will require the host to be rebooted once the restoration has been completed. This will cause any virtual machines on the host to be shut down. The host should be placed in the maintenance mode, and all running virtual machines should be vMotioned to other hosts if possible.

> A full documentation on the `vicfg-cfgbackup` vCLI command can be found in the vSphere documentation at `http://pubs.vmware.com/vsphere-55/topic/com.vmware.vcli.ref.doc/vicfg-cfgbackup.html`.

There's more...

An ESXi host configuration backup can also be performed using PowerCLI with the `Get-VMHostFirmware` PowerCLI cmdlet as shown in the following command line:

```
Get-VMHostFirmware -vmhost <hostname or IP Address> -BackupConfiguration
-DestinationPath<PathtoBackupLocation>
```

The following screenshot demonstrates a host configuration backup using PowerCLI and the `Get-VMHostFirmware` cmdlet:

```
PowerCLI C:\>
PowerCLI C:\>
PowerCLI C:\> Get-UMHostFirmware -vmhost 192.168.1.25 -BackupConfiguration -Dest
inationPath C:\Temp\

Host            Data
----            ----
192.168.1.25    C:\Temp\configBundle-192.168.1.25.tgz


PowerCLI C:\> _
```

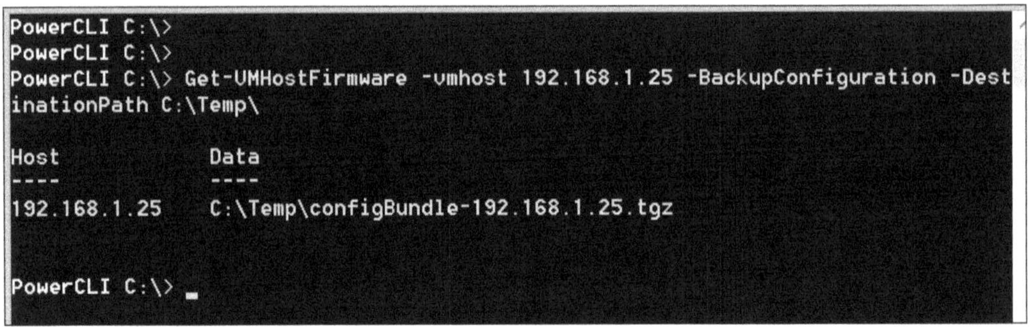

To restore the ESXi host configuration, the `Set-VMHostFirmware` PowerCLI cmdlet is used:

```
Set-VMHostFirmware -vmhost <hostname or IP Address> -Restore -SourcePath<
PathtoBackupLocation>
```

As with restoring the ESXi configuration using `vicfg-cfgbackup`, the host will be rebooted once the configuration is restored. The `Set-VMHostFirmware` cmdlet will not run against an ESXi host that has not been placed in the maintenance mode.

Configuring ESXi host logging

Having access to the ESXi host logs is required in order to troubleshoot or determine the root cause of an ESXi host failure. Redirecting host logs to persistent storage or to a Syslog server is especially important when a host has not been installed to persistent storage, for example, a stateless host deployed using vSphere Auto Deploy or a host that has been installed to a USB stick.

Logging may not seem to be a key component in disaster recovery. Having a proper backup of the host configuration allows a host to be quickly returned to a service, but if the root cause of the failure cannot be determined, preventing the failure from happening again cannot be guaranteed. Logs are the best source for performing analyses to determine the root cause of a failure and to determine the best course of action required to prevent future failures.

How to do it...

ESXi logs should be redirected to the persistent storage or sent to a central Syslog server in order to ensure that the logs are available for analysis after a host failure. The following process details how to configure ESXi logging:

1. To redirect host logs, select the host and edit **Advanced System Settings** on the **Manage** tab. Use the **Filter** box to display the Syslog settings, as shown in the following screenshot:

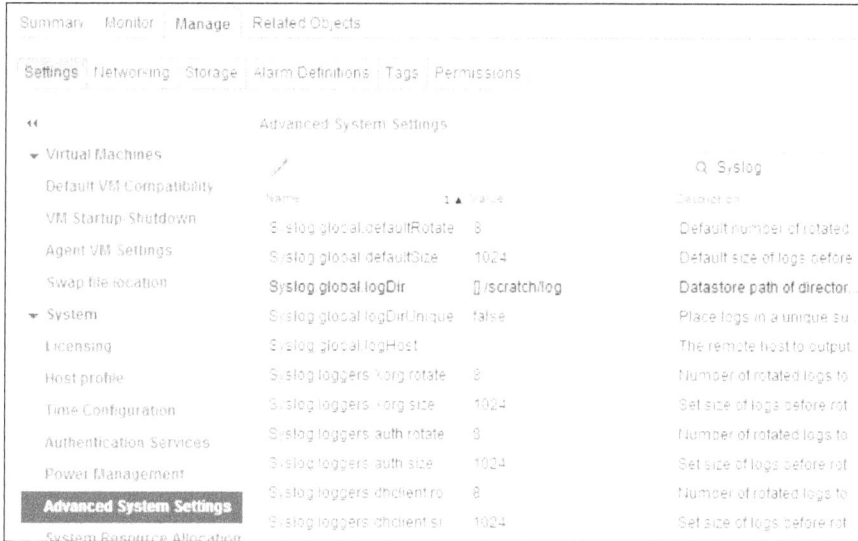

2. Edit the **Syslog.global.logDir** setting in order to set the datastore path to output the logs to. This can be set to a VMFS or NFS datastore, which has been configured on the host, as shown in the following screenshot:

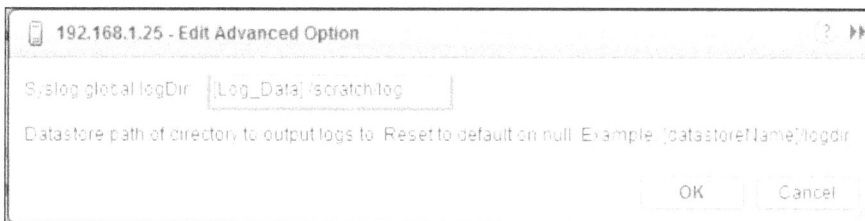

3. Edit the **Syslog.global.logDirUnique** setting to create a unique subdirectory for each host under **Syslog.global.logDir**. This setting is useful if logs from multiple hosts are being stored in the same directory. The following screenshot displays the enabling of the **Syslog.global.logDirUnique** setting by selecting the **Yes** option:

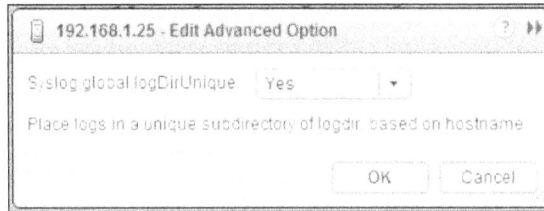

4. If the host logs are set to a central Syslog server, edit the **Syslog.global.logHost** setting and enter the FQDN or IP address of the Syslog server. The following screenshot shows the advanced configuration option for setting **Syslog.global.logHost**:

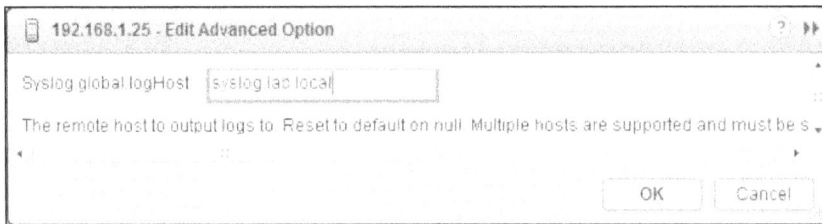

How it works...

When **Syslog.global.logDir** is configured, host logfiles will be stored in the configured path. The following screenshot shows an example of a host configured with **Syslog.global.logDir** set to **[datastore1] scratch/log** and **Syslog.global.logDirUnique** set to **Yes**.

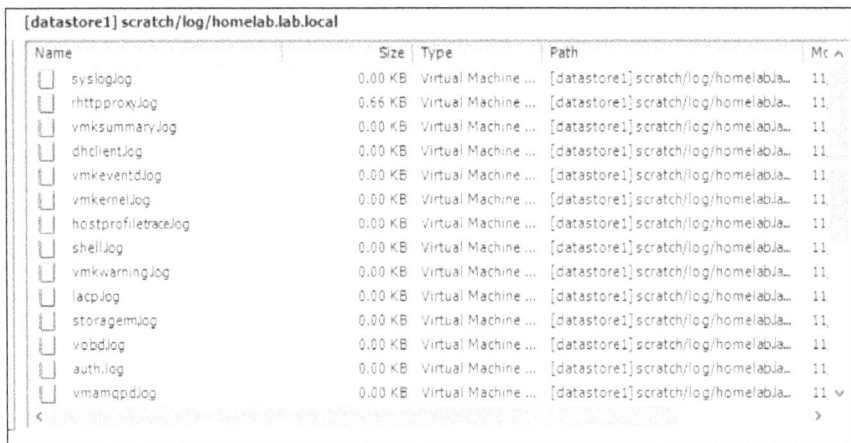

With **Syslog.global.logDirUnique** set to **Yes**, a subdirectory with the FQDN of the host is created to store the logfiles. If **Syslog.global.logHost** has been configured, the host logs are sent to a centralized Syslog server. The host logs can be sent to multiple Syslog servers by separating the servers with a comma. The ESXi host logs can be configured to be stored on persistent storage and to also be sent to a central Syslog server.

Backing up virtual distributed switch configurations

Virtual distributed switch configurations can be exported to a file. The file contains the switch configuration settings and can also contain information of the dvPortGroup configurations. This file can then be used to restore the virtual distributed switch configuration or to import the configuration into a different deployment.

> Virtual distributed switch import, export, and restore operations are available in the vSphere Web Client.

Virtual distributed switch configurations should be exported before making changes to the distributed virtual switches in a production environment in order to ensure that the switch can be restored to an operational state in the event of a configuration error.

How to do it...

Perform the following procedure to create a backup of the VDS configuration:

1. In the vSphere Web Client, right-click on the VDS to be exported. Navigate to **All vCenter Actions** | **Export Configuration...** as shown in the following screenshot:

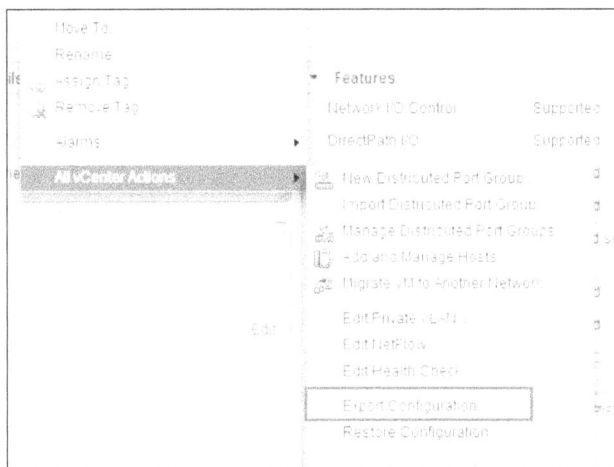

2. Select an option depending on whether you want to export the distributed switch and all of the port groups or the distributed switch only. Selecting the **Distributed switch only** option exports only the virtual distributed switch configuration and does not include any configurations for the port groups associated with the dvSwitch. Give the exported configurations a short description as illustrated in the following screenshot:

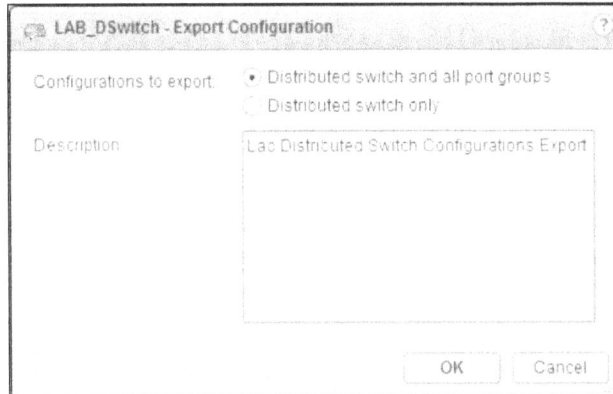

3. Select **Yes** when the **Confirm Configuration Export** dialog is displayed. The **Confirm Configuration Export** dialog box is shown in the following screenshot:

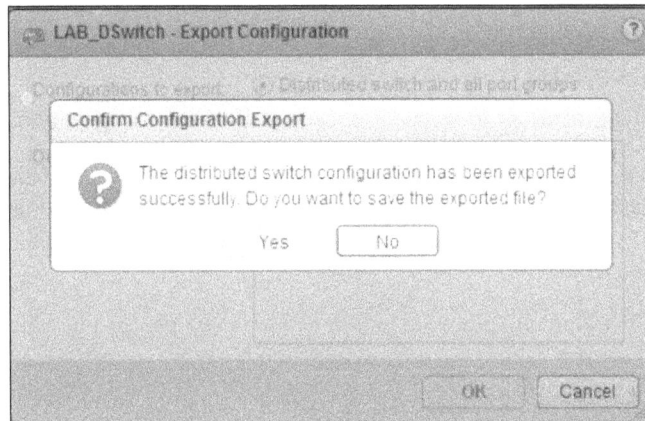

4. Select the local path to which you want to save the configuration, and specify a filename for the exported configuration, as shown in the following screenshot:

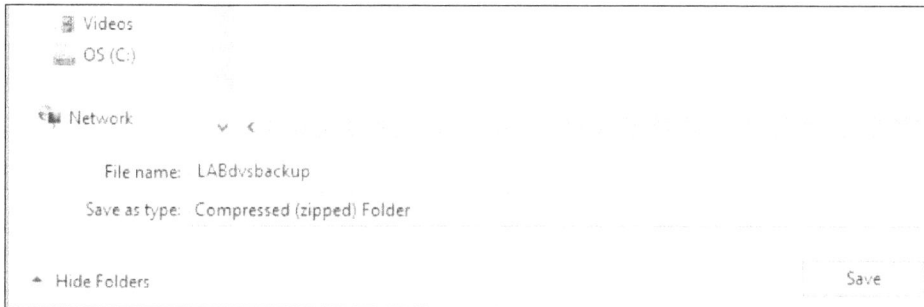

How it works...

Once exported, the configuration file will contain all of the settings for VDS and the dvPortgroup configurations. This file can then be used to restore the VDS configurations of an existing distributed switch or to import the configurations if VDS is accidently deleted or lost.

Restoring the VDS configuration from the exported configuration file is a simple process. Right-click on the VDS to be restored and navigate to **All vCenter Actions | Restore Configuration...**, as shown in the following screenshot:

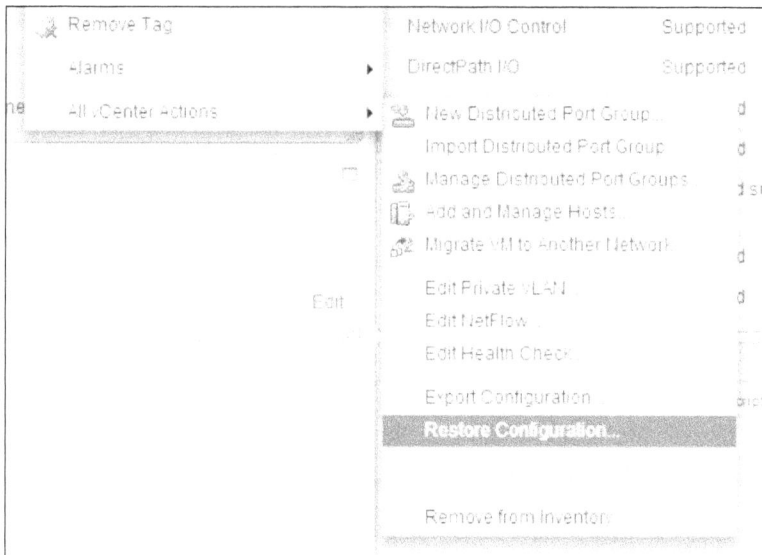

When restoring or importing a VDS from an exported configuration file, we can use one of the two options: **Restore distributed switch and all port groups** or **Restore distributed switch only**, as shown in the following screenshot:

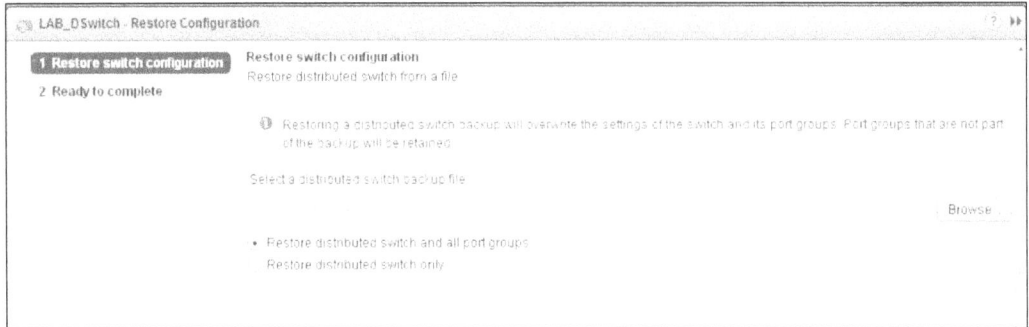

When using the **Restore distributed switch only** option, only the distributed switch configuration is restored. The dvPortGroups and their associated configurations are not restored. If the **Restore distributed switch and all port groups** option is selected, the virtual distributed switch configuration and the associated dvPortgroups are restored. Note that during the restore process, the current settings of the distributed virtual switch and the associated dvPortgroups will be overwritten.

Deploying VMware Data Protection

vSphere Data Protection (**VDP**) is an easy-to-deploy, Linux-based virtual appliance that leverages **EMC Avamar** to provide a disk-based backup of the virtual machines. Two deployment options are available. The first option is VDP, which is included free with VMware Essential Plus or a higher licensing, and the second is **VDP Advanced** (**VDPA**), which is a separately licensed product. VDP facilitates deduplicated, full virtual machine image backups. These backups can be replicated to a remote Avamar grid or to another VDP appliance. VDPA includes agents for the message-level backups of Microsoft Exchange and the database backups of Microsoft SQL Server.

How to do it...

In order to deploy VDP, perform the following steps:

1. Download the VMware Data Protection Appliance from http://www.vmware.com/go/download-vsphere.

2. Deploy the vSphere Data Protection Appliance from the OVA. Enter the appliance's network configuration information during the OVA deployment as shown in the following screenshot:

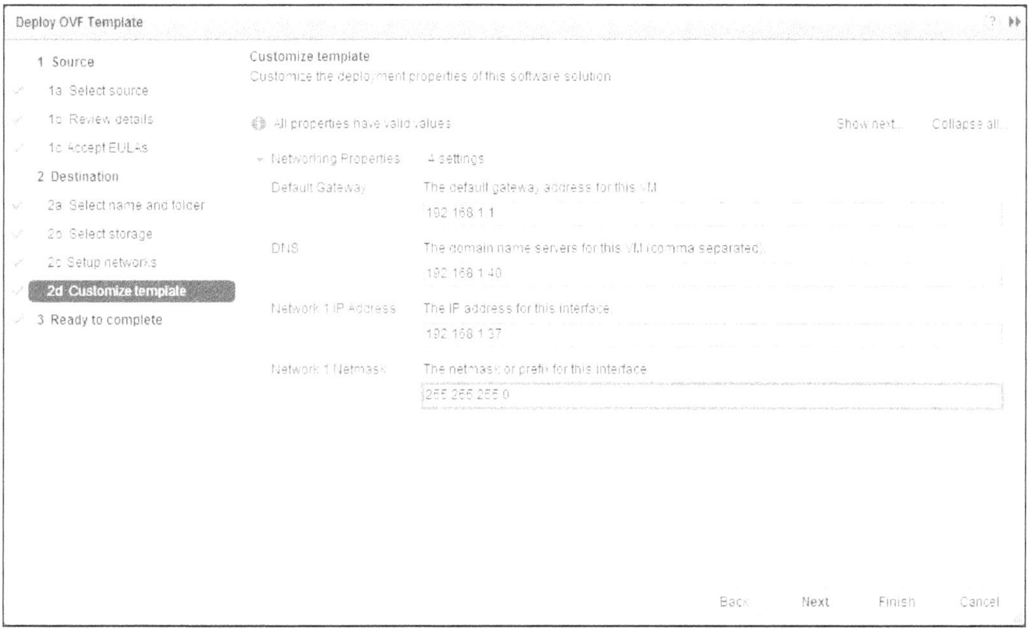

3. When the OVA deployment is complete and the VDP appliance is powered on, visit `https://<vdp-ip-address>:8543/vdp-configure` to complete the appliance's configuration. Log in to the appliance for the first time using the username `root` and the default password `changeme`.

4. Once you are logged in, the initial configuration wizard starts to configure the VDP appliance.

5. The first step performed by the wizard is verifying the network settings, as shown in the following screenshot:

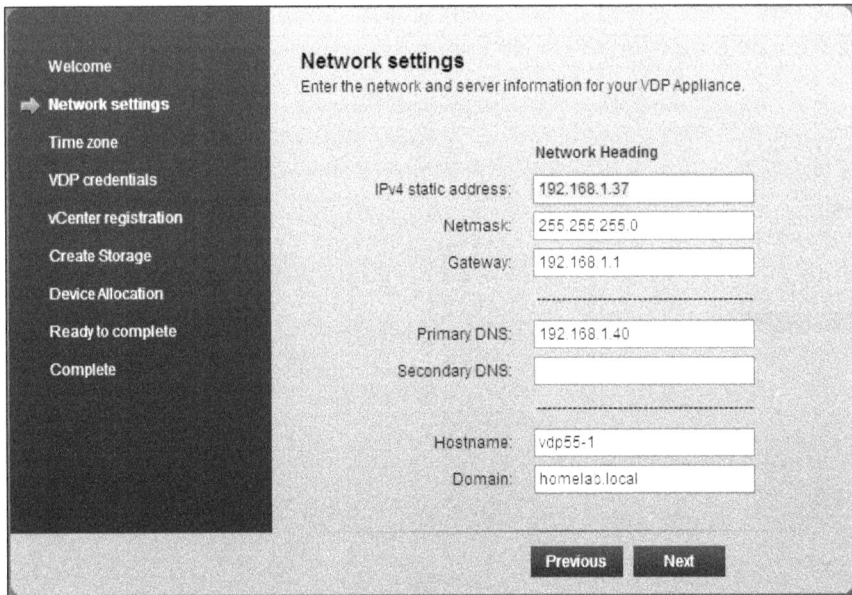

Network settings

Enter the network and server information for your VDP Appliance.

- Welcome
- → **Network settings**
- Time zone
- VDP credentials
- vCenter registration
- Create Storage
- Device Allocation
- Ready to complete
- Complete

Network Heading

IPv4 static address:	192.168.1.37
Netmask:	255.255.255.0
Gateway:	192.168.1.1
Primary DNS:	192.168.1.40
Secondary DNS:	
Hostname:	vdp55-1
Domain:	homelab.local

Previous   Next

> The wizard verifies whether the appliance's hostname can be resolved in DNS. Forward and reverse DNS entries will need to be configured before the network settings can be saved successfully.

6. The configuration wizard will then prompt you to choose the time zone. Select the time zone as shown in the following screenshot:

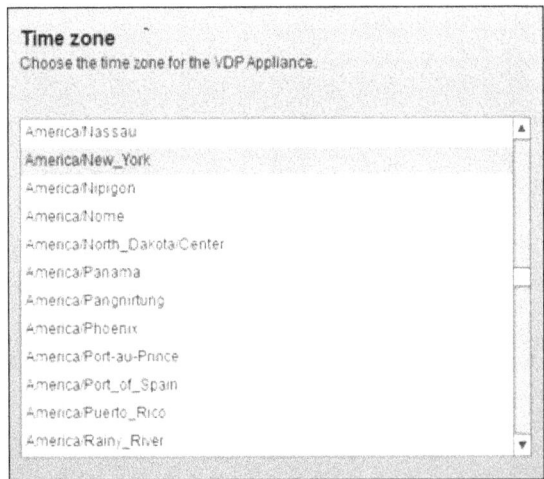

Time zone

Choose the time zone for the VDP Appliance.

America/Nassau
America/New_York
America/Nipigon
America/Nome
America/North_Dakota/Center
America/Panama
America/Pangnirtung
America/Phoenix
America/Port-au-Prince
America/Port_of_Spain
America/Puerto_Rico
America/Rainy_River

7. The default VDP password must be changed. Enter the VDP password, taking note of the password requirements. The wizard will place green checks next to the rules that the password meets. The password must meet all the password rules, as shown in the following screenshot:

VDP credentials
Enter a password for the VDP Appliance.

Passwords must have:
- ◯ Nine characters
- ◯ One upper case letter
- ◯ One lower case letter
- ◯ One number
- ◯ No special characters

Password: ●●●●●●●●●

Verify password: ●●●●●●●●●

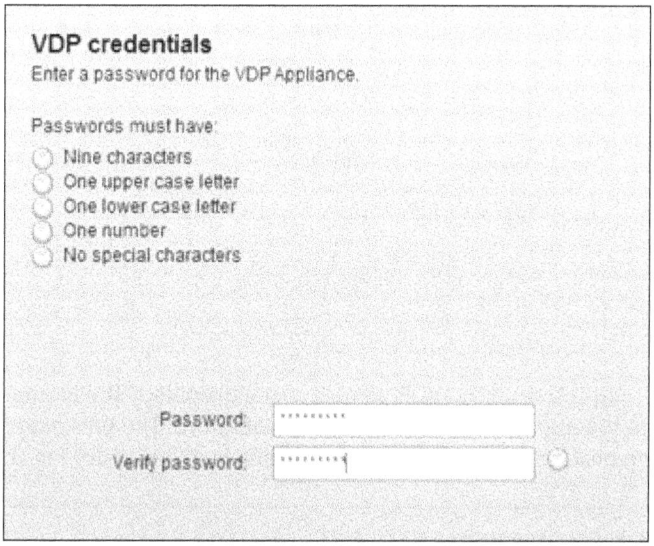

8. The VDP appliance is then registered with vCenter. Enter values for **vCenter username**, **vCenter password**, **vCenter FQDN or IP**, and **vCenter port**, as shown in the following screenshot:

vCenter registration
Identify the hostname or IP address of your vCenter server. Also provide a username and password for a user that has rights to register objects with the vCenter server.

vCenter username: administrator@vsphere.local

vCenter password: ●●●●●●●

vCenter FQDN or IP: vcva.homelab.local

vCenter port: 443

☑ Use vCenter for SSO authentication

Test Connection

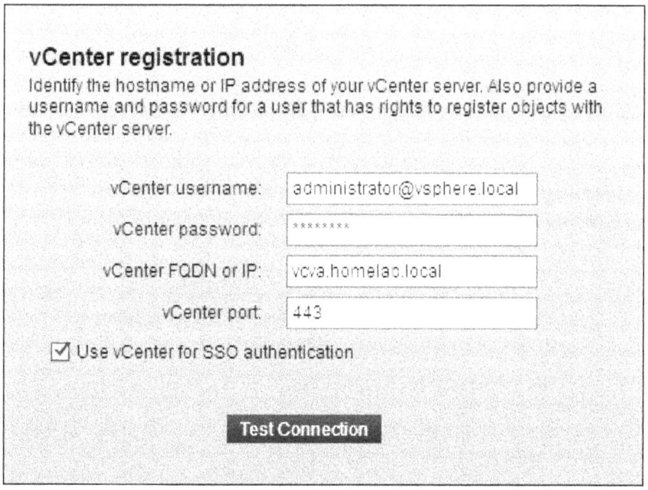

9. Create a new storage for the VDP backups. This can be configured from 0.5 TB to 2 TB per VDP appliance. The **Create Storage** dialog is displayed in the following screenshot:

Create Storage
Create new storage or attach existing VDP storage.

⦿ Create new storage

Capacity: | 0.5 | ⇕ | TiB

◯ Attach existing VDP storage

Note: It is highly recommended that you back up all the VDP storage which you intend on attaching to this appliance.

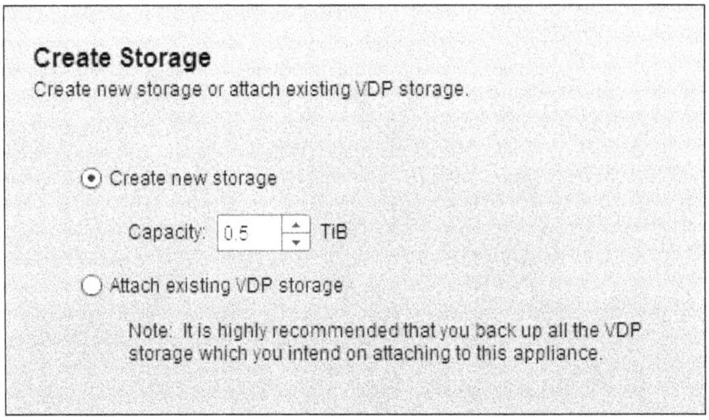

10. Choose where you want the VDP storage disks allocated. The storage disk can be stored with the appliance or on a specified datastore. The provisioning method for the storage disk can also be configured, as shown in the following screenshot:

Device Allocation
Allocate the VDP storage disks.

☑ Store With Appliance   Provision: | Thin | ▾

Datastores	Capacity	Provisioned	Free	Disks
datastore1	460.7 GiB	231.4 GiB	290.3 GiB	0 ⇕
MASSD	110.0 GiB	110.0 GiB	42.0 GiB	0 ⇕

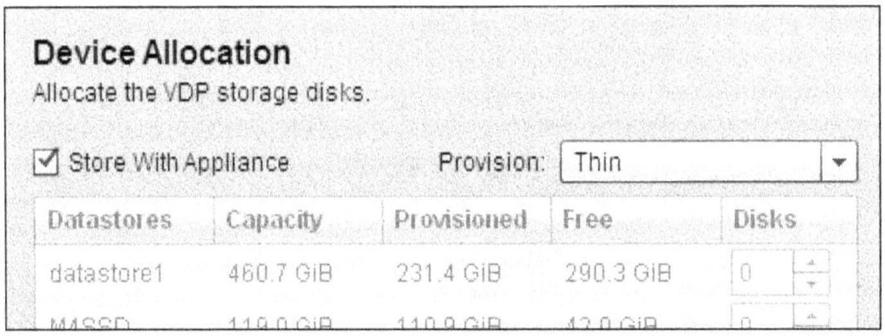

11. On completion of the VDP configuration, the following screen is shown:

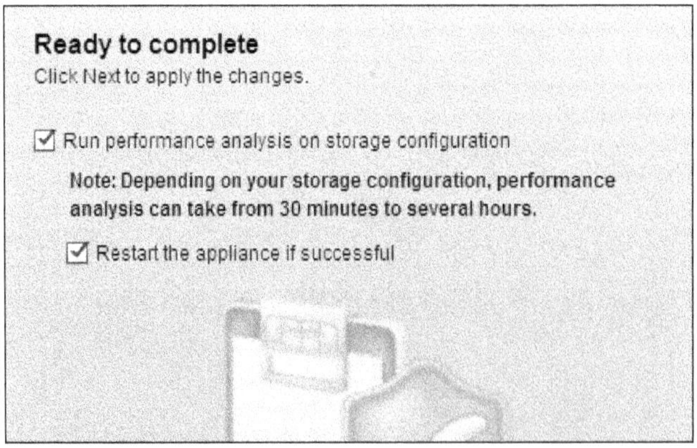

Ready to complete
Click Next to apply the changes.

☑ Run performance analysis on storage configuration

Note: Depending on your storage configuration, performance analysis can take from 30 minutes to several hours.

☑ Restart the appliance if successful

12. Select the **Run performance analysis on storage configuration** and **Restart the appliance if successful** checkboxes.

13. When you are prompted to start the storage configuration, select **Yes** to begin the process. A status window is displayed as the configuration is applied. The configuration will take some time to complete, 30 minutes or more, and the appliance will reboot once the configuration process has been completed successfully. The following screenshot shows the configuration status window:

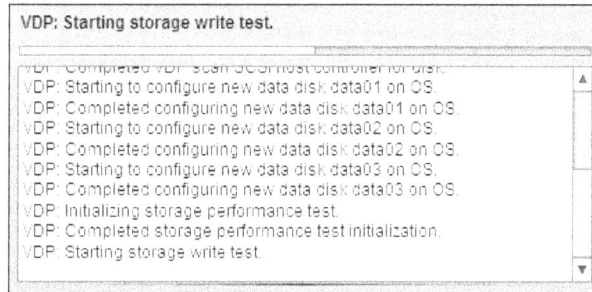

14. The progress can also be monitored using the **Tasks** tab in the vSphere Web Client as shown in the following screenshot:

15. Once the configuration has been completed and the VDP appliance restarts, the **vSphere Data Protection** management option will be available in the vSphere Web Client. The following screenshot shows the VDP connection screen in the vSphere Web Client:

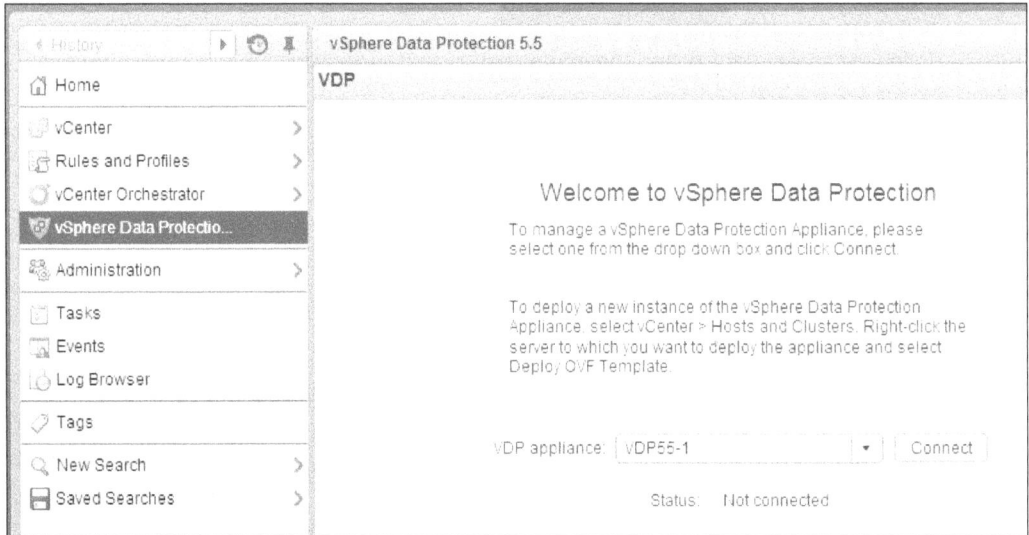

How it works...

During the VDP appliance OVA deployment, the initial network settings are configured which includes the network address of the appliance, the subnet mask, the default gateway, and the primary DNS.

Once the appliance has been deployed and powered on, the VDP configuration wizard is used to verify the network configurations, configure the hostname and domain, set the root password of the appliance, configure the timezone, and register the appliance with a vCenter server. The configuration of the storage for the virtual machine backups is also configured.

After the initial configuration and analysis has completed, the appliance will reboot and can then be managed using the vSphere Web Client. Backup jobs to protect virtual machines can then be created through the vSphere Web Client

Using VMware Data Protection to back up virtual machines

Virtual machine backups using the VDP appliance are created and managed using the vSphere Web Client connected to vCenter, where the VDP appliance has been registered.

How to do it...

Perform the following steps to create a backup job in order to protect virtual machines using VDP:

1. In the vSphere Web Client, select **vSphere Data Protection** and connect to the VDP appliance.

2. Select the **Backup** tab, and from the **Backup job actions** menu, select **New**, as shown in the following screenshot:

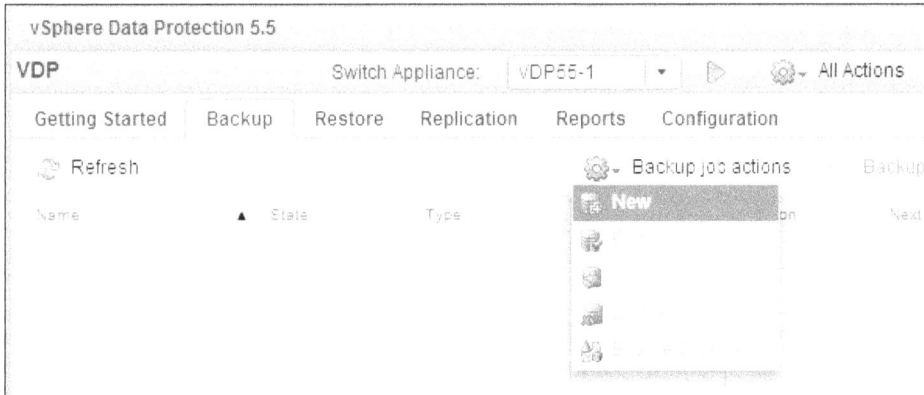

3. Select the type of backup to be performed: either a **Full Image**, which is a complete backup of the virtual machine including all the disks and configurations, or **Individual Disks**, which are individual **virtual machine disks** (**VMDKs**), as shown in the following screenshot:

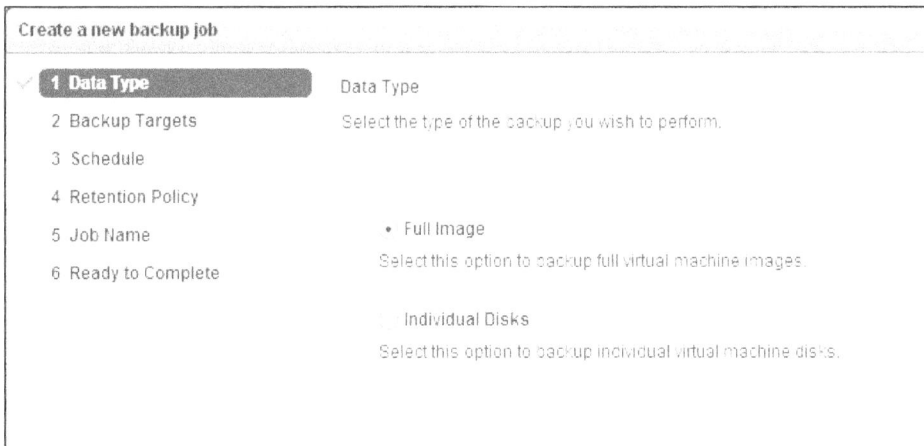

4. Select the backup targets. Targets can be vCenter inventory objects including datacenters, clusters, resource pools, or individual virtual machines. The following screenshot illustrates selecting two individual virtual machines to be a part of this backup job:

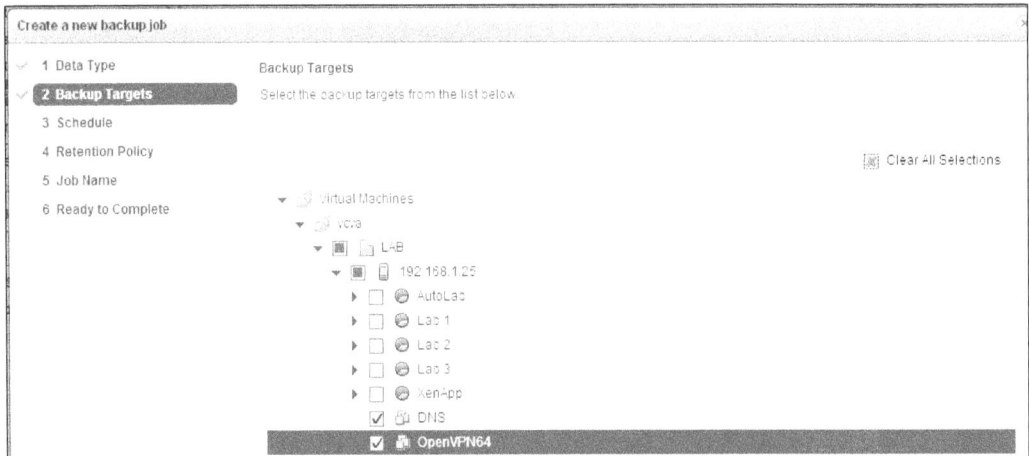

5. Create a schedule of the backup job. The **Schedule** determines how often and when the backup job will run. The following screenshot demonstrates a daily schedule with the start time of 8:00 P.M.:

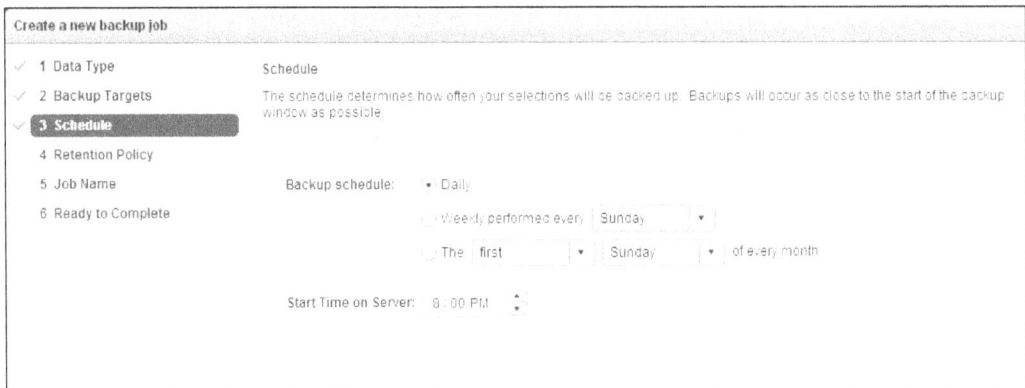

6. Set a retention policy for the backup job. **Retention Policy** determines for how long the backups are retained. In the following screenshot, the retention policy has been set to 30 days:

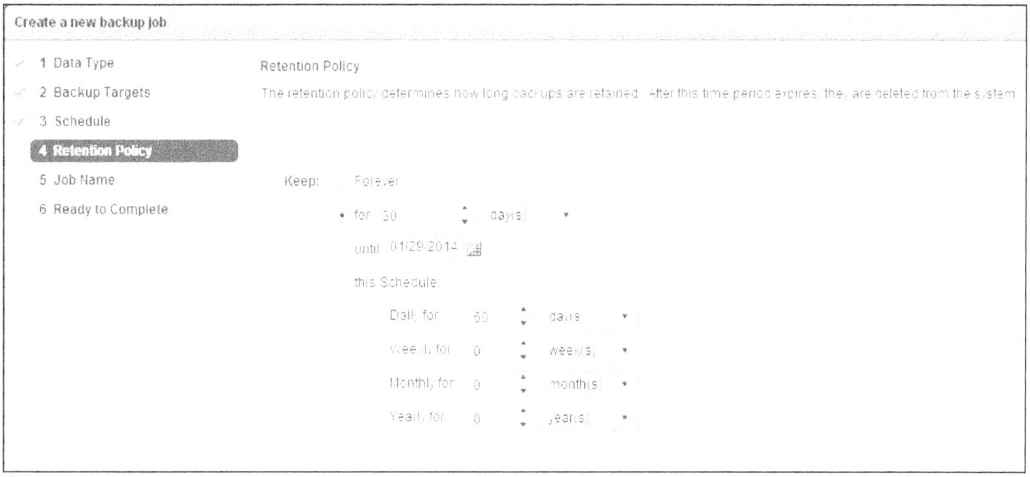

7. Set a job name for the backup job. It can be helpful if the name is a short description of the backup job, as shown in the following screenshot:

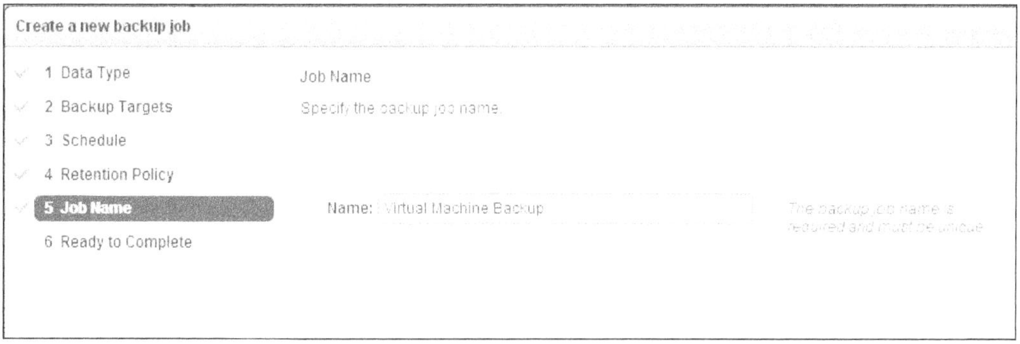

8. A **Ready to Complete** screen is shown to allow the configuration settings to be reviewed, as shown in the following screenshot:

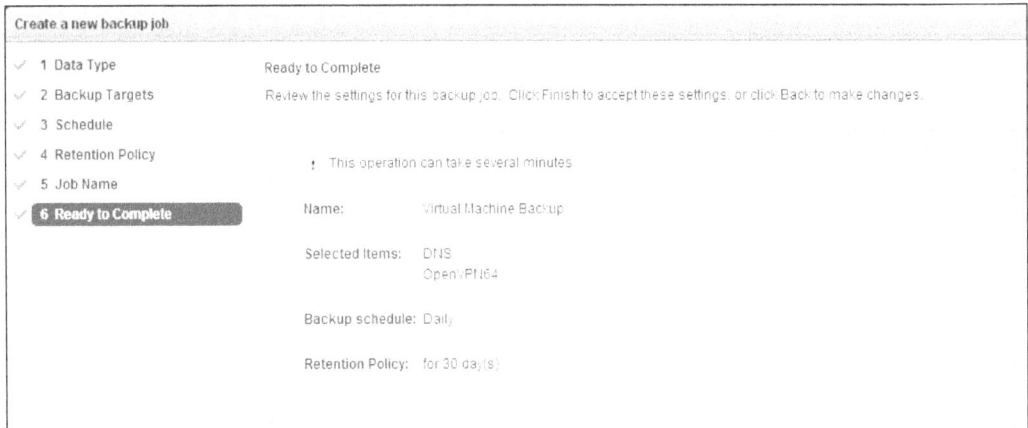

9. Once completed, the backup job is created and will run according to the configured schedule.

How it works...

Backup jobs are created in order to back up virtual machines or groups of virtual machines. Backup jobs include the backup targets, the backup schedule, and the backup retention policy.

The best RPO that can be obtained for a single backup job is 24 hours because only a single daily backup can be configured. If the RPO for a specific virtual machine or a group of virtual machines is less than 24 hours, multiple backup jobs will need to be created. For example, if the RPO for a virtual machine is 6 hours, four daily backup jobs configured to start at 12:00 A.M., 6:00 A.M., 12:00 P.M., and 6:00 P.M. would need to be created to meet the RPO.

Once the backup jobs have run, the virtual machines can be restored to their original location or to a different location. Restoring to a different location provides a way to test the virtual machine backups without impacting the running virtual machine.

File-level restores can also be performed by connecting to the VDP appliance from the backup target. To access file-level restores, visit `https://vdp-appliance-ip:8543/flr` from the virtual machine that has been backed up. The file-level restore client is shown in the following screenshot:

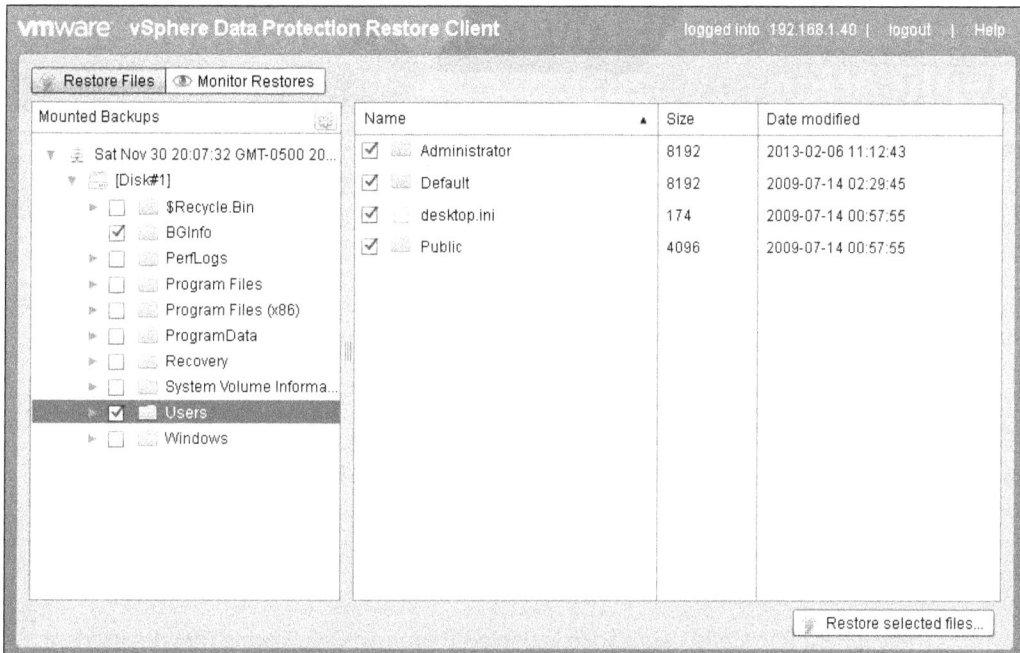

The health of the appliance, current usage, and status of the backup jobs can be monitored using the **Reports** tab, as shown in the following screenshot:

Replicating virtual machines with vSphere Replication

vSphere Replication is included for free with vSphere Essentials Plus or higher. vSphere Replication allows virtual machines to be replicated between sites or between datastores on the same site. vSphere Replication leverages **Change Block Tracking** (**CBT**) to only replicate changes between the source virtual machines and the replication target.

vSphere Replication appliances are deployed at each site participating in replication. Multiple vSphere Replication appliances can be deployed to improve replication performance.

How to do it...

To deploy vSphere Replication and configure a virtual machine for replication, perform the following steps:

1. Download the vSphere Replication appliance from `http://www.vmware.com/go/download-vsphere`.

2. The vSphere Replication appliance is deployed from an OVA. During OVA deployment, the initial configuration of the administrator password, the database, and the management network IP address are configured as shown in the following screenshot:

3. Once the vSphere Replication appliance has been deployed, it can be managed from the vSphere Web Client as shown in the following screenshot:

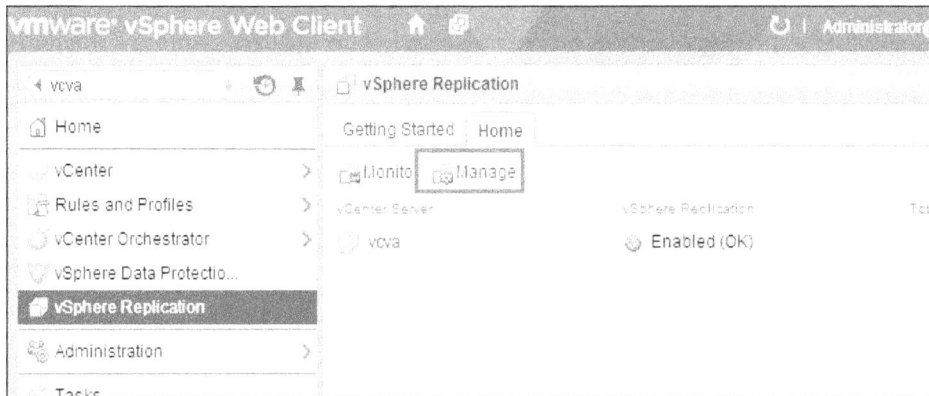

4. Replication can now be configured for virtual machines. To enable replication, right-click on the virtual machine to be replicated. Then, navigate to **All vSphere Replication Actions | Configure Replication** from the menu, as shown in the following screenshot:

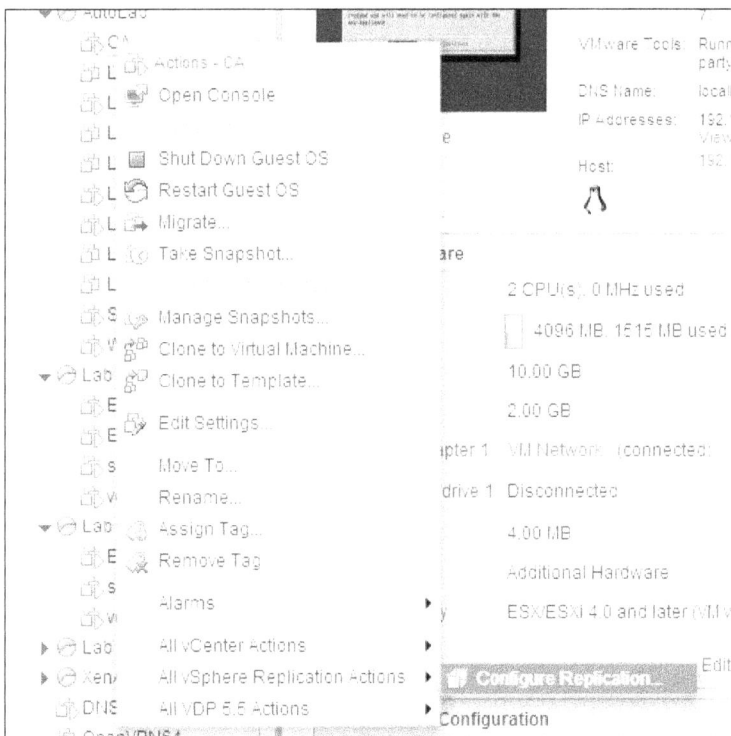

5. The replication wizard walks through the configuration of **Target site**, **Replication server**, **Target location**, and **Replication options**. The following screenshot displays the **Configure Replication** wizard for a virtual machine:

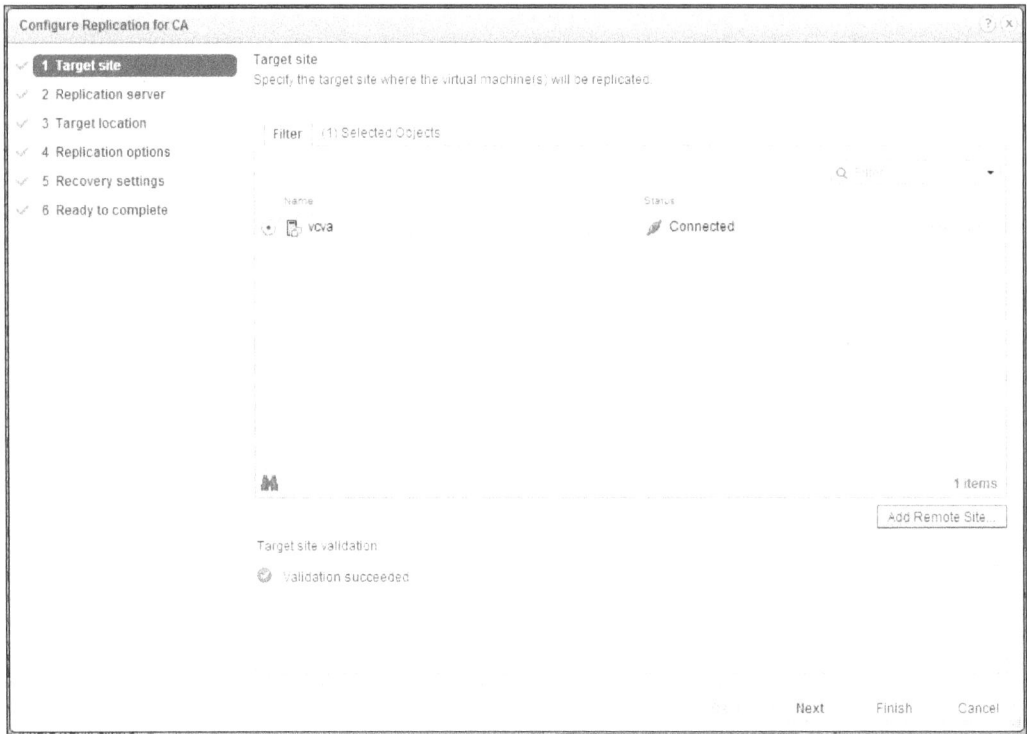

6. The **Recovery settings** menu allows you to configure **Recovery Point Objective (RPO)**, time between replications, and the number of **Point in time instances** to keep of the replicated virtual machine. The best RPO that can be realized with vSphere Replication is 15 minutes. The following screenshot shows the configuration of an RPO of 15 minutes for the selected virtual machine:

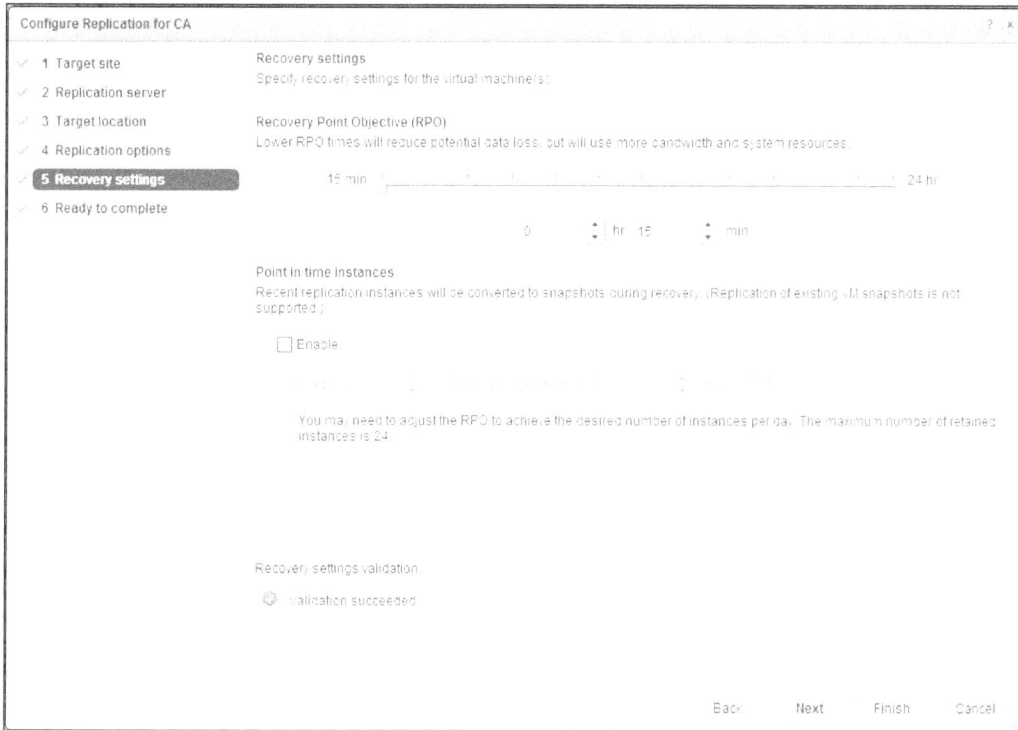

7. Once replication for a virtual machine has been configured, the replication can be monitored in the vSphere Web Client. The following screenshot shows the status of **Initial Full Sync** on a virtual machine that has been configured for replication:

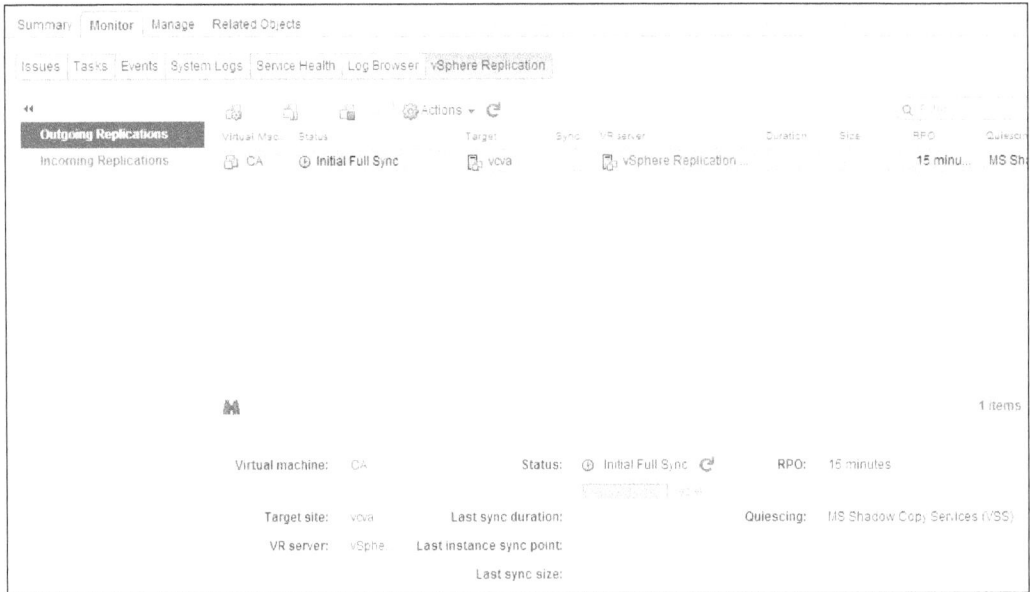

How it works...

After the initial synchronization has been completed, the vSphere kernel tracks the writes to the protected virtual machine and transfers only the blocks that have changed. The following diagram illustrates the traffic flow for a virtual machine replicated with vSphere Replication:

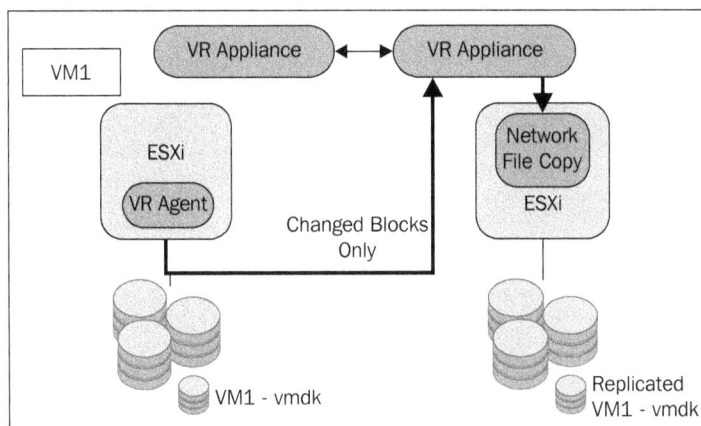

Here, VM1 has been configured for replication. Changed blocks are tracked and transferred to the target vSphere Replication appliance.

Once a replication has been set up, it can be recovered from the **vSphere Replication** management by selecting the replicated virtual machine and choosing **Recover**, as shown in the following screenshot:

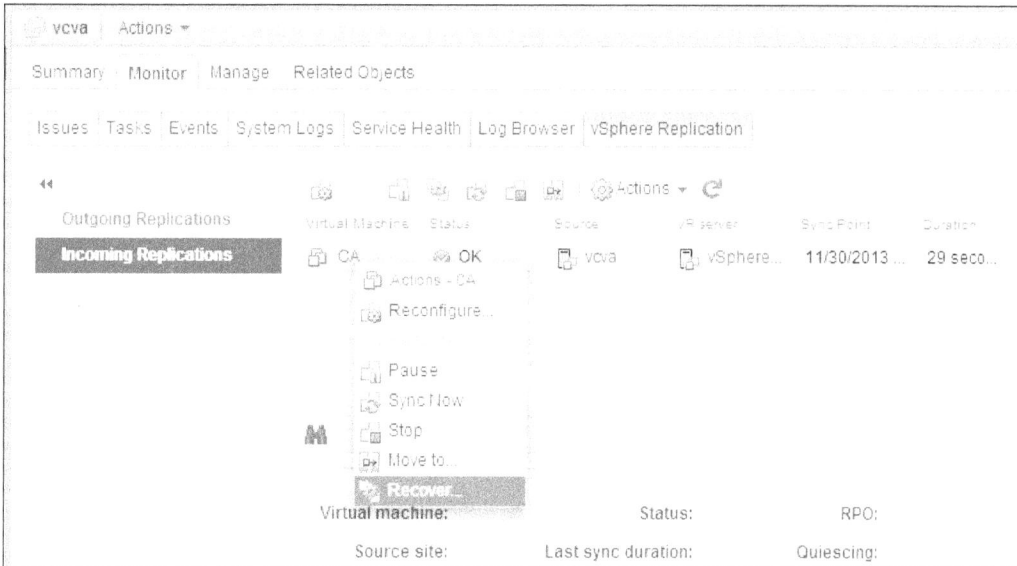

Protecting the virtual datacenter with Site Recovery Manager

Site Recovery Manager (**SRM**) is a VMware product that provides a framework for automating the protection and failover between VMware virtualized datacenters. SRM is licensed as a separate product. Licensing is per VM protected and there are two license editions: Standard and Enterprise. The **Standard Edition** provides for the protection of up to 75 virtual machines, and the **Enterprise Edition** can protect an unlimited number of virtual machines.

A complete book can be dedicated to the implementation and use of SRM. This book is just meant to be a quick overview of the configuration and capabilities of SRM. More information on the implementation and use of SRM can be found in the SRM documentation at `http://www.vmware.com/support/pubs/srm_pubs.html`.

How to do it...

Protecting the datacenter using SRM is accomplished through the following process:

1. Identify the requirements of Site Recovery Manager.
2. Deploy Site Recovery Manager at the protected and recovery sites.
3. Configure connections between the protected and recovery sites.
4. Establish virtual machine replication between the protected and recovery sites.
5. Create resource mapping between the protected and recovery sites.
6. Create protection groups containing the virtual machines to be protected.
7. Configure recovery plans to automate the recovery of virtual machines.
8. Test the recovery plan to ensure that it will operate as expected.

How it works...

SRM does not provide for the protection of virtual machines. It provides a way to easily automate and manage the protection and failover of virtual machines. The SRM service runs on a Windows server and requires a supported database. Supported databases for the deployed SRM version can be found on the product and solution interoperability matrix at `http://partnerweb.vmware.com/comp_guide2/sim/interop_matrix.php`.

Virtual machines can be replicated between sites using either vSphere Replication or array-based replication. If array-based replication is used, a supported **Storage Replication Adapter** (**SRA**) is installed on the SRM servers at each site. SRA communicates with the array to control replication flow during normal, failover, and failback operations.

vSphere Replication can be deployed independently, or it can be deployed as part of the SRM installation. vSphere Replication connectivity between sites can be configured and managed from within SRM.

> SRM configuration and management can only be done using the thick vSphere Client. It cannot be managed using the vSphere Web Client.

The following diagram illustrates a basic SRM architecture using both vSphere Replication and array-based replication between the protected and recovery sites.

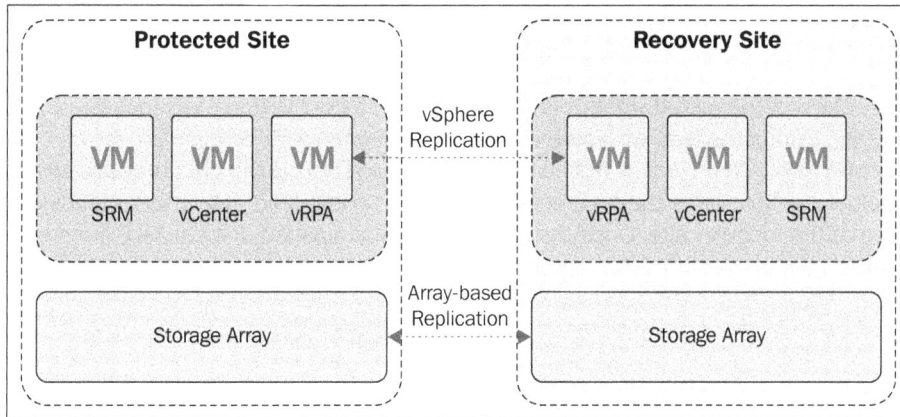

Compute resources (datacenters, clusters, and resource pools) and network resources on the protected site are mapped to the resources at the recovery site. For example, the port group named *Production VM Network* at the protected site is mapped to a port group named *Failover VM Network* at the recovery site. The resource must exist at the recovery site before they can be mapped. A placeholder datastore is configured to hold the protected virtual machine configuration files at the recovery site.

Protection groups are created and contain virtual machines that are protected. When virtual machines are added to a protection group, a placeholder configuration file is created at the recovery site on the placeholder datastore. Protection groups can be used to group virtual machines that should be recovered together to ensure that workload dependencies are met. For example, an application that includes a virtual machine running a web frontend and another virtual machine running the support database can be placed in a protection group to ensure that all of the workload dependencies are recovered when a failover is initiated.

Recovery plans contain protection groups. Multiple recovery plans can be created, and a protection group can be included in more than one recovery plan. For example, a recovery plan can be created for a single protection group to facilitate recovery, or a single application and another recovery plan can be created to include all the configured protection groups in order to facilitate the recovery of the entire site.

As part of the recovery plan, the virtual machine startup order can be configured with virtual machine network options. If the virtual machine network configuration (IP address or DNS servers) needs to be changed during recovery, the virtual machine network options are set on the individual virtual machines in the recovery plan. VMware Tools must be installed on the virtual machines if network changes are required.

A recovery plan can be tested without impacting the protected virtual machines by running a recovery test. During the test, an isolated vSwitch—a vSwitch with no uplinks—will be created at the recovery site. When virtual machines are recovered during the test, they are connected to this isolated switch. Once the test recovery has been completed, the virtual machine can be verified at the recovery site. Once the test has been completed and verified, the cleanup operation can be run to return the virtual machines to a protected state.

11
The Design Documentation

In this chapter, we will cover the following topics:

- ▶ Creating the architecture design document
- ▶ Writing an implementation plan
- ▶ Developing an installation guide
- ▶ Creating a validation test plan
- ▶ Writing operational procedures
- ▶ Presenting the design
- ▶ Implementing the design

Introduction

The design documentation provides written documentation of the design factors and the choices the architect has made in the design to satisfy the business and technical requirements.

The design documentation also aids in the implementation of the design. In many cases where the design architect is not responsible for the implementation, the design documents ensure the successful implementation of the design by the implementation engineer.

> Once you have created the documentation for a few designs, you will be able to develop standard processes and templates to aid in the creation of design documentation.

Documentation can vary from project to project. Many consulting companies and resellers have standard documentation templates that they use when designing solutions. A properly documented design should include the following information:

- Architecture design
- Implementation plan
- Installation guide
- Validation test plan
- Operational procedures

This information can be included in a single document or separated into different documents.

VMware provides Service Delivery Kits to VMware partners. These kits can be found on the VMware Partner University portal at `http://www.vmware.com/go/partneruniversity`, which provides documentation templates that can be used as a foundation for creating design documents. If you do not have access to these templates, example outlines are provided in this chapter to assist you in developing your own design documentation templates.

The final steps of the design process include gaining customer approval to begin implementation of the design and the implementation of the design.

Creating the architecture design document

The architecture design document is a technical document describing the components and specifications required to support the solution and ensure that the specific business and technical requirements of the design are satisfied.

> An excellent example of an architecture design document is the *Cloud Infrastructure Architecture Case Study White Paper* article that can be found at `http://www.vmware.com/files/pdf/techpaper/cloud-infrastructure-achitecture-case-study.pdf`.

The architect creates the architecture design document to document the design factors and the specific choices that have been made to satisfy those factors. The document serves as a way for the architect to show his work when making design decisions. The architecture design document includes the conceptual, logical, and physical designs.

How to do it...

The architecture design document should include the following information:

- ▶ Purpose and overview
    - ❏ Executive summary
    - ❏ Design methodology
- ▶ Conceptual design
- ▶ Logical management, storage, compute, and network design
- ▶ Physical management, storage, compute, and network design

How it works...

The *Purpose and Overview* section of the architecture design includes the *Executive Summary* section. The *Executive Summary* section provides a high-level overview of the design and the goals the design will accomplish, and defines the purpose and scope of the architecture design document.

The following is an example executive summary in the *Cloud Infrastructure Architecture Case Study White Paper*:

> *Executive Summary: This architecture design was developed to support a virtualization project to consolidate 100 existing physical servers on to a VMware vSphere 5.x virtual infrastructure. The primary goals this design will accomplish are to increase operational efficiency and to provide high availability of customer-facing applications.*

> *This document details the recommended implementation of a VMware virtualization architecture based on specific business requirements and VMware recommended practices. The document provides both logical and physical design considerations for all related infrastructure components including servers, storage, networking, management, and virtual machines.*

> *The scope of this document is specific to the design of the virtual infrastructure and the supporting components.*

The purpose and overview section should also include details of the design methodology the architect has used in creating the architecture design. This should include the processes followed to determine the business and technical requirements along with definitions of the infrastructure qualities that influenced the design decisions.

Design factors, requirements, constraints, and assumptions are documented as part of the conceptual design. *Chapter 3, The Design Factors* provides details on the key factors included as part of the conceptual design. To document the design factors, use a table to organize them and associate them with an ID that can be easily referenced.

The following table illustrates an example of how to document the design requirements:

ID	Requirement
R001	Consolidate the existing 100 physical application servers down to five servers
R002	Provide capacity to support growth for 25 additional application servers over the next five years
R003	Server hardware maintenance should not affect application uptime
R004	Provide *N+2* redundancy to support a hardware failure during normal and maintenance operations

The conceptual design should also include tables documenting any constraints and assumptions. A high-level diagram of the conceptual design can also be included.

Details of the logical design are documented in the architecture design document. The logical design of management, storage, network, and compute resources should be included. When documenting the logical design document, any recommended practices that were followed should be included. Also include references to the requirements, constraints, and assumptions that influenced the design decisions.

> When documenting the logical design, show your work to support your design decisions. Include any formulas used for resource calculations and provide detailed explanations of why design decisions were made.

An example table outlining the logical design of compute resource requirements is as follows:

Parameter	Specification
Current CPU resources required	100 GHz
*CPU growth	25 GHz
CPU required (75 percent utilization)	157 GHz
Current memory resources required	525 GB
*Memory growth	131 GB
Memory required (75 percent utilization)	821 GB
Memory required (25 percent TPS savings)	616 GB
*CPU and memory growth of 25 additional application servers (R002)	

Similar tables will be created to document the logical design for storage, network, and management resources.

The physical design documents have the details of the physical hardware chosen along with the configurations of both the physical and virtual hardware. Details of vendors and hardware models chosen and the reasons for decisions made should be included as part of the physical design. The configuration of the physical hardware is documented along with the details of why specific configuration options were chosen. The physical design should also include diagrams that document the configuration of physical resources, such as physical network connectivity and storage layout.

A sample outline of the architecture design document is as follows:

- **Cover page**: It includes the customer and project names
- **Document version log**: It contains the log of authors and changes made to the document
- **Document contacts**: It includes the subject matter experts involved in the creation of the design
- **Table of contents**: It is the index of the document sections for quick reference
- **List of tables**: It is the index of tables included in the document for quick reference
- **List of figures**: It is the index of figures included in the document for quick reference
- **Purpose and overview**: This section consists of an executive summary to provide an overview of the design and the design methodology followed in creating the design
- **Conceptual design**: It is the documentation of the design factors: requirements, constraints, and assumptions
- **Logical design**: It has the details of the logical management, storage, network, and compute design
- **Physical design**: It contains the details of the selected hardware and the configuration of the physical and virtual hardware

Writing an implementation plan

The implementation plan documents the requirements necessary to complete the implementation of the design.

The implementation plan defines the project roles and defines what is expected of the customer and what they can expect during the implementation of the design.

This document is sometimes referred to as the **statement of work**. It defines the key points of contact, the requirements that must be satisfied to start the implementation, any project documentation deliverables, and how changes to the design and implementation will be handled.

How to do it...

The implementation plan should include the following information:

- Purpose statement
- Project contacts
- Implementation requirements
- Overview of implementation steps
- Definition of project documentation deliverables
- Implementation of change management

How it works...

The purpose statement defines the purpose and scope of the document. The purpose statement of the implementation plan should define what is included in the document and provide a brief overview of the goals of the project. The purpose statement is simply an introduction so that someone reading the document can gain a quick understanding of what the document contains.

The following is an example purpose statement:

> *This document serves as the implementation plan and defines the scope of the virtualization project. This document identifies points of contact for the project, lists implementation requirements, provides a brief description of each of the document deliverables, deliverables, and provides an overview of the implementation process for the data-center virtualization project.*

> *The scope of this document is specific to the implementation of the virtual data-center implementation and the supporting components as defined in the Architecture Design.*

Key project contacts, their roles, and their contact information should be included as part of the implementation plan document. These contacts include customer stakeholders, project managers, project architects, and implementation engineers.

The following is a sample table that can be used to document project contacts for the implementation plan:

Role	Name	Contact information
Customer project sponsor		
Customer technical resource		
Project manager		
Design architect		
Implementation engineer		
QA engineer		

Support contacts for hardware and software used in the implementation plan may also be included in the table, for example, contact numbers for VMware support or other vendor support.

Implementation requirements contain the implementation dependencies to include the access and facility requirements. Any hardware, software, and licensing that must be available to implement the design is also documented here.

Access requirements include the following:

▶ Physical access to the site.

▶ Credentials necessary for access to resources. These include active directory credentials and VPN credentials (if remote access is required).

Facility requirements include the following:

▶ Power and cooling to support the equipment that will be deployed as part of the design

▶ Rack space requirements

Hardware, software, and licensing requirements include the following:

▶ vSphere licensing

▶ Windows or other operating system licensing

▶ Other third-party application licensing

▶ Software (ISO, physical media, and so on)

▶ Physical hardware (hosts, array, network switches, cables, and so on)

A high-level overview of the steps required to complete the implementation is also documented. The details of each step are not a part of this document; only the steps that need to be performed will be included. For example:

1. Procurement of hardware, software, and licensing.
2. Scheduling of engineering resources.
3. Verification of access and facility requirements.
4. Performance of an inventory check for the required hardware, software, and licensing.
5. Installation and configuration of storage array.
6. Rack, cable, and burn-in of physical server hardware.
7. Installation of ESXi on physical servers.
8. Installation of vCenter Server.
9. Configuration of ESXi and vCenter.
10. Testing and verification of implementation plan.
11. Migration of physical workloads to virtual machines.
12. Operational verification of the implementation plan.

The implementation overview may also include an implementation timeline documenting the time required to complete each of the steps.

Project documentation deliverables are defined as part of the implementation plan. Any documentation that will be delivered to the customer once the implementation has been completed should be detailed here. Details include the name of the document and a brief description of the purpose of the document.

The following table provides example descriptions of the project documentation deliverables:

Document	Description
Architecture design	This is a technical document describing the vSphere components and specifications required to achieve a solution that addresses the specific business and technical requirements of the design.
Implementation plan	This identifies implementation roles and requirements. It provides a high-level map of the implementation and deliverables detailed in the design. It documents change management procedures.
Installation guide	This document provides detailed, step-by-step instructions on how to install and configure the products specified in the architecture design document.

Document	Description
Validation test plan	This document provides an overview of the procedures to be executed post installation to verify whether or not the infrastructure is installed correctly. It can also be used at any point subsequent to the installation to verify whether or not the infrastructure continues to function correctly.
Operational procedures	This document provides detailed, step-by-step instructions on how to perform common operational tasks after the design is implemented.

How changes are made to the design, specifically changes made to the design factors, must be well documented. Even a simple change to a requirement or an assumption that cannot be verified can have a tremendous effect on the design and implementation. The process for submitting a change, researching the impact of the change, and approving the change should be documented in detail.

The following is an example outline for an implementation plan:

- ▶ **Cover page**: It includes the customer and project names
- ▶ **Document version log**: It contains the log of authors and changes made to the document
- ▶ **Document contacts**: It includes the subject matter experts involved in the creation of the design
- ▶ **Table of contents**: It is the index of document sections for quick reference
- ▶ **List of tables**: It is the index of tables included in the document for quick reference
- ▶ **List of figures**: It is the index of figures included in the document for quick reference
- ▶ **Purpose statement**: It defines the purpose of the document
- ▶ **Project contacts**: It is the documentation of key project points of contact
- ▶ **Implementation requirements**: It provides the access, facilities, hardware, software, and licensing required to complete the implementation
- ▶ **Implementation overview**: It is the overview of the steps required to complete the implementation
- ▶ **Project deliverables**: It consists of the documents that will be provided as deliverables once implementation has been completed

Developing an installation guide

The installation guide provides step-by-step instructions for the implementation of the architecture design. This guide should include detailed information about how to implement and configure all the resources associated with the virtual datacenter project.

In many projects, the person creating the design is not the person responsible for implementing the design. The installation guide outlines the steps necessary to implement the physical design outlined in the architecture design document.

The installation guide should provide details about the installation of all components, including the storage and network configurations required to support the design. In a complex design, multiple installation guides may be created to document the installation of the various components required to support the design. For example, separate installation guides may be created for the storage, network, and vSphere installation and configuration.

How to do it...

The installation guide should include the following information:

- Purpose statement
- Assumption statement
- Step-by-step instructions to implement the design

How it works...

The purpose statement simply states the purpose of the document. The assumption statement describes any assumptions the document's author has made. Commonly, an assumption statement simply states that the document has been written, assuming that the reader is familiar with virtualization concepts and the architecture design.

The following is an example of a basic purpose and assumption statement that can be used for an installation guide:

> Purpose: This document provides a guide for installing and configuring the virtual infrastructure design defined in the Architecture Design.

> Assumptions: This guide is written for an implementation engineer or administrator who is familiar with vSphere concepts and terminologies. The guide is not intended for administrators who have no prior knowledge of vSphere concepts and terminology.

The installation guide should include details on implementing all areas of the design. It should include configuration of the storage array, physical servers, physical network components, and vSphere components. The following are just a few examples of installation tasks to include instructions for:

- Storage array configurations
- Physical network configurations
- Physical host configurations
- ESXi installation

- vCenter Server installation and configuration
- Virtual network configuration
- Datastore configuration
- High availability, distributed resource scheduler, storage DRS, and other vSphere components installation and configuration

The installation guide should provide as much detail as possible. Along with the step-by-step procedures, screenshots can be used to provide installation guidance.

The following screenshot is an example taken from an installation guide that details enabling and configuring the Software iSCSI adapter:

5.3 Configure Storage

1. Enable the Software iSCSI HBA.
    - Select **Storage Adapters** in the **Hardware** menu.
    - Select **Add** to create the Software iSCSI HBA
    - Select the new Software iSCSI HBA and select **Properties**.
    - In the iSCSI initiator properties select **Configure** to set the **iSCSI Name** and **iSCSI Alias**.
    - Select the **Network Configuration** tab and **Add** the iSCSI-A VMkernel

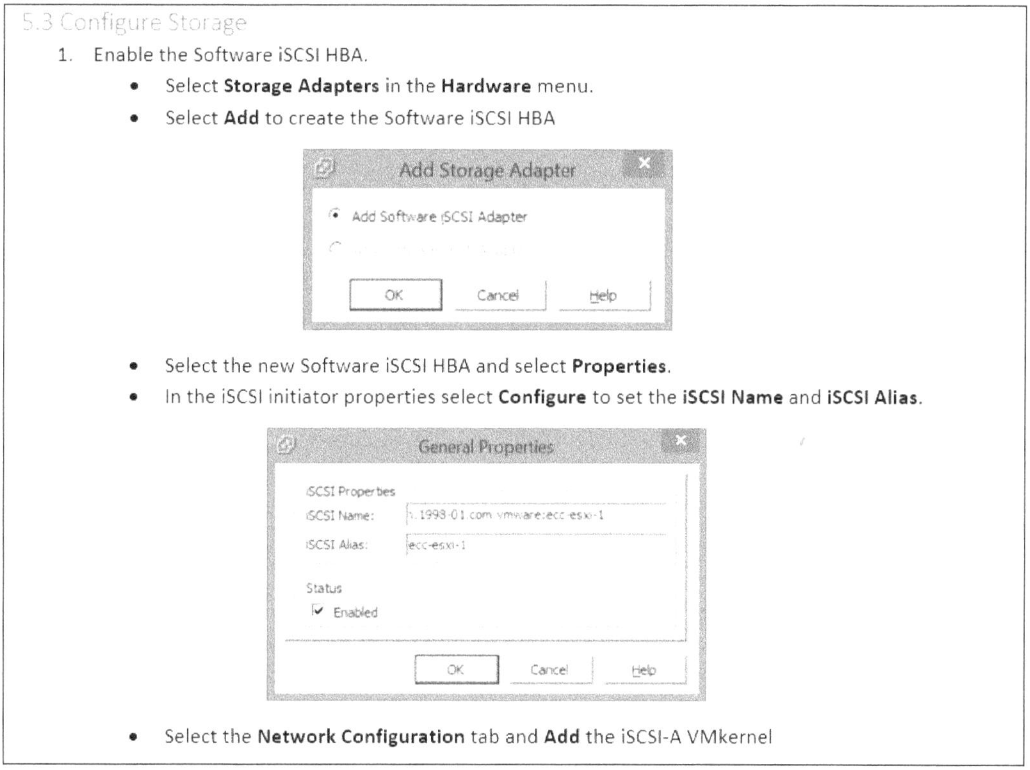

The following is an example outline for an installation guide:

- **Cover page**: It includes the customer and project names
- **Document version log**: It contains the log of authors and changes made to the document
- **Document contacts**: It includes the subject matter experts involved in the creation of the design

- ▸ **Table of contents**: It is the index of document sections for quick reference
- ▸ **List of tables**: It is the index of tables included in the document for quick reference
- ▸ **List of figures**: It is the index of figures included in the document for quick reference
- ▸ **Purpose statement**: It defines the purpose of the document
- ▸ **Assumption statement**: It defines any assumptions made in creating the document
- ▸ **Installation guide**: It provides the step-by-step installation instructions to be followed when implementing the design

Creating a validation test plan

The validation test plan documents how the implementation will be verified. It documents the criteria that must be met to determine the success of the implementation and the test procedures that should be followed when validating the environment. The criteria and procedures defined in the validation test plan determine whether or not the design requirements have been successfully met.

How to do it...

The validation test plan should include the following information:

- ▸ Purpose statement
- ▸ Assumption statement
- ▸ Success criteria
- ▸ Test procedures

How it works...

The purpose statement defines the purpose of the validation test plan and the assumption statement documents any assumptions the author of the plan has made in developing the test plan. Typically, the assumptions are that the testing and validation will be performed by someone who is familiar with the concepts and the design.

The following is an example of a purpose and assumption statement for a validation test plan:

Purpose*: This document contains testing procedures to verify that the implemented configurations specified in the Architecture Design document successfully addresses the customer requirements.*

Assumptions*: This document assumes that the person performing these tests has a basic understanding of VMware vSphere and is familiar with the accompanying design documentation. This document is not intended for administrators or testers who have no prior knowledge of vSphere concepts and terminology.*

The success criteria determines whether or not the implemented design is operating as expected. More importantly, these criteria determine whether or not the design requirements have been met. Success is measured based on whether or not the criteria satisfies the design requirements.

The following table shows some examples of success criteria defined in the validation test plan:

Description	Measurement
Members of the active directory group vSphere administrators are able to access vCenter as administrators	Yes/No
Access is denied to users outside the vSphere administrators active directory group	Yes/No
Access to a host using the vSphere Client is permitted when lockdown mode is disabled	Yes/No
Access to a host using the vSphere Client is denied when lockdown mode is enabled	Yes/No
Cluster resource utilization is less than 75 percent.	Yes/No

If the success criteria are not met, the design does not satisfy the design factors. This can be due to a misconfiguration or error in the design. Troubleshooting will need to be done to identify the issue or modifications to the design may need to be made.

Test procedures are performed to determine whether or not the success criteria have been met. Test procedures should include testing of usability, performance, and recoverability. Test procedures should include the test description, the tasks to perform the test, and the expected results of the test.

The following table provides some examples of usability testing procedures:

Test description	Tasks to perform test	Expected result
vCenter administrator access	Use the vSphere Web Client to access the vCenter Server. Log in as a user who is a member of the vSphere administrators AD group.	Administrator access to the inventory of the vCenter Server
vCenter access: No permissions	Use the vSphere Web Client to access the vCenter Server. Log in as a user who is not a member of the vSphere administrators AD group.	Access is denied
Host access: lockdown mode disabled	Disable lockdown mode through the DCUI. Use the vSphere Client to access the host and log in as root.	Direct access to the host using the vSphere Client is successful

Test description	Tasks to perform test	Expected result
Host access: lockdown mode enabled	Re-enable lockdown mode through the DCUI. Use the vSphere Client to access the host and log in as root.	Direct access to the host using the vSphere Client is denied

The following table provides some examples of reliability testing procedures:

Test description	Tasks to perform test	Expected result
Host storage path failure	Disconnect a vmnic providing IP storage connectivity from the host	The disconnected path fails, but I/O continues to be processed on the surviving paths. A network connectivity alarm should be triggered and an e-mail should be sent to the configured e-mail address.
Host storage path restore	Reconnect the vmnic providing IP storage connectivity	The failed path should become active and begin processing the I/O. Network connectivity alarms should clear.
Array storage path failure	Disconnect one network connection from the active SP	The disconnected paths fail on all hosts, but I/O continues to be processed on the surviving paths.
Management network redundancy	Disconnect the active management network vmnic	The stand-by adapter becomes active. Management access to the host is not interrupted. A loss-of-network redundancy alarm should be triggered and an e-mail should be sent to the configured e-mail address.

These are just a few examples of test procedures. The actual test procedures will depend on the requirements defined in the conceptual design.

The following is an example outline of a validation test plan:

- **Cover page**: It includes the customer and project names
- **Document version log**: It contains the log of authors and changes made to the document
- **Document contacts**: It includes the subject matter experts involved in the creation of the design
- **Table of contents**: It is the index of document sections for quick reference
- **List of tables**: It is the index of tables included in the document for quick reference

- **List of figures**: It is the index of figures included in the document for quick reference

- **Purpose statement**: It defines the purpose of the document

- **Assumption statement**: It defines any assumptions made in creating the document

- **Success criteria**: It is a list of criteria that must be met to validate the successful implementation of the design

- **Test Procedures**: It is a list of test procedures to follow, including the steps to follow and the expected results

Writing operational procedures

The operational-procedure document provides the detailed, step-by-step procedures required for the successful operation of the implemented virtual data-center design. These procedures should include monitoring and troubleshooting, virtual machine deployment, environment startup and shutdown, patching and updating, and any other details that may be required for the successful operation of the implemented design.

How to do it...

The operational procedures should include the following information:

- Purpose statement

- Assumption statement

- Step-by-step procedure for daily operations

- Troubleshooting and recovery procedures

How it works...

As with other design documents, the purpose statement defines the purpose of the operational-procedures document. The assumption statement details any assumptions the author of the plan made in developing the procedures.

Purpose: *This document contains detailed step-by-step instructions on how to perform common operational tasks. This document provides a guide to performing common tasks associated with management, monitoring, troubleshooting, virtual machine deployment, updating, and recovery.*

Assumptions: *This document assumes that an administrator who uses these procedures is familiar with VMware vSphere concepts and terminology.*

The operational procedure document provides step-by-step procedures for common tasks that will need to be performed by the administrator of the environment. Examples of procedures to include are as follows:

- Accessing the environment
- Monitoring resource usage and performance
- Deploying new virtual machines
- Patching ESXi hosts
- Updating VMware tools and virtual-machine hardware

The operational procedure document should also describe troubleshooting and recovery. Examples of these procedures include the following:

- Monitoring alarms
- Exporting log bundles
- Restoring a virtual machine from a backup
- Environment shutdown and startup

The following screenshot is an example taken from an operational-procedures document that details the process for exporting a log bundle:

5. Exporting a vCenter Log Bundle

When a service request is submitted to VMware for support, VMware Support may require the system logs to troubleshoot the reported issue.

1. To export system logs right-click the vCenter Server inventory object and select **All vCenter Actions -> Export System Logs**.
2. Select the hosts and vCenter logs to include in the log bundle.

3. Select the logs to export. In most cases the default selections will be used unless otherwise stated by VMware Support. Click **Generate Log Bundle** to begin the log export.

4. After the log bundle has been generated click **Download Log Bundle** to download the logs.
5. Choose a location to save the log export. A zipped archive containing the exported logs will be downloaded to location selected.

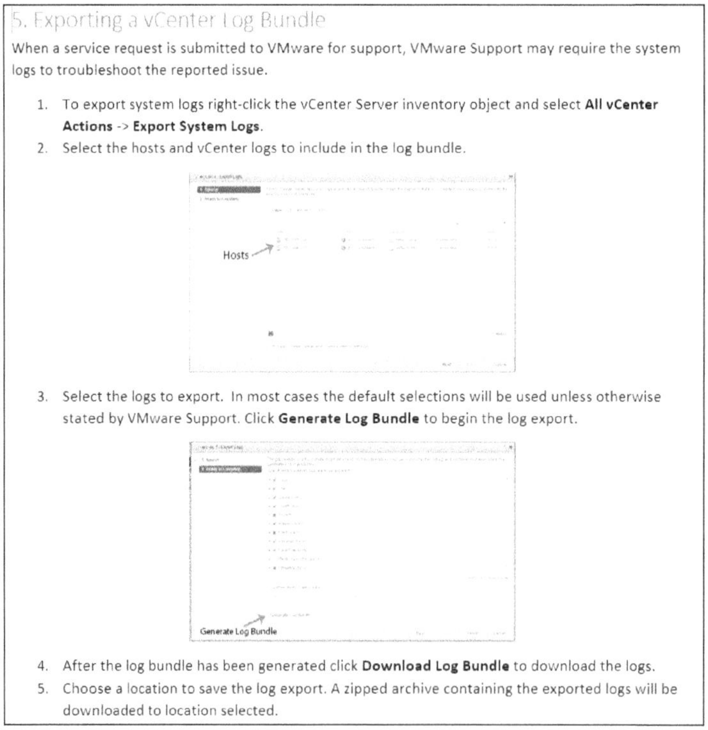

The following is an example outline of an operational-procedure document:

- **Cover page**: It includes the customer and project names
- **Document version log**: It contains the log of authors and changes made to the document
- **Document contacts**: It includes the subject matter experts involved in the creation of the design
- **Table of contents**: It is the index of document sections for quick reference
- **List of tables**: It is the index of tables included in the document for quick reference
- **List of figures**: It is the index of figures included in the document for quick reference
- **Purpose statement**: It defines the purpose of the document
- **Assumption statement**: It defines any assumptions made when creating the document
- **Operational procedures**: These are the step-by-step procedures for the day-to-day access, monitoring, and operation of the environment
- **Troubleshooting and recovery procedures**: These are the step-by-step procedures for troubleshooting issues and recovering from a failure

Presenting the design

Typically, once the design has been completed, it is presented to the customer for approval before implementation.

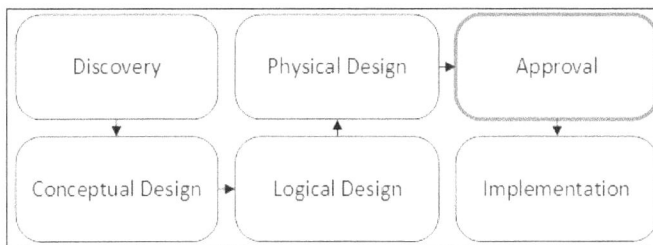

In order to obtain customer approval, typically, a high-level presentation is given to the project stakeholders to provide details on how the design satisfies the requirements and the benefits associated with the design.

> If you are not comfortable giving presentations, check out `http://www.toastmasters.org/`. Toastmasters can help you develop presentation skills and build confidence when speaking in front of people.

How to do it...

Presenting the design to stakeholders is a simple, but important, part of the design process:

1. Develop a presentation.
2. Present the design to the customer.

How it works...

The presentation should include the following information:

▸ An overview of the design methodology

▸ An overview of the discovery process

▸ The design factors: requirements, constraints, and assumptions

▸ A high-level overview of the logical and physical design

Remember to tailor your presentation to your audience. Keep the presentation at a high level, but be ready to provide details about the technical and business decisions made to support the design.

When presenting the design, explain the key design decisions and how they satisfy the requirements. Cover the entire design, but keep the presentation brief. Be ready to answer questions about the design and the reasons behind the design decisions.

Implementing the design

The final step of the design process is the implementation of the design.

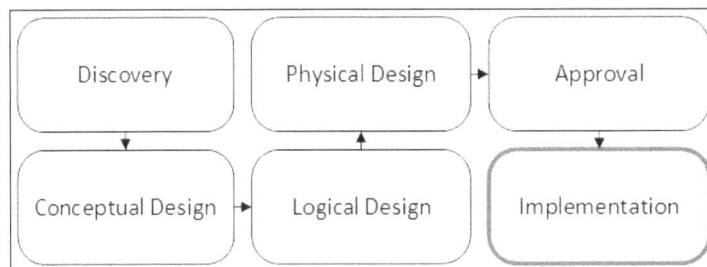

Implementation takes the design from paper and puts it into practice. If time has been taken to create and correctly document a solid design, its implementation will be the easiest part of the process.

How to do it...

The following steps are part of the design implementation:

1. Implementation of the documented design.
2. Validation and testing.
3. Review and delivery.

How it works...

Implement the design as documented in the architecture design. The implementation plan provides a guide to the implementation process, while the installation guide provides the details about performing the installation. The validation test plan is then used to test and validate the implementation against the design requirements.

Once the design has been successfully implemented, the design should be reviewed with the customer to identify any lessons learned for next steps. The documented deliverables are then provided to the customer.

Good luck.

Index

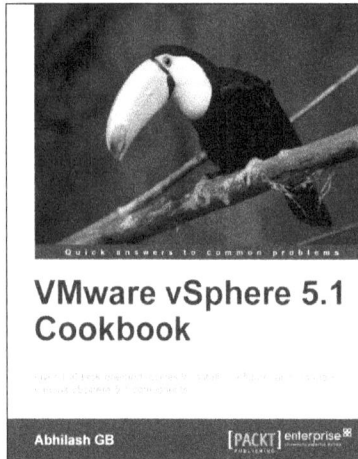

VMware vSphere 5.1 Cookbook

ISBN: 978-1-84968-402-6   Paperback: 466 pages

Over 130 task-oriented recipes to install, configure, and manage various vSphere 5.1 components

1. Install and configure vSphere 5.1 core components

2. Learn important aspects of vSphere such as administration, security, and performance

3. Configure vSphere Management Assistant (vMA) to run commands/scripts without the need to authenticate every attempt

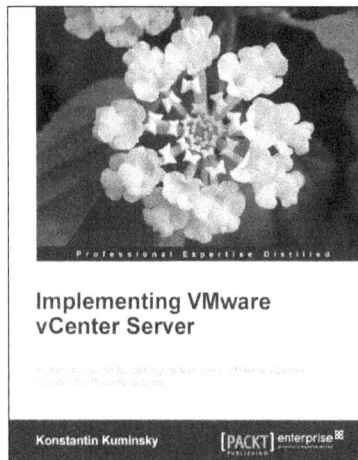

Implementing VMware vCenter Server

ISBN: 978-1-84968-998-4   Paperback: 324 pages

A practical guide for deploying and using VMware vCenter, suitable for IT professionals

1. Gain in-depth knowledge of the VMware vCenter features, requirements, and deployment process

2. Manage hosts, virtual machines, and learn storage management in VMware vCenter server

3. Overview of VMware vCenter Operations Manager and VMware vCenter Orchestrator

Please check **www.PacktPub.com** for information on our titles

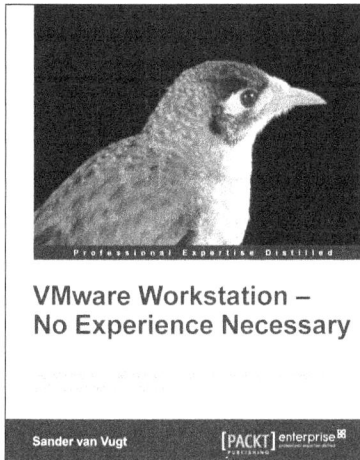

VMware Workstation – No Experience Necessary

ISBN: 978-1-84968-918-2   Paperback: 136 pages

Get started with VMware Workstation to create virtual machines and a virtual testing platform

1. Create virtual machines on Linux and Windows hosts

2. Create advanced test labs that help in getting back to any Virtual Machine state in an easy way

3. Share virtual machines with others, no matter which virtualization solution they're using

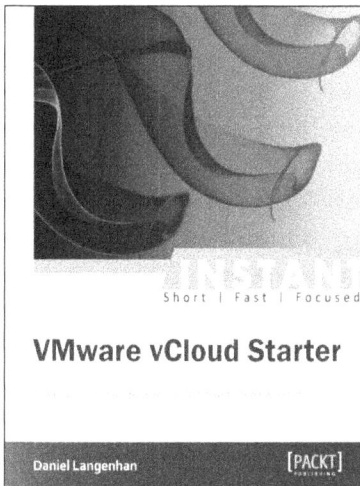

Instant VMware vCloud Starter

ISBN: 978-1-84968-996-0   Paperback: 76 pages

A practical, hands-on guide to get started with VMware vCloud

1. Learn something new in an Instant! A short, fast, focused guide delivering immediate results

2. Deploy and operate a VMware vCloud in your own demo kit

3. Understand the basics about the cloud in general and why there is such a hype

4. Build and use templates to quickly deploy complete environments

Please check **www.PacktPub.com** for information on our titles

www.ingramcontent.com/pod-product-compliance
Lightning Source LLC
Chambersburg PA
CBHW061400210326
41598CB00035B/6051